2009 SUPPLEMENT

SEXUALITY, GENDER, AND THE LAW

SECOND EDITION

by

WILLIAM N. ESKRIDGE, JR.
John A. Garver Professor of Jurisprudence
Yale Law School

NAN D. HUNTER
Professor of Law
Georgetown Law Center

FOUNDATION PRESS
2009

THOMSON REUTERS

© 2005, 2007 THOMSON REUTERS/FOUNDATION PRESS
© 2009 By THOMSON REUTERS/FOUNDATION PRESS

     195 Broadway, 9th Floor
     New York, NY 10007
     Phone Toll Free 1–877–888–1330
     Fax (212) 367–6799
     foundation–press.com
Printed in the United States of America

ISBN 978–1–59941–638–0

ACKNOWLEDGMENTS

We appreciate the **excellent** research assistance of Darsana Srinivasan (Yale Law School, Class of 2007); Diana Rusk (Yale Law School, Class of 2009); Baolu Lan (Yale Law School, Class of 2009); and Patricia Page (Yale Law School Personal Assistant). Without their help and expert guidance, we could not have produced this Supplement in time for use in academic year 2009–10.

                              WNE, Jr.
                              NDH

*

TABLE OF CONTENTS

*

TABLE OF CONTENTS FOR COLLEGE EDITION

TABLE OF CASES

Principal cases are in bold type. Non-principal cases are in roman type. References are to Pages.

2009 SUPPLEMENT

SEXUALITY, GENDER, AND THE LAW

*

CHAPTER 1

PRIVACY AND THE STATE

SECTION 2

STATE REGULATION OF SEX OUTSIDE OF MARRIAGE

Page 99. Replace Williams v. Pryor (2001), with the following Case:

Williams v. Pryor, 378 F.3d 1232 (11th Cir. 2004). Alabama added a provision to its obscenity law that prohibited sale or distribution of "any device designed or marketed as useful primarily for the stimulation of human genital organs." Ala. Code § 13A–12–200.2(a)(1) (Supp. 1998). The law does not prohibit the possession or private use of such devices, nor does it prohibit Alabama citizens from purchasing such items out-of-state and bringing them back to Alabama. Moreover, the statute permits the sale of ordinary vibrators and body massagers that, although useful as sexual aids, are not "designed or marketed ... primarily" for that particular purpose. Finally, the statute exempts sales of sexual devices "for a bona fide medical, scientific, educational, legislative, judicial, or law enforcement purpose."

The ACLU challenged the law on privacy grounds. In *Williams v. Pryor*, 240 F.3d 944 (11th Cir. 2001), the Eleventh Circuit ruled that, on a facial challenge to the law, at least some persons—minors—lacked a fundamental right of access to such devices. "The State's interest in public morality is a legitimate interest rationally served by the statute. The crafting and safeguarding of public morality has long been an established part of the States' plenary police power to legislate and indisputably is a legitimate government interest under rational basis scrutiny. A statute banning the commercial distribution of sexual devices is rationally related to this interest. Alabama argues 'a ban on the sale of sexual devices and related orgasm stimulating paraphernalia is rationally related to a legitimate legislative interest in discouraging prurient interests in autonomous sex' and that 'it is enough for a legislature to reasonably believe that commerce in the pursuit of orgasms by artificial means for their own sake is detrimental to the health and morality of the State.' The criminal proscription on the distribution of sexual devices certainly is a rational means for eliminating commerce in the devices, which itself is a rational means for making the acquisition and use of the devices more difficult. Moreover, incremental steps are not a defect in legislation under rational basis scrutiny, so Alabama did not act irrationally by prohibiting only the commercial distribution of sexual devices, rather than prohibiting their possession or use or by directly proscribing masturbation with or without a sexual device. Thus, we hold the Alabama sexual devices distribution criminal statute is constitutional under rational basis scrutiny because it is rationally related to at least one legitimate State interest."

The Court of Appeals remanded for the district judge to consider the as-applied challenges by four women, two married and two once-married but then single, who used such devices to enhance their intimate relationships with men. On remand, the district court ruled that the statute was invalid as applied to those plaintiffs, ruling that the adult plaintiffs had a fundamental right to sexual privacy and that the state had demonstrated no compelling state interest to justify "prohibit[ing] plaintiffs from purchasing sexual devices for use within the confines of their private, adult, consensual, sexual relationships." *Williams v. Pryor*, 220 F. Supp. 2d 1257, 1259–1260 (N.D. Ala. 2002). After *Lawrence*, the Eleventh Circuit reversed the district court, in an opinion by **Judge Birch**.

"The ACLU invokes 'privacy' and 'personal autonomy' as if such phrases were constitutional talismans. In the abstract, however, there is no fundamental right to either. See, e.g., *Glucksberg* (Casebook, pp. 74–76) (fundamental rights are 'not simply deduced from abstract concepts of personal autonomy'). Undoubtedly, many fundamental rights currently recognized under Supreme Court precedent touch on matters of personal autonomy and privacy. However, '[t]hat many of the rights and liberties protected by the Due Process Clause sound in personal autonomy does not warrant the sweeping conclusion that any and all important, intimate, and personal decisions are so protected.' *Id.* Such rights have been denominated 'fundamental' not simply because they implicate deeply personal and private considerations, but because they have been identified as 'deeply rooted in this Nation's history and tradition and implicit in the concept of ordered liberty, such that neither liberty nor justice would exist if they were sacrificed.' *Id.*

"Nor, contrary to the ACLU's assertion, have the Supreme Court's substantive-due-process precedents recognized a free-standing 'right to sexual privacy.' The Court has been presented with repeated opportunities to identify a fundamental right to sexual privacy—and has invariably declined. See, e.g., *Carey v. Population Servs. Int'l,* 431 U.S. 678, 688 n.5 (1977) (noting that the Court 'has not definitively answered the difficult question whether and to what extent the Constitution prohibits state statutes regulating private consensual sexual behavior among adults, and we do not purport to answer that question now'). Although many of the Court's 'privacy' decisions have implicated sexual matters, see, e.g., *Casey* (abortion); *Carey* (contraceptives), the Court has never indicated that the mere fact that an activity is sexual and private entitles it to protection as a fundamental right. * * *

"The dissent in turn argues that the right recognized in *Lawrence* was a longstanding right that preexisted *Lawrence,* thus obviating the need for any *Glucksberg*-type fundamental rights analysis. But the dissent never identifies the source, textual or precedential, of such a preexisting right to sexual privacy. It does cite *Griswold, Eisenstadt, Roe,* and *Carey.* However, although these precedents recognize various substantive rights *closely related* to sexual intimacy, none of them recognize the overarching right to sexual privacy asserted here. *Griswold* (marital privacy and contraceptives); *Eisenstadt* (equal protection extension of Griswold); *Roe* (abortion); *Carey* (contraceptives). As we noted above, in the most recent of these decisions, *Carey,* the Court specifically observed that it had not answered the question of whether there is a constitutional right to private sexual conduct. Moreover, nearly two decades later, the *Glucksberg* Court, listing the current catalog of fundamental rights, did not include such a right."

Judge Birch drew from *Glucksberg* a two-step approach to identifying fundamental rights protected by the Due Process Clause: First, the Court must carefully describe the right in question. Then, it must determine whether it has historically been protected in our legal culture. The right in question is not only the right to buy or sell the sexual devices described by the statute, but also to use them. Cf. *Glucksberg* (right of physician to assist in suicide also involves the right of the person to receive such assistance). Judge Birch then asked whether such a right was deeply rooted in our legal traditions. He found it was not and criticized the district judge's approach: "The first error relates back to the district court's overbroad framing of the asserted right in question. Having framed the relevant right as a generalized 'right to sexual privacy,' the district court's history and tradition analysis consisted largely of an irrelevant exploration of the history of sex in America. Second, we find that this analysis placed too much weight on contemporary practice and attitudes with respect to sexual conduct and sexual devices. Third, rather than look for a history and tradition of *protection* of the asserted right, the district court asked whether there was a history and tradition of state *non-interference* with the right."

"The district court—rather than requiring a showing that the right to use sexual devices is 'deeply rooted in this Nation's history and tradition'— looked for a showing that *proscriptions* against sexual devices are deeply rooted in history and tradition. Under this approach, the freedom to smoke, to pollute, to engage in private discrimination, to commit marital rape—at one time or another—all could have been elevated to fundamental-rights status. Moreover, it would create the perverse incentive for legislatures to regulate every area within their plenary power for fear that their restraint in any area might give rise to a right of constitutional proportions.

"Beyond these obvious objections, the most significant flaw in the district court's analysis is its misreading of *Glucksberg*. Admittedly, the *Glucksberg* Court, in declining to extend constitutional protection to assisted suicide, cited the extensive history of laws forbidding or discouraging suicide. But the context of this inquiry was the Court's attempt to determine whether a right to suicide, and particularly assisted suicide, was deeply rooted in American history and tradition. Naturally, prohibitions on suicide were particularly competent evidence of the absence of such a history and tradition. The *Glucksberg* Court, however, never suggested that the reviewing court must find a history of proscription of a given activity before declining to recognize a new constitutional right to engage in that activity. Id. (rejecting the analogy between the constitutionally-protected right to refuse unwanted medical treatment and the asserted right to assisted suicide, noting that the former right 'has never enjoyed similar legal protection').

"Not only does the record before us fail to evidence such a deeply rooted right, but it suggests that, to the extent that sex toys historically have attracted the attention of the law, it has been in the context of proscription, not protection." Judge Birch's chief example was the Comstock laws. "The federal Comstock Act of 1873 was a criminal statute directed at 'the suppression of Trade in and Circulation of obscene Literature and Articles of immoral Use.' Act of March 3, 1873, ch. 258, § 2, 17 Stat. 599 (1873). The Act prohibited importation of and use of the mails for transporting, among other things, 'every article or thing intended or adapted for any indecent or immoral use.' *United States v. Chase*, 135 U.S. 255, 257 (1890). Various states also enacted similar statutes prohibiting the sale of such articles."

Judge Barkett dissented. She read *Lawrence* as reaffirming a "right to sexual privacy." *Lawrence*'s opening passage says: "Liberty protects the person from unwarranted government intrusions into a dwelling or other private places. In our tradition the State is not omnipresent in the home. And there are other spheres of our lives and existence, outside the home, where the State should not be a dominant presence ... The instant case involves liberty of the person both in its spatial and more transcendent dimensions."

"Beginning with *Griswold*, the *Lawrence* Court found that its prior decisions confirmed 'that the protection of liberty under the Due Process Clause has a substantive dimension of fundamental significance in defining the rights of the person' and 'that the right to make certain decisions regarding sexual conduct extends beyond the marital relationship.' Id. (summarizing *Griswold, Eisenstadt, Roe,* and *Carey*)."

"When the Court announced it was overruling *Bowers,* Justice Kennedy said the Court's prior holdings had already made 'abundantly clear' that individuals have a substantive due process right to make decisions 'concerning the intimacies of their physical relationship[s], even when not intended to produce offspring.' The *Lawrence* Court therefore concluded that '*Bowers* was not correct when it was decided.'

"Given these statements in *Lawrence*, I fail to understand the majority's reliance on a footnote from the Supreme Court's 1977 decision in *Carey*, where the Court indicated in dicta that it had not 'definitively answered' the extent to which the Due Process Clause protects the private sexual conduct of consenting adults. Obviously, *Carey* does not resolve in any way the meaning of a case that comes twenty-six years later. Nor does it prevent *Lawrence* from answering the very question posed in *Carey*'s footnote. *Lawrence* does precisely this in affirming the right of consenting adults to make private sexual decisions. * * *

"[T]he *Lawrence* Court held that the petitioners' 'right to liberty under the Due Process Clause gives them the full right to engage in their [private sexual] conduct without intervention of the government.' The Court could not have been more clear that the petitioners' right to engage in private sexual conduct has its textual locus in the Due Process Clause." Judge Barkett suggested that Judge Birch made the same mistake *Bowers* had made, by framing the liberty interest too specifically and therefore missing the relevance of the Court's privacy precedents and the nation's legal traditions. Judge Barkett also rejected the majority's suggestion that she was pulling together "scattered dicta"; to the contrary, her analysis of the liberty interest was based upon the *Lawrence* Court's emphatic framing of the matter and the key reason the Court declared that *Bowers* had been wrong the day it was decided.

"In narrowly framing the right at issue, the majority also errs in its use of history. The majority claims that under *Glucksberg*, the district court was wrong to rely on a history and tradition of state non-interference with the private sexual lives of adults as a basis to recognize a right to sexual privacy. According to the majority, *Glucksberg* requires that there be a long-standing history of affirmative legal protection of specific conduct before a right can be recognized under the Due Process Clause.

"Contrary to the majority's claim, neither *Glucksberg* nor any other relevant Supreme Court precedent supports the requirement that there must be a history of affirmative legislative protection before a right can be judicially protected. The majority simply invents this requirement, effectively redefining the doctrine of substantive due process to protect only those rights that are already explicitly protected by law. Such a requirement ignores not only *Lawrence* but also a complete body of Supreme Court jurisprudence. Had the Supreme Court required affirmative governmental protection of an asserted liberty interest, all of the Court's privacy cases would have been decided differently. For instance, there was no lengthy tradition of protecting abortion and the use of contraceptives, yet both were found to be protected by a right to privacy under the Due Process Clause. In its analysis, the trial court here correctly considered the history of non-interference by government. Its analysis was expressly validated by *Lawrence*, in which there was no history of affirmatively protecting the right to engage in consensual sodomy. * * * Therefore, the majority is plainly incorrect that there must be a history and tradition of laws protecting the right to use sex toys. * * *

"The majority states that *Lawrence* held that sodomy laws fail rational-basis review. However, the majority neglects to address whether Alabama's statute has a rational basis even though Alabama relies upon the same justification for criminalizing private sexual activity rejected by *Lawrence*—public morality. In *Lawrence*, Texas had explicitly relied upon public morality as a rational basis for its sodomy law. *Lawrence* summarily rejected Texas's argument, holding that the sodomy law 'further[ed] no legitimate state interest which can justify its intrusion into the personal and private life of the individual.' In *Williams II*, this Court previously upheld Alabama's law on rational basis grounds, relying on the now defunct *Bowers* to conclude that public morality provides a legitimate state interest. Obviously, now that *Bowers* has been overruled, this proposition is no longer good law and we must, accordingly, revisit our holding in *Williams II*. * * * "

NOTE ON THE SEX TOY CASES

In light of Judge Barkett's analysis, is it fair to say that the majority simply refuses to apply *Lawrence* to anything not covered by the facts of that case? If so, that would appear to be insubordinate conduct reminiscent of southern appeals court decisions in the desegregation cases. If not, what is the basis on which the majority might fairly distinguish *Lawrence*? (Or the contraception and abortion cases, which are also wrongly decided under the majority's "look to a specific tradition protecting *this* conduct.")

The Supreme Court denied review in *Williams* and in another case involving a similar debate between Judges Birch and Barkett, over the constitutionality of Florida's gay adoption ban (*Lofton*, Chapter 2 of this Supplement). How should the Supreme Court's denial of certiorari (which has no value as precedent) in these cases be understood?

Confusing the matter further, the Fifth Circuit declared a Texas law essentially identical to the Alabama law to be unconstitutional. The state defendants did not seek Supreme Court review in the Texas case, *infra*, so the contradictory holdings stand.

Reliable Consultants, Inc. v. Earle

U.S. Court of Appeals for the Fifth Circuit, 2008.
517 F.3d 738, rehearing denied, 538 F.3d 355.

... The State's primary justifications for the statute are "morality based." The asserted interests include "discouraging prurient interests in autonomous sex and the pursuit of sexual gratification unrelated to procreation and prohibiting the commercial sale of sex."

These interests in "public morality" cannot constitutionally sustain the statute after *Lawrence*. To uphold the statute would be to ignore the holding in *Lawrence* and allow the government to burden consensual private intimate conduct simply by deeming it morally offensive. In *Lawrence*, Texas's only argument was that the anti-sodomy law reflected the moral judgment of the legislature. The Court expressly rejected the State's rationale by adopting Justice Stevens' view in *Bowers v. Hardwick* as "controlling" and quoting Justice Stevens' statement that " 'the fact that the governing majority in a State has traditionally viewed a particular practice as immoral is not a sufficient reason for upholding a law prohibiting the practice.' " Thus, if in *Lawrence* public morality was an insufficient justification for a law that restricted "adult consensual intimacy in the home," then public morality also cannot serve as a rational basis for Texas's statute, which also regulates private sexual intimacy.

Perhaps recognizing that public morality is an insufficient justification for the statute after *Lawrence*, the State asserts that an interest the statute serves is the "protection of minors and unwilling adults from exposure to sexual devices and their advertisement." It is undeniable that the government has a compelling interest in protecting children from improper sexual expression. However, the State's generalized concern for children does not justify such a heavy-handed restriction on the exercise of a constitutionally protected individual right. Ultimately, because we can divine no rational connection between the statute and the protection of children, and because the State offers none, we cannot sustain the law under this justification.

The alleged governmental interest in protecting "unwilling adults" from exposure to sexual devices is even less convincing. The Court has consistently refused to burden individual rights out of concern for the protection of "unwilling recipients." Furthermore, this asserted interest bears no rational relation to the restriction on sales of sexual devices because an adult cannot buy a sexual device without making the affirmative decision to visit a store and make the purchase. . . .

Just as in *Lawrence*, the State here wants to use its laws to enforce a public moral code by restricting private intimate conduct. The case is not about public sex. It is not about controlling commerce in sex. It is about controlling what people do in the privacy of their own homes because the State is morally opposed to a certain type of consensual private intimate conduct. This is an insufficient justification for the statute after *Lawrence*.

It follows that the Texas statute cannot define sexual devices themselves as obscene and prohibit their sale. . . .

Witt v. Department of the Air Force

U.S. Court of Appeals for the Ninth Circuit, 2008.
527 F.3d 806.

■ GOULD, CIRCUIT JUDGE:

Plaintiff–Appellant Major Margaret Witt . . . alleges that 10 U.S.C. § 654, commonly known as the "Don't Ask, Don't Tell" policy ("DADT"), violates substantive due process, the Equal Protection Clause, and procedural due process. She seeks to enjoin DADT's enforcement. The district court dismissed the suit . . . for failure to state a claim. We reverse and remand in part, and affirm in part.

I

Major Witt entered the Air Force in 1987. She was commissioned as a Second Lieutenant that same year and promoted to First Lieutenant in 1989, to Captain in 1991, and to Major in 1999. In 1995, she transferred from active to reserve duty and was assigned to McChord Air Force Base in Tacoma, Washington.

By all accounts, Major Witt was an outstanding Air Force officer. . . . Major Witt was made an Air Force "poster child" in 1993, when the Air Force featured her in recruitment materials; photos of her appeared in Air Force promotional materials for more than a decade.

Major Witt was in a committed and long-term relationship with another woman from July 1997 through August 2003. Major Witt's partner was never a member nor a civilian employee of any branch of the armed forces, and Major Witt states that she never had sexual relations while on duty or while on the grounds of any Air Force base. During their relationship, Major Witt and her partner shared a home in Spokane, Washington, about 250 miles away from McChord Air Force Base. While serving in the Air Force, Major Witt never told any member of the military that she was homosexual.

[Investigations of allegations that Major Witt is a lesbian began in 2004, and culminated in her discharge from the Air Force in 2007.]

To evaluate Major Witt's substantive due process claim, we first must determine the proper level of scrutiny to apply. In previous cases, we have applied rational basis review to DADT and predecessor policies. However, Major Witt argues that *Lawrence v. Texas* effectively overruled those cases by establishing a fundamental right to engage in adult consensual sexual acts. The Air Force disagrees. Having carefully considered *Lawrence* and the arguments of the parties, we hold that *Lawrence* requires something more than traditional rational basis review and that remand is therefore appropriate. . . .

Major Witt argues that *Lawrence* recognized a fundamental right to engage in private, consensual, homosexual conduct and therefore requires us to subject DADT to heightened scrutiny. The Air Force argues that *Lawrence* applied only rational basis review, and that the Ninth Circuit's [earlier] decisions [upholding DADT] remain binding law. . . . Because *Lawrence* is, perhaps intentionally so, silent as to the level of scrutiny that it applied, both parties draw upon language from *Lawrence* that supports their views. . . .

The parties urge us to pick through *Lawrence* with a fine-toothed comb and to give credence to the particular turns of phrase used by the Supreme Court that best support their claims. But given the studied limits of the verbal analysis in *Lawrence*, this approach is not conclusive. Nor does a review of our circuit precedent answer the question; as the Court of Appeals for the Armed Forces stated in *United States v. Marcum*, [60 M.J. 198 (C.A.A.F. 2004)] "[a]lthough particular sentences within the Supreme Court's opinion may be culled in support of the Government's argument, other sentences may be extracted to support Appellant's argument." In these ambiguous circumstances, we analyze *Lawrence* by considering what the Court actually did, rather than by dissecting isolated pieces of text. In so doing, we conclude that the Supreme Court applied a heightened level of scrutiny in *Lawrence*.

We cannot reconcile what the Supreme Court did in *Lawrence* with the minimal protections afforded by traditional rational basis review. First, the Court overruled *Bowers v. Hardwick*, an earlier case in which the Court had upheld a Georgia sodomy law under rational basis review. If the Court was undertaking rational basis review, then *Bowers* must have been wrong because it failed under that standard; namely, it must have lacked "any reasonably conceivable state of facts that could provide a rational basis for the classification." *FCC v. Beach Commc'ns, Inc.*, 508 U.S. 307, 313 (1993). But the Court's criticism of *Bowers* had nothing to do with the basis for the law; instead, the Court rejected *Bowers* because of the "Court's own failure to appreciate the extent of the liberty at stake."

The criticism that the Court in *Bowers* had misapprehended "the extent of the liberty at stake" does not sound in rational basis review. Under rational basis review, the Court determines whether governmental action is so arbitrary that a rational basis for the action cannot even be conceived post hoc. If the Court was applying that standard . . . , it had no reason to consider the extent of the liberty involved. Yet it did, ultimately concluding that the ban on homosexual sexual conduct sought to "control a personal relationship that, whether or not entitled to formal recognition in the law, is within the liberty of persons to choose without being punished as criminals." This is inconsistent with rational basis review.

Second, the cases on which the Supreme Court explicitly based its decision in *Lawrence* are based on heightened scrutiny. . . .

Third, the *Lawrence* Court's rationale for its holding—the inquiry analysis that it was applying—is inconsistent with rational basis review. The Court declared: "The Texas statute furthers no legitimate state interest which can justify its intrusion into the personal and private life of the individual." Were the Court applying rational basis review, it would not identify a legitimate state interest to "justify" the particular intrusion of liberty at issue in *Lawrence*; regardless of the liberty involved, any hypothetical rationale for the law would do.

We therefore conclude that *Lawrence* applied something more than traditional rational basis review. This leaves open the question whether the Court applied strict scrutiny, intermediate scrutiny, or another heightened level of scrutiny. . . . [W]e hesitate to apply strict scrutiny when the Supreme Court did not discuss narrow tailoring or a compelling state interest in *Lawrence*, and we do not address the issue here.

Instead, we look to another recent Supreme Court case that applied a heightened level of scrutiny to a substantive due process claim—a scrutiny that resembles and expands upon the analysis performed in *Lawrence*. In *Sell v. United States*, 539 U.S. 166, 179 (2003), the Court considered whether the Constitution permits the government to forcibly administer antipsychotic drugs to a mentally-ill defendant in order to render that defendant competent to stand trial. The Court held that the defendant has a "significant constitutionally protected liberty interest" at stake, so the drugs could be administered forcibly "only if the treatment is medically appropriate, is substantially unlikely to have side effects that may undermine the fairness of the trial, and, taking account of less intrusive alternatives, is necessary significantly to further important governmental trial-related interests."

Although the Court's holding in *Sell* is specific to the context of forcibly administering medication, the scrutiny employed by the Court to reach that holding is instructive. The Court recognized a "significant" liberty interest—the interest "in avoiding the unwanted administration of antipsychotic drugs"—and balanced that liberty interest against the "legitimate" and "important" state interest "in providing appropriate medical treatment to reduce the danger that an inmate suffering from a serious mental disorder represents to himself or others." To balance those two interests, the Court required the state to justify its intrusion into an individual's recognized liberty interest against forcible medication—just as *Lawrence* determined that the state had failed to "justify its intrusion into the personal and private life of the individual."

The heightened scrutiny applied in *Sell* consisted of four factors: First, a court must find that important governmental interests are at stake....

Courts, however, must consider the facts of the individual case in evaluating the Government's interest.... Special circumstances may lessen the importance of that interest....

Second, the court must conclude that involuntary medication will significantly further those concomitant state interests....

Third, the court must conclude that involuntary medication is necessary to further those interests. The court must find that any alternative, less intrusive treatments are unlikely to achieve substantially the same results....

Fourth, ... the court must conclude that administration of the drugs is medically appropriate....

The fourth factor is specific to the medical context of *Sell*, but the first three factors apply equally here. We thus take our direction from the Supreme Court and adopt the first three heightened-scrutiny *Sell* factors as the heightened scrutiny balancing analysis required under *Lawrence*. We hold that when the government attempts to intrude upon the personal and private lives of homosexuals, in a manner that implicates the rights identified in *Lawrence*, the government must advance an important governmental interest, the intrusion must significantly further that interest, and the intrusion must be necessary to further that interest. In other words, for the third factor, a less intrusive means must be unlikely to achieve substantially the government's interest.

In addition, we hold that this heightened scrutiny analysis is as-applied rather than facial. "This is the preferred course of adjudication since it enables courts to avoid making unnecessarily broad constitutional judgments." *City of Cleburne v. Cleburne Living Ctr. Inc.* ... *Sell* required courts to "consider the facts of the individual case in evaluating the Government's interest Under this review, we must determine not whether DADT has some hypothetical, post hoc rationalization in general, but whether a justification exists for the application of the policy as applied to Major Witt. This approach is necessary to give meaning to the Supreme Court's conclusion that liberty gives substantial protection to adult persons in deciding how to conduct their private lives in matters pertaining to sex...."

Here, applying heightened scrutiny to DADT in light of current Supreme Court precedents, it is clear that the government advances an important governmental interest. ... However, it is unclear on the record before us whether DADT, as applied to Major Witt, satisfies the second and third factors. The Air Force attempts to justify the policy by relying on congressional findings regarding "unit cohesion" and the like, but that does not go to whether the application of DADT specifically to Major Witt significantly furthers the government's interest and whether less intrusive means would achieve substantially the government's interest. Remand therefore is required for the district court to develop the record on Major Witt's substantive due process claim. Only then can DADT be measured against the appropriate constitutional standard.

We next turn to Major Witt's Equal Protection Clause claim. She argues that DADT violates equal protection because the Air Force has a mandatory rule discharging those who engage in homosexual activities but not those "whose presence may also cause discomfort among other service members," such as child molesters. However, [an earlier Ninth Circuit decision] held that DADT does not violate equal protection under rational basis review, and that holding was not disturbed by *Lawrence*, which declined to address equal protection. We thus affirm the district court's dismissal of Major Witt's equal protection claims. . . .

Witt v. Department of the Air Force

U.S. Court of Appeals for the Ninth Circuit, 2008.
548 F.3d 1264.

■ O'SCANNLAIN, CIRCUIT JUDGE, dissenting from the denial of rehearing en banc, joined by BEA, M. SMITH, JR., and N.R. SMITH, CIRCUIT JUDGES:

This is the first case in which a federal appellate court has allowed a member of the armed services to bring a substantive due process challenge to the congressionally enacted "Don't Ask, Don't Tell" homosexual personnel policy for the military. With respect, I believe that our three-judge panel has erroneously reversed a district court order dismissing such suit and remanded for further fact-finding under an unsanctioned and malleable standard of review. . . .

After careful but, I respectfully submit, misguided consideration, the panel concluded that *Lawrence* introduced a new requirement of some kind of heightened scrutiny. The *Lawrence* opinion itself does not prescribe such scrutiny or even mention that it applied heightened scrutiny of any kind. Lacking a standard of review, the panel imported a multi-factor balancing test from another Supreme Court case, *Sell v. United States*, that it thought enunciated a standard of review appropriate to *Lawrence*. In *Sell*, a case involving the government's forcible administration of anti-psychotic drugs to a mentally ill defendant, the Court did develop a four-factor test, but only on the basis of prior cases with similar facts (deriving a standard from *Washington v. Harper*, [494 U.S. 210 (1990)] which considered "whether a judicial hearing is required before the State may treat a mentally ill prisoner with anti-psychotic drugs against his will" and *Riggins v. Nevada*, [504 U.S. 127 (1992)], which reversed State convictions because the defendant was unconstitutionally forced to take an anti-psychotic drug during trial). The *Sell* Court explicitly tied its test to those cases where the government had "involuntarily . . . administer[ed] antipsychotic drugs to a mentally ill defendant facing serious criminal charges in order to render that defendant competent to stand trial."

Notwithstanding the inapposite origin of the *Sell* test, the *Witt* panel adapted it to its own purposes. In *Witt*'s modified version, the inquiry requires "that when the government attempts to intrude upon the personal and private lives of homosexuals, in a manner that implicates the rights identified in *Lawrence*, the government must advance an important governmental interest, the intrusion must significantly further that interest, and the intrusion must be necessary to further that interest.... In addition, we hold that this heightened scrutiny analysis is as-applied rather than facial."
. . .

My first objection to *Witt* is to its application of *Lawrence* in the first place. ... [T]he occasional generality of the analysis does not mean that *Lawrence* applies to any statute that affects homosexual conduct to the exclusion of the rest of the case law on substantive due process. Such is common sense, and our sister circuits have recognized it. See, e.g., *Muth v. Frank*, 412 F.3d 808, 817 (7th Cir.2005) ("*Lawrence* ... did not announce ... a fundamental right, protected by the Constitution, for adults to engage in all manner of consensual sexual conduct...."); *Lofton v. Sec'y of the Dep't of Children Family Servs.*, 358 F.3d 804, 817 (11th Cir.2004) (noting that "the shared homosexuality component" does not alone require application of *Lawrence*); *United States v. Marcum* (same)....

... The *Witt* panel professed its desire to focus on what the *Lawrence* Court did rather than to "dissect[ ] isolated pieces of text," and yet *Witt*'s analysis derives almost entirely from *Lawrence*'s dicta. What *Lawrence* did was to strike down an outlier criminal statute punishing private, consensual homosexual conduct in the home....

Crucially, as if to anticipate challenges like the one before the *Witt* panel, *Lawrence* concludes by limiting its holding to the facts of the case. ... [T]he most relevant limitation here is that the opinion did not apply itself to cases involving "public conduct" or require that "the government ... give formal recognition to any relationship that homosexual persons seek to enter," *Lawrence*. If one combines the holding with this self-imposed limitation, one comes to the inexorable conclusion that a *Lawrence* case requires, at least, a criminal sanction on private conduct. Put in the negative, *Lawrence* did not deal with laws addressed to public conduct or non-criminal statutes....

Once one keeps these limits in mind, it becomes apparent that *Witt* strayed far beyond the proper reach of *Lawrence*. The case before the panel involved both public conduct and a non-criminal statute. The opinion makes much of the fact that the homosexual acts for which, in part, Major Witt was dismissed occurred in the privacy of the couple's shared home. But nothing in the "Don't Ask, Don't Tell" policy forbids anyone from doing anything in the home on pain of criminal or even of civil penalties. Indeed, the whole point of the policy is to keep such private behavior private. If no one asks and no one tells, no one in the military cares. "Don't Ask, Don't Tell" is about how the military manages its personnel; the policy only matters if an employee's homosexual conduct or acknowledgment of homosexuality becomes public. What happened in this case, and what must happen for "Don't Ask, Don't Tell" to apply, is that homosexual conduct, originally private or not, became public. And *Lawrence* simply does not apply to non-criminal public conduct. . . .

■ KLEINFELD, CIRCUIT JUDGE, dissenting from the denial of rehearing en banc, joined by BEA, CIRCUIT JUDGE:

. . . Even under . . . a broad and aggressive interpretation of *Lawrence*, the panel would still be mistaken. The reason why is that the general constitutional right to sexual liberty competes against the especially high level of deference we are required to extend to Congress and the President regarding military affairs, and few liberties prevail against that deference. . . .

It is not our business to decide whether Congress and the President were correct or mistaken in their judgment about homosexuality and military effectiveness. I intimate no view of my own. Many homosexuals have been excellent soldiers, as is evidently the case with Major Witt, and some militaries seem to function fine with homosexuals in the ranks. On the other hand, further injecting passions of love and jealousy into the emotional maelstrom of armed nineteen year olds who may soon die for their country may reasonably be seen by Congress and the President as too risky, especially when combined with minority sexual orientations.

I cannot tell just what the panel intends for the district court to do on remand. The panel remanded the case to the district court to determine whether, under a heightened level of scrutiny, application of this law to Major Witt "significantly furthers the government's interest." Congress and the President concluded that it does, because the rule is general, for the entire military. The panel cannot mean that the district court should repeat the extensive congressional hearings that preceded adoption of the law, to determine whether the court agrees with the policy adopted. But the panel does not say what sort of evidence the district court is supposed to consider, or precisely what factual question the evidence is supposed to answer.

Do model officers such as Major Witt get an exception to the rule? Popular officers? Officers whose units appear to have suffered no decline in morale and unit cohesion? The panel does not justify making any of these things matter. . . .

Regardless of what liberties the Constitution guarantees for civilians, the military context changes the analysis. . . .

NOTES ON THE NEW NINTH CIRCUIT STANDARD

As the dissent correctly notes, the *Witt* decision marked the first federal appellate court to explicitly hold that *Lawrence v. Texas* was grounded in heightened scrutiny. Do you agree with the analogy to the *Sell* case? Can you articulate a more persuasive basis for finding that heightened scrutiny was in play in *Lawrence*?

As this Supplement goes to press, the *Witt* case goes back to the district court, on remand from this ruling. The decision whether to seek certiorari in the Supreme Court fell to the new Obama Justice Department, and it elected not to. Do you think this was a smart decision from the administration's perspective? What scenarios for change does it enable?

Page 112.   Add the following Case and Notes at the end of Section 2:

Alberto R. Gonzalez v. Leroy Carhart et al.

United States Supreme Court, 2007.
550 U.S. 124, 127 S.Ct. 1610, 167 L.Ed.2d 480.

[In the usual second-trimester abortion procedure, "dilation and evacuation" (D&E), the doctor dilates the cervix and then inserts surgical instruments into the uterus in order to separate portions of the fetus and remove them one by one. A variation of the standard D&E, usually termed an "intact D&E," and sometimes called "dilation and extraction" (D&X), requires a doctor to extract the fetus intact or largely intact with only a few passes, pulling out its entire body instead of ripping it apart. In order to allow the head to pass through the cervix, the doctor typically pierces or crushes the skull. The Supreme Court in *Stenberg v. Carhart*, 530 U.S. 914 (2000), overturned a Nebraska "partial-birth abortion" law that banned intact D&E procedures and, possibly, some regular D&E procedures as well. The Court found two constitutional problems: first, the law was vague as to what procedures it actually criminalized, and second there was no exception to protect the health of the mother.

[After *Stenberg*, Congress passed a national Partial–Birth Abortion Ban Act of 2003. The federal statute prohibits "knowingly perform[ing] a partial-birth abortion ... that is [not] necessary to save the life of a mother." There is no exclusion for the mother's health. The statute defines a partial birth abortion as a procedure in which the doctor: "(A) deliberately and intentionally vaginally delivers a living fetus until, in the case of a head-first presentation, the entire fetal head is outside the [mother's] body ..., or, in the case of breech presentation, any part of the fetal trunk past the navel is outside the [mother's] body ..., for the purpose of performing an overt act that the person knows will kill the partially delivered living fetus"; and "(B) performs the overt act, other than completion of delivery, that kills the fetus."]

■ JUSTICE KENNEDY delivered the opinion of the Court.

[I. As he and Justice Thomas had done in their *Stenberg* dissenting opinions, Justice Kennedy started his *Carhart* majority with a detailed description of the D&E and intact D&E (or D&X) procedures. Justice

Kennedy started with an "abortion doctor's clinical description," followed by "another description from a nurse who witnessed the same method performed on a 26–week fetus and who testified before the Senate Judiciary Committee:"

> Dr. Haskell went in with forceps and grabbed the baby's legs and pulled them down into the birth canal. Then he delivered the baby's body and the arms—everything but the head. The doctor kept the head right inside the uterus.

> The baby's little fingers were clasping and unclasping, and his little feet were kicking. Then the doctor stuck the scissors in the back of his head, and the baby's arms jerked out, like a startle reaction, like a flinch, like a baby does when he thinks he is going to fall.

> The doctor opened up the scissors, stuck a high-powered suction tube into the opening, and sucked the baby's brains out. Now the baby went completely limp....

> He cut the umbilical cord and delivered the placenta. He threw the baby in a pan, along with the placenta and the instruments he had just used.

Based upon testimony such as this, Congress found that "[a] moral, medical, and ethical consensus exists that the practice of performing a partial-birth abortion ... is a gruesome and inhumane procedure that is never medically necessary and should be prohibited." Congressional Findings, 117 Stat. 1202, notes following 18 U.S.C. § 1531.]

II.   The principles set forth in the joint opinion in [*Casey*] did not find support from all those who join the instant opinion. Whatever one's views concerning the *Casey* joint opinion, it is evident a premise central to its conclusion—that the government has a legitimate and substantial interest in preserving and promoting fetal life—would be repudiated were the Court now to affirm the judgments of the Courts of Appeals. * * *

We assume the following principles for the purposes of this opinion. Before viability, a State "may not prohibit any woman from making the ultimate decision to terminate her pregnancy." *Casey* (plurality opinion). It also may not impose upon this right an undue burden, which exists if a regulation's "purpose and effect is to place a substantial obstacle in the path of a woman seeking an abortion before the fetus obtains viability." On the other hand, "[r]egulations which do no more than create a structural mechanism by which the State, or the parent or the guardian of a minor, may express profound respect for the life of the unborn are permitted, if they are not a substantial obstacle to the woman's exercise of the right to choose." *Casey*, in short, struck a balance. The balance was central to its holding. We now apply its standard to the cases at bar. * * *

[III.B]   Respondents contend * * * the Act is unconstitutionally vague on its face. "As generally stated, the void-for-vagueness doctrine requires that a penal statute define the criminal offense with sufficient definiteness that ordinary people can understand what conduct is prohibited and in a manner that does not encourage arbitrary and discriminatory enforcement." *Kolender v. Lawson,* 461 U.S. 352, 357 (1983). The Act satisfies both requirements.

The Act provides doctors "of ordinary intelligence a reasonable opportunity to know what is prohibited." *Grayned v. City of Rockford,* 408 U.S. 104, 108 (1972). Indeed, it sets forth "relatively clear guidelines as to prohibited conduct" and provides "objective criteria" to evaluate whether a doctor has performed a prohibited procedure. *Posters 'N Things v. United States,* 511 U.S. 513, 525–26 (1994). Unlike the statutory language in *Stenberg* that prohibited the delivery of a " 'substantial portion' " of the fetus—where a doctor might question how much of the fetus is a substantial portion—the Act defines the line between potentially criminal conduct on the one hand and lawful abortion on the other. Doctors performing D&E will know that if they do not deliver a living fetus to an anatomical landmark they will not face criminal liability.

This conclusion is buttressed by the intent that must be proved to impose liability. The Court has made clear that scienter requirements alleviate vagueness concerns. Because a doctor performing a D&E will not face criminal liability if he or she delivers a fetus beyond the prohibited point by mistake, the Act cannot be described as "a trap for those who act in good faith." *Colautti v. Franklin,* 439 U.S. 379, 395 (1979).

Respondents likewise have failed to show that the Act should be invalidated on its face because it encourages arbitrary or discriminatory enforcement. Just as the Act's anatomical landmarks provide doctors with objective standards, they also "establish minimal guidelines to govern law enforcement." *Smith v. Goguen,* 415 U.S. 566, 574 (1974). * * * The Act is not vague.

[C]   We next determine whether the Act imposes an undue burden, as a facial matter, because its restrictions on second-trimester abortions are too broad. A review of the statutory text discloses the limits of its reach. The Act prohibits intact D&E; and, notwithstanding respondents' arguments, it does not prohibit the D&E procedure in which the fetus is removed in parts. * * *

The Act excludes most D&Es in which the fetus is removed in pieces, not intact. If the doctor intends to remove the fetus in parts from the outset, the doctor will not have the requisite intent to incur criminal liability. A doctor performing a standard D&E procedure can often "tak[e] about 10–15 'passes' through the uterus to remove the entire fetus." Removing the fetus in this manner does not violate the Act because the doctor will not have delivered the living fetus to one of the anatomical landmarks or committed an additional overt act that kills the fetus after partial delivery. § 1531(b)(1).

A comparison of the Act with the Nebraska statute struck down in *Stenberg* confirms this point. The statute in *Stenberg* prohibited " 'deliberately and intentionally delivering into the vagina a living unborn child, or a substantial portion thereof, for the purpose of performing a procedure that the person performing such procedure knows will kill the unborn child and does kill the unborn child.' " The Court concluded that this statute encompassed D&E because "D&E will often involve a physician pulling a 'substantial portion' of a still living fetus, say, an arm or leg, into the vagina prior to the death of the fetus." The Court also rejected the limiting interpretation urged by Nebraska's Attorney General that the statute's reference to a "procedure" that " 'kill[s] the unborn child' " was to a distinct procedure, not to the abortion procedure as a whole. [Justice Kennedy concluded that the language of the new statute avoided these concerns.]

[IV. Finally, Justice Kennedy considered the *Casey*-based argument that the Act imposed a substantial obstacle to late-term but pre-viability abortions.]

[A]   The Act's purposes are set forth in recitals preceding its operative provisions. A description of the prohibited abortion procedure demonstrates the rationale for the congressional enactment. The Act proscribes a method of abortion in which a fetus is killed just inches before completion of the birth process. Congress stated as follows: "Implicitly approving such a brutal and inhumane procedure by choosing not to prohibit it will further coarsen society to the humanity of not only newborns, but all vulnerable and innocent human life, making it increasingly difficult to protect such life." Congressional Findings. The Act expresses respect for the dignity of human life. * * *

Respect for human life finds an ultimate expression in the bond of love the mother has for her child. The Act recognizes this reality as well. Whether to have an abortion requires a difficult and painful moral decision. *Casey.* While we find no reliable data to measure the phenomenon, it seems unexceptionable to conclude some women come to regret their choice to abort the infant life they once created and sustained. See Brief for Sandra Cano et al. As *Amici Curiae.* Severe depression and loss of esteem can follow. See *ibid.*

In a decision so fraught with emotional consequence some doctors may prefer not to disclose precise details of the means that will be used, confining themselves to the required statement of risks the procedure entails. From one standpoint this ought not to be surprising. Any number of patients facing imminent surgical procedures would prefer not to hear all details, lest the usual anxiety preceding invasive medical procedures become the more intense. This is likely the case with the abortion procedures here in issue.

It is, however, precisely this lack of information concerning the way in which the fetus will be killed that is of legitimate concern to the State.

Casey (plurality opinion). The State has an interest in ensuring so grave a choice is well informed. It is self-evident that a mother who comes to regret her choice to abort must struggle with grief more anguished and sorrow more profound when she learns, only after the event, what she once did not know: that she allowed a doctor to pierce the skull and vacuum the fast-developing brain of her unborn child, a child assuming the human form.

It is a reasonable inference that a necessary effect of the regulation and the knowledge it conveys will be to encourage some women to carry the infant to full term, thus reducing the absolute number of late-term abortions. The medical profession, furthermore, may find different and less shocking methods to abort the fetus in the second trimester, thereby accommodating legislative demand. The State's interest in respect for life is advanced by the dialogue that better informs the political and legal systems, the medical profession, expectant mothers, and society as a whole of the consequences that follow from a decision to elect a late-term abortion.

It is objected that the standard D&E is in some respects as brutal, if not more, than the intact D&E, so that the legislation accomplishes little. What we have already said, however, shows ample justification for the regulation. Partial-birth abortion, as defined by the Act, differs from a standard D&E because the former occurs when the fetus is partially outside the mother to the point of one of the Act's anatomical landmarks. It was reasonable for Congress to think that partial-birth abortion, more than standard D&E, "undermines the public's perception of the appropriate role of a physician during the delivery process, and perverts a process during which life is brought into the world." Congressional Findings. There would be a flaw in this Court's logic, and an irony in its jurisprudence, were we first to conclude a ban on both D&E and intact D&E was overbroad and then to say it is irrational to ban only intact D&E because that does not proscribe both procedures. In sum, we reject the contention that the congressional purpose of the Act was "to place a substantial obstacle in the path of a woman seeking an abortion." *Casey* (plurality opinion).

[B] The Act's furtherance of legitimate government interests bears upon, but does not resolve, the next question: whether the Act has the effect of imposing an unconstitutional burden on the abortion right because it does not allow use of the barred procedure where " 'necessary, in appropriate medical judgment, for [the] preservation of the . . . health of the mother.' " [W]hether the Act creates significant health risks for women has been a contested factual question. The evidence presented in the trial courts and before Congress demonstrates both sides have medical support for their position.

[For example, "abortion doctors" testified that intact D&E is safer for the pregnant woman, because it poses less risk of cervical laceration or uterine perforation and of leaving fetal material in the uterus. On the other hand, Justice Kennedy pointed to trial and congressional testimony "by other doctors" that D&E is "always" a safe alternative to intact D&E.

"There is documented medical disagreement whether the Act's prohibition would ever impose significant health risks on women."]

The question becomes whether the Act can stand when this medical uncertainty persists. The Court's precedents instruct that the Act can survive this facial attack. The Court has given state and federal legislatures wide discretion to pass legislation in areas where there is medical and scientific uncertainty.

This traditional rule is consistent with *Casey*, which confirms the State's interest in promoting respect for human life at all stages in the pregnancy. Physicians are not entitled to ignore regulations that direct them to use reasonable alternative procedures. The law need not give abortion doctors unfettered choice in the course of their medical practice, nor should it elevate their status above other physicians in the medical community. * * *

Medical uncertainty does not foreclose the exercise of legislative power in the abortion context any more than it does in other contexts. The medical uncertainty over whether the Act's prohibition creates significant health risks provides a sufficient basis to conclude in this facial attack that the Act does not impose an undue burden.

The conclusion that the Act does not impose an undue burden is supported by other considerations. Alternatives are available to the prohibited procedure. As we have noted, the Act does not proscribe D&E. One District Court found D&E to have extremely low rates of medical complications. In addition the Act's prohibition only applies to the delivery of "a living fetus." 18 U.S.C. § 1531(b)(1)(A). If the intact D&E procedure is truly necessary in some circumstances, it appears likely an injection that kills the fetus is an alternative under the Act that allows the doctor to perform the procedure. * * *

In reaching the conclusion the Act does not require a health exception we reject certain arguments made by the parties on both sides of these cases. On the one hand, the Attorney General urges us to uphold the Act on the basis of the congressional findings alone. Although we review congressional factfinding under a deferential standard, we do not in the circumstances here place dispositive weight on Congress' findings. The Court retains an independent constitutional duty to review factual findings where constitutional rights are at stake.

As respondents have noted, and the District Courts recognized, some recitations in the Act are factually incorrect. Whether or not accurate at the time, some of the important findings have been superseded. Two examples suffice. Congress determined no medical schools provide instruction on the prohibited procedure. The testimony in the District Courts, however, demonstrated intact D&E is taught at medical schools. Congress also found there existed a medical consensus that the prohibited procedure is never medically necessary. The evidence presented in the District Courts contradicts that conclusion. Uncritical deference to Congress' factual findings in these cases is inappropriate.

On the other hand, relying on the Court's opinion in *Stenberg*, respondents contend that an abortion regulation must contain a health exception "if 'substantial medical authority supports the proposition that banning a particular procedure could endanger women's health.'" As illustrated by respondents' arguments and the decisions of the Courts of Appeals, *Stenberg* has been interpreted to leave no margin of error for legislatures to act in the face of medical uncertainty.

A zero tolerance policy would strike down legitimate abortion regulations, like the present one, if some part of the medical community were disinclined to follow the proscription. This is too exacting a standard to impose on the legislative power, exercised in this instance under the Commerce Clause, to regulate the medical profession. Considerations of marginal safety, including the balance of risks, are within the legislative competence when the regulation is rational and in pursuit of legitimate ends. When standard medical options are available, mere convenience does not suffice to displace them; and if some procedures have different risks than others, it does not follow that the State is altogether barred from imposing reasonable regulations. The Act is not invalid on its face where there is uncertainty over whether the barred procedure is ever necessary to preserve a woman's health, given the availability of other abortion procedures that are considered to be safe alternatives.

[V]   The considerations we have discussed support our further determination that these facial attacks should not have been entertained in the first instance. In these circumstances the proper means to consider exceptions is by as-applied challenge. The Government has acknowledged that pre-enforcement, as-applied challenges to the Act can be maintained. This is the proper manner to protect the health of the woman if it can be shown that in discrete and well-defined instances a particular condition has or is likely to occur in which the procedure prohibited by the Act must be used. In an as-applied challenge the nature of the medical risk can be better quantified and balanced than in a facial attack. * * *

Respondents have not demonstrated that the Act, as a facial matter, is void for vagueness, or that it imposes an undue burden on a woman's right to abortion based on its overbreadth or lack of a health exception. For these reasons the judgments of the Courts of Appeals for the Eighth and Ninth Circuits are reversed.

[■ JUSTICE THOMAS, joined by JUSTICE SCALIA, concurred in Justice Kennedy's opinion. They reiterated their view that "the Court's abortion jurisprudence, including *Casey* and *Roe v. Wade*, has no basis in the Constitution." Justice Thomas also noted that the parties had not raised the question of whether the statute exceeded Congress's Article I powers and, therefore, that the validity of Congress's exercising jurisdiction over this issue was not before the Court.]

■ JUSTICE GINSBURG, with whom JUSTICE STEVENS, JUSTICE SOUTER, and JUSTICE BREYER join, dissenting. * * *

Today's decision is alarming. It refuses to take *Casey* and *Stenberg* seriously. It tolerates, indeed applauds, federal intervention to ban nationwide a procedure found necessary and proper in certain cases by the American College of Obstetricians and Gynecologists (ACOG). It blurs the line, firmly drawn in *Casey*, between previability and postviability abortions. And, for the first time since *Roe*, the Court blesses a prohibition with no exception safeguarding a woman's health.

I dissent from the Court's disposition. Retreating from prior rulings that abortion restrictions cannot be imposed absent an exception safeguarding a woman's health, the Court upholds an Act that surely would not survive under the close scrutiny that previously attended state-decreed limitations on a woman's reproductive choices. * * *

[I]   As *Casey* comprehended, at stake in cases challenging abortion restrictions is a woman's "control over her own destiny." * * * [L]egal challenges to undue restrictions on abortion procedures do not seek to vindicate some generalized notion of privacy; rather, they center on a woman's autonomy to determine her life's course, and thus to enjoy equal citizenship stature. See, e.g., Siegel, Reasoning from the Body: A Historical Perspective on Abortion Regulation and Questions of Equal Protection, 44 Stan. L. Rev. 261 (1992); Law, Rethinking Sex and the Constitution, 132 U. Pa.L. rev. 955, 1002–28 (1984).

In keeping with this comprehension of the right to reproductive choice, the Court has consistently required that laws regulating abortion, at any stage of pregnancy and in all cases, safeguard a woman's health. *Stenberg*.

[Justice Ginsburg noted that the federal statute had no health exception, based upon incorrect assumptions, such as the congressional finding that "[t]here is no credible medical evidence that partial-birth abortions are safe or are safer than other abortion procedures." Yet ACOG and other medical associations attested to Congress and the trial courts that "intact D&E carries meaningful safety advantages over other methods." Intact D&E minimizes the number of times a physician must insert instruments through the cervix and into the uterus, a minimization that helps the woman avoid risks of tearing and infection. Intact D&E reduces the risk that fetal material will be left in the uterus, which can cause infection, hemorrhage, and infertility. Intact D&E diminishes the chances of exposing the woman's tissues to sharp bony fragments sometimes resulting from dismemberment of the fetus. Intact D&E takes less operating time, thereby reducing risks of complications relating to anesthesia. Justice Ginsburg maintained that there was no reasonable basis to believe otherwise, as reflected in the trial records.]

[II.]   The Court offers flimsy and transparent justifications for upholding a nationwide ban on intact D&E *sans* any exception to safeguard a women's health. Today's ruling, the Court declares, advances "a premise central to [*Casey*'s] conclusion"—*i.e.,* the Government's "legitimate and substantial interest in preserving and promoting fetal life." But the Act scarcely furthers that interest: The law saves not a single fetus from destruction, for it targets only a *method* of performing abortion. And surely the statute was not designed to protect the lives or health of pregnant women. In short, the Court upholds a law that, while doing nothing to "preserv[e] ... fetal life," bars a woman from choosing intact D&E although her doctor "reasonably believes [that procedure] will best protect [her]." * * *

Ultimately, the Court admits that "moral concerns" are at work, concerns that could yield prohibitions on any abortion. Notably, the concerns expressed are untethered to any ground genuinely serving the Government's interest in preserving life. By allowing such concerns to carry the day and case, overriding fundamental rights, the Court dishonors our precedent.

Revealing in this regard, the Court invokes an antiabortion shibboleth for which it concededly has no reliable evidence: Women who have abortions come to regret their choices, and consequently suffer from "[s]evere depression and loss of esteem." Because of women's fragile emotional state and because of the "bond of love the mother has for her child," the Court worries, doctors may withhold information about the nature of the intact D&E procedure. The solution the Court approves, then, is *not* to require doctors to inform women, accurately and adequately, of the different procedures and their attendant risks. Instead, the Court deprives women of the right to make an autonomous choice, even at the expense of their safety.

This way of thinking reflects ancient notions about women's place in the family and under the Constitution—ideas that have long since been discredited.

Though today's majority may regard women's feelings on the matter as "self-evident," this Court has repeatedly confirmed that "[t]he destiny of the woman must be shaped ... on her own conception of her spiritual imperatives and her place in society." *Casey.* * * *

[III] If there is anything at all redemptive to be said of today's opinion, it is that the Court is not willing to foreclose entirely a constitutional challenge to the Act. "The Act is open," the Court states, "to a proper as-applied challenge in a discrete case." But the Court offers no clue on what a "proper" lawsuit might look like. Nor does the Court explain why the injunctions ordered by the District Courts should not remain in place, trimmed only to exclude instances in which another procedure would safeguard a woman's health at least equally well. Surely the Court cannot mean that no suit may be brought until a woman's health is immediately jeopardized by the ban on intact D&E. A woman "suffer[ing] from medical complications," needs access to the medical procedure at once and cannot wait for the judicial process to unfold.

The Court appears, then, to contemplate another lawsuit by the initiators of the instant actions. In such a second round, the Court suggests, the challengers could succeed upon demonstrating that "in discrete and well-defined instances a particular condition has or is likely to occur in which the procedure prohibited by the Act must be used." One may anticipate that such a preenforcement challenge will be mounted swiftly, to ward off serious, sometimes irremediable harm, to women whose health would be endangered by the intact D&E prohibition. * * *

[IV]   As the Court wrote in *Casey*, "overruling *Roe*'s central holding would not only reach an unjustifiable result under principles of *stare decisis*, but would seriously weaken the Court's capacity to exercise the judicial power and to function as the Supreme Court of a Nation dedicated to the rule of law."

Though today's opinion does not go so far as to discard *Roe* or *Casey*, the Court, differently constituted than it was when we last considered a restrictive abortion regulation, is hardly faithful to our earlier invocations of the "rule of law" and the "principles of *stare decisis*." * * *

* * * In candor, the Act, and the Court's defense of it, cannot be understood as anything other than an effort to chip away at a right declared again and again by this Court—and with increasing comprehension of its centrality to women's lives. * * *

NOTES ON *CARHART* AND THE PRIVACY RIGHT

1. *Is There a Core to the Privacy Right?* Carefully review the analytical give-and-take between the majority and the dissenters. Does Justice Kennedy have persuasive answers to Justice Ginsburg's arguments that the Court is departing from precedent in various ways, including *Stenberg*'s holding that state limits on previability abortion methods include a mother's health exception, *Casey*'s holding that the state cannot impose undue burdens on women seeking previability abortions, and perhaps even *Roe*'s apparent holding that morality alone cannot justify restrictions on a woman's right to choose? All of these earlier cases are, of course, distinguishable (Kennedy's main response), but the question remains whether the Court is departing from reasoning essential to these precedents. How does a Justice neutrally determine that?

Justice Ginsburg's dissenting opinion essentially accuses the majority—five politically and religiously conservative males—of writing their morality into the Constitution. Implicit in the context within which her opinion was read in open Court was the suggestion that a Court that once included two women would not have ruled this way. Justice O'Connor was in the *Stenberg* majority, while her replacement, Justice Alito, was in the *Carhart* majority.

As in *Carhart,* women may still have a "liberty" to choose abortions, but not after viability and, now, not the safest procedure for late-term (previability) abortions. The Court responds that *Casey* set a "balance," and the woman's liberty is just one prong of that balance. Justice Ginsburg worries: If women's possible regret and state concern for the sanctity of life can trump women's liberty to choose intact D&E, why can these concerns also not trump women's ability to choose D&E itself, which destroys the fetus (or baby) in gruesome ways and therefore also triggers regrets.

What *principle* now governs a woman's "liberty" to choose abortions after *Carhart*?

Recall Judge Bork's criticism of the privacy right as having no legal core, because it is not based upon any constitutional text or legal tradition (Casebook, pp. 20–23). It will mean whatever five Justices want it to mean, based upon their own moral philosophy *or* public opinion (most states adopted laws that went beyond the federal statute *Carhart* sustained) *or* simply their own feelings of *disgust.* Although we have edited the majority opinion's extensive description of the intact D&E procedure, the nurse's description of it in our excerpt conveys to you the palpable disgust that Justice Kennedy must feel toward the procedure. Bluntly, intact D&E looks too much like infanticide for the nurse and Justice Kennedy to find it acceptable.

2. *The Relationship of* Carhart *to* Lawrence. There are some similarities between *Carhart* and *Lawrence,* now the two most-discussed constitutional privacy decisions in the new millennium. Justice Kennedy, the author of five-Justice majority opinions in both cases, overrules (*Lawrence*) or narrowly construes (*Carhart*) recent precedents; abandons the "fundamental rights" rhetoric and treats privacy as simply a due process "liberty" that can be regulated in a number of ways, but not "too much"; and follows the moral consensus reached by large majorities of the states, which had repealed their sodomy laws (*Lawrence*) or adopted partial-birth abortion statutes (*Carhart*).

The differences between the two opinions are more notable, however. Paradoxically, the differences might help us understand the limits of *Lawrence* as well as the normative problems with *Carhart.*

First, equal citizenship plays a key role in *Lawrence,* as a reason to give the privacy right bite, while it is not only ignored but rhetorically inverted in *Carhart.* Justice Ginsburg's dissent not only emphasizes the relationship of abortion choice to women's equal citizenship, but also charges that the Court's rhetoric reveals a slanted perspective. Women appear in the majority opinion as body parts (Justice Kennedy has more to say about "uteruses" and "cervixes" than women as workers and family planners) operated upon by "abortion doctors." In the one passage where women appear as subjects rather than objects, Justice Kennedy presents them as decision-makers prone to regret the abortion procedure.

This does *not* mean that *Carhart* returns women to a period where their "natural" role as domestics prevented or impeded their participation in public life—any more than *Lawrence* means that the state can never discriminate against lesbians, gay men, bisexuals, and transgendered people. (This latter point is a reading of *Lawrence* that may be normatively attractive, but it is clearly *not* a reading to which the Court has committed itself.) Both *Carhart* and *Lawrence* are about how much majoritarian social attitudes must yield to personal liberty decisions that group members feel they need to carry out their life projects. Because it is overruling a decision that denied gay people any equal treatment (*Bowers*), *Lawrence* can honestly present itself as egalitarian, but that does not mean that the Court would go "all the way" to marriage for gay rights. Likewise, *Roe* can be imagined as an egalitarian decision (as the Court did in *Casey*), but *Carhart* indicates the Court will not go "all the way" in this regard either.

Second, morality plays a strikingly different role in the two cases. *Lawrence* announces that sectarian morality cannot justify invading gay people's privacy—but *Carhart* says that the same kind of natural law morality can require women seeking late-term abortions to fall back on riskier procedures. Justice Kennedy does not see these different roles of morality to be inconsistent. Recall that he co-authored the Joint Opinion in *Casey*, so he has put himself on record that women's abortion choices cannot be completely foreclosed by moral views. From his point of view, *Lawrence* is analogous to *Casey*. *Carhart*, then, might be analogous to a decision upholding choices that Justice Kennedy believes are not central to the lives of homosexuals. In other words, *Carhart* makes it clear that, for the current Court, public morality remains relevant as a limitation on the privacy right. The limitation is floating and indeterminate—but so is the privacy right.

Third, disgust plays a different role in the two cases. In *Lawrence*, Justice Kennedy says nothing about what actually goes on in the homosexual bedroom, while his *Carhart* opinion lays out the process of partial-birth abortion from the perspective of a nurse who views it as killing a helpless baby. Most readers will be disgusted by what they read in Part I of *Carhart*, only the most dedicated homophobe would be disgusted by the sanitized presentation of gay relationships in *Lawrence*. This is the deepest and most disturbing difference between the two opinions. It is apparent that the *Bowers* majority found homosexual relations disgusting and were unable to see any human connection there—and that directly generated the result in *Bowers*. See William Eskridge, Jr., *Dishonorable Passions: Sodomy Law in America, 1861–2003* (forthcoming 2008) (detailed account of *Bowers*). It appears that the majority Justices (and at least one dissenter, Justice Thomas) found nothing particularly disgusting about homosexual relations in *Lawrence*. But Justices Kennedy and Thomas, unfazed by anal sex in one case, are horrified by what they consider infanticide in the other.

All three points are related. Social scientists have found that people's moral opinions are shaped by what "disgusts" them, and public morality is shaped by creating disgusting images and associating them with certain people (homosexuals) or practices (sodomy) or both (the homosexual is always a disgusting sodomite). Reflecting modern social attitudes, *Lawrence* disrupts that process for homosexuals and sodomy, but *Carhart* initiates a new process that partially reverses what *Roe v. Wade* and *Casey* were trying to do, namely, disaggregate women's life choices from folk images of abortion as infanticide. Where this is going is determined by social attitudes and politics (including who the next Justices will be), not by law, strictly speaking.

3. *Overlapping Justifications for Abortion Restrictions.* Notice how pro-life legal as well as political rhetoric has changed since *Roe v. Wade.* Most pro-life Americans believe their position is required by religious faith and God's commands in Scripture and Church doctrine. The Roman Catholic Church has long considered any kind of abortion, however early in the pregnancy and however performed, to be the moral equivalent of murder; from the Church's point of view, the fetus is a human being, *Imago Dei* (in the Image of God), from the point of insemination. Protestant Churches were long neutral on this issue, but in the decade after *Roe v. Wade* many of them formulated doctrinal positions similar to that of the Catholic Church.

Nineteenth century abortion laws were justified by medical science as necessary to "protect" the health of the mother. The first part of Chapter 1 documents the power of medical arguments in Sanger's birth control movement and in *Roe v. Wade*; many feminists, including Justice Ginsburg, are ambivalent about the prominent role of doctors in the creation of an abortion-protective jurisprudence. In *Carhart*, both sides rely heavily on medical discourse. The "medical" nature of the discourse in *Carhart* explicitly overlaps with and subsumes the underlying moral discourse. In one of the most heartfelt passages, Justice Kennedy's opinion quotes from a nurse's description of partial-birth abortion, where the doctor "grabbed the baby's legs," and then "the baby's body and arms," and then stuck scissors into the head, "and the baby's arms jerked out, like a startle reaction, like a flinch, like a baby does when he thinks he is going to fall." The "baby went limp" when the doctor "sucked the baby's brains out." It is impossible to see where morality ends and medicine starts; the two are inextricably intertwined. However characterized, this discourse exercised a powerful hold on Justice Kennedy.

The last layer of argumentation is civic republican, the rhetoric of deliberation. Critics of *Roe v. Wade* have long maintained that constitutionalizing abortion choice takes a loaded moral issue out of the deliberative legislative process. *Carhart* illustrates a feature of the debate that the informed consent laws also reflected: focus on decisionmaking *regret.* The individual *woman*, the mother, often regrets the decision, Justice Kennedy informs the country, and this is a state justification for barring a particularly grisly method of abortion choice. This is an important, but by no means new, modernization of pro-life rhetoric. See Reva Siegel, "The New

Politics of Abortion: An Equality Analysis of Woman–Protecting Abortion Restrictions," 2007 *U. Ill. L. Rev.* 992.

NOTE ON OPERATION OUTCRY

The argument that women regret abortions has been an important theme of the pro-life social movement since the 1980s, if not before. (Informed consent and mandatory counseling laws of the 1970s as well as 1980s rested at least in part on this idea.) As early as 1981, pro-life thinkers were referring to *post-abortion syndrome*, a variant of post-traumatic stress disorder. Although post-abortion syndrome was rejected as a medical concept by pro-life Surgeon General C. Everett Koop and has never been recognized by a professional medical association, it has achieved a robust status as folk wisdom for many Americans. See Emily Bazelon, "Is There a Post–Abortion Syndrome?," *N.Y. Times Magazine,* Jan. 21, 2007.

Even though medical opinion remained skeptical, the concept of abortion-regret was a potentially powerful feature of a new identity politics. David Reardon argued in *Making Abortion Rare* (1986) that the pro-life movement would not prevail with ordinary Americans so long as it limited its arguments to the sanctity of fetal life. "We must change the abortion debate so that we are arguing with our opponents on their own turf, on the issue of defending the interests of women." An increasing number of pro-life leaders and organizations have taken up this call and argued against abortion as a matter of women's own mental health.

Founded in Texas, the Justice Foundation (now with chapters in 22 states) created *Operation Outcry* as a project "to end legal abortion by exposing the truth about its devastating impact on women and families. We believe this will be accomplished through prayer and with testimonies of mothers who have taken the life of their own unborn babies and of others who have suffered harm from abortion." (Source: www.operationoutcry. org.) Operation Outcry has collected sworn affidavits from thousands of women, most of whom have submitted their testimonies through the operation's website. These sworn affidavits were the factual basis for an abortion ban adopted by the South Dakota Legislature in 2005 (later revoked) and for the *amicus* brief Justice Kennedy credited in *Carhart.*

The methodology of Operation Outcry bears some similarity to the consciousness-raising method of some feminist political campaigns, such as the anti-porn campaigns in Minneapolis and Indianapolis in the early 1980s. It has thus far attracted little support within mainstream medical science. "The best studies available on psychological responses to unwanted pregnancy terminated by abortion in the United States suggest that severe negative reactions are rare, and they parallel those following other normal life stresses." N.E. Adler et al., "Psychological Factors in Abortion: A Review," *American Psychologist*, Oct. 1992, 1194, 1202. Does the lack of an *empirical* basis mean that this evidence cannot suffice as a basis for state policy?

CHAPTER 2

EQUALITY CHALLENGES TO STATE SEX AND SEXUALITY DISCRIMINATIONS

SECTION 1

SEX DISCRIMINATIONS

Page 215.   Insert the following Case and Note right before Problem 2–3:

Alberto R. Gonzalez v. Leroy Carhart et al.
United States Supreme Court, 2007.
— U.S. —, 127 S.Ct. 1610, 167 L.Ed.2d 480.

[Excerpted in Chapter 1 of this Supplement]

NOTE ON *CARHART* AND THE COURT'S SEX DISCRIMINATION JURISPRUDENCE

Justices Kennedy and Ginsburg take completely different stances as regards the equality features of the Partial–Birth Abortion Act of 2003. Justice Ginsburg views this as a case about women's citizenship and implicating the Court's sex discrimination jurisprudence, epitomized by her own opinion in the VMI Case (Casebook, pp. 192–202). Unlike the VMI Case, *Carhart* does not evaluate a law that explicitly discriminates on the basis of sex. But abortion laws do operate uniquely and exclusively on only one sex, namely, women. Moreover, abortion laws generally, and the partial-birth abortion law in particular, operate disproportionately on young, poor, and working class pregnant women. Such women are more likely to have abortions later in their pregnancies. Lawrence Finer et al., "Timing of Steps and Reasons for Delays in Obtaining Abortions in the United States," 74 *Contraception* 334 (2006). By removing a relatively safer choice (intact D&E) for late-term abortions, *Carhart* makes the process especially dangerous and stressful for younger and less wealthy women, including women of color disproportionately.

Consistent with *Casey* (now the Court's leading statement on abortion) and *Nguyen* (the recent case where citizenship was, literally, gendered), *Carhart* reflects a new post-*Loving* approach to equality jurisprudence on the part of the Justices. Without overruling the tiered approach to equal protection reflected in *Loving* (strict scrutiny for race-based classifications) and *Craig* (intermediate scrutiny for sex-based classifications), *Nguyen* and *Carhart* reflect a sliding scale approach akin to but more institutionally conservative than the analogous approach Justice Marshall advocated long ago in *San Antonio Independent School District v. Rodriguez*, 411 U.S. 1 (1973) (Casebook, pp. 173–74).

The new equality jurisprudence considers (1) the nature of the impact of a suspicious classification, with classifications having a race- or sex-based discriminatory effect being treated much more leniently than those which are explicitly race- or sex-based; (2) the importance of liberties denied to the class subject to the discrimination; and (3) the weightiness of the state justifications, including institutional and political justifications. There is plenty of room for disagreement applying such a sliding scale, as reflected in *Carhart*, but this is probably the prevailing approach within the Court. Consider this point as you read the sexual orientation cases in Section 2 of this chapter, especially *Romer v. Evans* (Casebook, pages 259–71) and *Lawrence v. Texas* (Casebook, pages 78–91 and 274–79), and then the lower court cases applying or (typically) declining to apply the pro-gay rights rulings in those landmark Supreme Court cases.

SECTION 2

SEXUAL ORIENTATION DISCRIMINATIONS

Page 282. Insert the following Case and Note before Problem 2–5:

Steven Lofton et al. v. Secretary of the Department of Children and Social Services et al.

United States Court of Appeals for the Eleventh Circuit, 2004.
358 F.3d 804, *petition for en banc review denied,* 377 F.3d 1275.

■ JUDGE BIRCH

Since 1977, Florida's adoption law has contained a codified prohibition on adoption by any "homosexual" person. 1977 Fla. Laws, ch. 77–140, § 1, Fla. Stat. § 63.042(3) (2002). For purposes of this statute, Florida courts have defined the term "homosexual" as being "limited to applicants who are known to engage in current, voluntary homosexual activity," thus drawing "a distinction between homosexual orientation and homosexual activity." *Fla. Dep't of Health & Rehab. Servs.*, 627 So.2d 1210, 1215 (Fla. Dist. Ct. App. 1993), aff'd in relevant part, 656 So. 2d 902, 903 (Fla. 1995). During the past twelve years, several legislative bills have attempted to repeal the statute, and three separate legal challenges to it have been filed in the Florida courts. To date, no attempt to overturn the provision has succeeded. We now consider the most recent challenge to the statute.

[Steven Lofton and his life partner Roger Croteau, both pediatric nurses, have adopted six HIV-positive children in the last 20 years. One of them, identified by the Court as "John Doe," was born in 1991, and sero-converted after about a year in Lofton and Croteau's care. In September of 1994, Lofton filed an application to adopt Doe but refused to answer the application's inquiry about his sexual preference and also failed to disclose Croteau as a member of his household. After Lofton refused requests from the Department of Children and Families ("DCF") to supply the missing information, his application was rejected pursuant to the homosexual adoption provision.]

[Judge Birch carefully analyzed Florida's adoption law scheme, which trains closely on the "best interests of the child."] Because of the primacy of the welfare of the child, the state can make classifications for adoption purposes that would be constitutionally suspect in many other arenas. For example, Florida law requires that, in order to adopt any child other than a special needs child, an individual's primary residence and place of employment must be located in Florida. Fla. Stat. § 63.185. In screening adoption applicants, Florida considers such factors as physical and mental health, income and financial status, duration of marriage, housing, and neighborhood, among others. Fla. Admin. Code Ann. Rule 65C–16.005(3) (2003). Similarly, Florida gives preference to candidates who demonstrate a commitment to "value, respect, appreciate, and educate the child regarding his or her racial and ethnic heritage." Id. Moreover, prospective adoptive parents are required to sign an affidavit of good moral character. Id. Many of these preferences and requirements, if employed outside the adoption arena, would be unlikely to withstand constitutional scrutiny.

[Lofton and the other challengers made three arguments: The homosexual exclusion violated their due process rights to family integrity and sexual intimacy, and was a classification abridging the Equal Protection Clause. The Court rejected all three arguments.]

[*The Family Integrity Argument.*] Although the text of the Constitution contains no reference to familial or parental rights, Supreme Court precedent has long recognized that "the Due Process Clause of the Fourteenth Amendment protects the fundamental right of parents to make decisions concerning the care, custody, and control of their children." [*Troxel v. Nebraska*, 530 U.S. 57, 66 (2000) (Casebook, pp. 1178–82).] A corollary to this right is the "private realm of family life which the state cannot enter that has been afforded both substantive and procedural protection." *Smith v. Org. of Foster Families for Equal. & Reform,* 431 U.S. 816, 842 (1977). Historically, the Court's family-and parental-rights holdings have involved biological families. See, e.g., *Troxel*; *Wisconsin v. Yoder,* 406 U.S. 205 (1972); *Stanley v. Illinois,* 405 U.S. 645 (1972); *Pierce v. Soc'y of Sisters,* 268 U.S. 510 (1925); *Meyer v. Nebraska,* 262 U.S. 390 (1923). The Court itself has noted that "the usual understanding of 'family' implies biological relationships, and most decisions treating the relation between parent and child have stressed this element." *Smith.* Appellants, however, seize on a few lines of dicta from *Smith,* in which the Court acknowledged that "biological relationships are not [the] exclusive determination of the existence of a family," and noted that "adoption, for instance, is recognized as the legal equivalent of biological parenthood." Extrapolating from *Smith,* appellants argue that parental and familial rights should be extended to individuals such as foster parents and legal guardians and that the touchstone of this liberty interest is not biological ties or official legal recognition, but the emotional bond that develops between and among individuals as a result of shared daily life.

We do not read *Smith* so broadly. In *Smith,* the Court considered whether the appellee foster families possessed a constitutional liberty interest in "the integrity of their family unit" such that the state could not disrupt the families without procedural due process. Although the Court found it unnecessary to resolve that question, Justice Brennan, writing for the majority, did note that the importance of familial relationships stems not merely from blood relationships, but also from "the emotional attachments that derive from the intimacy of daily association." The *Smith* Court went on, however, to discuss the "important distinctions between the foster family and the natural family," particularly the fact that foster families have their genesis in state law. The Court stressed that the parameters of whatever potential liberty interest such families might possess would be defined by state law and the justifiable expectations it created. * * *

* * * Here, we find that under Florida law neither a foster parent nor a legal guardian could have a justifiable expectation of a permanent relationship with his or her child free from state oversight or intervention. Under Florida law, foster care is designed to be a short-term arrangement while the state attempts to find a permanent adoptive home. For instance, Florida law permits foster care as a "permanency option" only for children at least fourteen years of age, Fla. Stat. § 39.623(1), and DCF may remove a foster child anytime that it believes it to be in the child's best interests, id. § 409.165(3)(f). Similarly, legal guardians in Florida are subject to ongoing judicial oversight, including the duty to file annual guardianship reports and annual review by the appointing court, id. § § 744.361–372, and can be removed for a wide variety of reasons, id. § 744.474 (permitting removal of a guardian for such causes as incapacity, illness, substance abuse, conviction of a felony, failure to file annual guardianship reports, and failure to fulfill guardianship education requirements). In both cases, the state is not interfering with natural family units that exist independent of its power, but is regulating ones created by it. Lofton and Houghton entered into relationships to be a foster parent and legal guardian, respectively, with an implicit understanding that these relationships would not be immune from state oversight and would be permitted to continue only upon state approval. The emotional connections between Lofton and his foster child and between Houghton and his ward originate in arrangements that have been subject to state oversight from the outset. We conclude that Lofton, Doe, Houghton, and Roe could have no justifiable expectation of permanency in their relationships. Nor could Lofton and Houghton have developed expectations that they would be allowed to adopt, in light of the adoption provision itself.

[*Burden on Fundamental Right to Private Sexual Intimacy*] Laws that burden the exercise of a fundamental right require strict scrutiny and are sustained only if narrowly tailored to further a compelling government interest. Appellants argue that the Supreme Court's recent decision in *Lawrence v. Texas* (Casebook, pp. 78–91), which struck down Texas's sodomy statute, identified a hitherto unarticulated fundamental right to private sexual intimacy. They contend that the Florida statute, by disallowing adoption to any individual who chooses to engage in homosexual conduct, impermissibly burdens the exercise of this right.

We begin with the threshold question of whether *Lawrence* identified a new fundamental right to private sexual intimacy. *Lawrence*'s holding was that substantive due process does not permit a state to impose a criminal prohibition on private consensual homosexual conduct. The effect of this holding was to establish a greater respect than previously existed in the law for the right of consenting adults to engage in private sexual conduct. Nowhere, however, did the Court characterize this right as "fundamental." Nor did the Court locate this right directly in the Constitution, but instead treated it as the by-product of several different constitutional principles and liberty interests.

[Judge Birch then distinguished *Lawrence*, quoting language at the end of Justice Kennedy's opinion, that the Texas case did not involve minors and so forth.] Here, the involved actors are not only consenting adults, but minors as well. The relevant state action is not criminal prohibition, but grant of a statutory privilege. And the asserted liberty interest is not the negative right to engage in private conduct without facing criminal sanctions, but the affirmative right to receive official and public recognition. Hence, we conclude that the *Lawrence* decision cannot be extrapolated to create a right to adopt for homosexual persons.

[*Equal Protection* Because the Court found neither a fundamental right nor a suspect classification, the Court evaluated the ban of homosexual adoption along rational basis lines.] Cognizant of the narrow parameters of our review, we now analyze the challenged Florida law. Florida contends that the statute is only one aspect of its broader adoption policy, which is designed to create adoptive homes that resemble the nuclear family as closely as possible. Florida argues that the statute is rationally related to Florida's interest in furthering the best interests of adopted children by placing them in families with married mothers and fathers. Such homes, Florida asserts, provide the stability that marriage affords and the presence of both male and female authority figures, which it considers critical to optimal childhood development and socialization. In particular, Florida emphasizes a vital role that dual-gender parenting plays in shaping sexual and gender identity and in providing heterosexual role modeling. Florida argues that disallowing adoption into homosexual households, which are necessarily motherless or fatherless and lack the stability that comes with marriage, is a rational means of furthering Florida's interest in promoting adoption by marital families. * * *

[T]he state has a legitimate interest in encouraging this optimal family structure by seeking to place adoptive children in homes that have both a mother and father. Florida argues that its preference for adoptive marital families is based on the premise that the marital family structure is more stable than other household arrangements and that children benefit from the presence of both a father and mother in the home. Given that appellants have offered no competent evidence to the contrary, we find this premise to be one of those "unprovable assumptions" that nevertheless can provide a legitimate basis for legislative action. *Paris Adult Theatre I v. Slaton,* 413 U.S. 49, 62–63 (1973). Although social theorists from Plato to Simone de Beauvoir have proposed alternative child-rearing arrangements, none has proven as enduring as the marital family structure, nor has the accumulated wisdom of several millennia of human experience discovered a superior model. See, e.g., Plato, *The Republic,* Bk. V, 459d–461e; Simone de Beauvoir, *The Second Sex* (H. M. Parshley trans., Vintage Books 1989) (1949). Against this "sum of experience," it is rational for Florida to conclude that it is in the best interests of adoptive children, many of whom come from troubled and unstable backgrounds, to be placed in a home anchored by both a father and a mother.

[The challengers claimed that the classification (homosexual) was not reasonably related to this goal.] Appellants note that Florida law permits adoption by unmarried individuals and that, among children coming out the Florida foster care system, 25% of adoptions are to parents who are currently single. Their argument is that homosexual persons are similarly situated to unmarried persons with regard to Florida's asserted interest in promoting married-couple adoption. According to appellants, this disparate treatment lacks a rational basis and, therefore, disproves any rational connection between the statute and Florida's asserted interest in promoting adoption into married homes. Citing *City of Cleburne v. Cleburne Living Ctr. Inc.,* 473 U.S. 432 (1985), appellants argue that the state has not satisfied *Cleburne*'s threshold requirement that it demonstrate that homosexuals pose a unique threat to children that others similarly situated in relevant respects do not. * * *

This case is distinguishable from *Cleburne.* The Florida legislature could rationally conclude that homosexuals and heterosexual singles are not "similarly situated in relevant respects." It is not irrational to think that heterosexual singles have a markedly greater probability of eventually establishing a married household and, thus, providing their adopted children with a stable, dual-gender parenting environment. Moreover, as the state noted, the legislature could rationally act on the theory that heterosexual singles, even if they never marry, are better positioned than homosexual individuals to provide adopted children with education and guidance relative to their sexual development throughout pubescence and adolescence. In a previous challenge to Florida's statute, a Florida appellate court observed:

> Whatever causes a person to become a homosexual, it is clear that the state cannot know the sexual preferences that a child will exhibit as an adult. Statistically, the state does know that a very high percentage of children available for adoption will develop heterosexual preferences. As a result, those children will need education and guidance after puberty concerning relationships with the opposite sex. In our society, we expect that parents will provide this education to teenagers in the home. These subjects are often very embarrassing for teenagers and

some aspects of the education are accomplished by the parents telling stories about their own adolescence and explaining their own experiences with the opposite sex. It is in the best interests of a child if his or her parents can personally relate to the child's problems and assist the child in the difficult transition to heterosexual adulthood. Given that adopted children tend to have some developmental problems arising from adoption or from their experiences prior to adoption, it is perhaps more important for adopted children than other children to have a stable heterosexual household during puberty and the teenage years.

Cox, 627 So. 2d at 1220. * * *

Appellants cite recent social science research and the opinion of mental health professionals and child welfare organizations as evidence that there is no child welfare basis for excluding homosexuals from adopting. They argue that the cited studies show that the parenting skills of homosexual parents are at least equivalent to those of heterosexual parents and that children raised by homosexual parents suffer no adverse outcomes. Appellants also point to the policies and practices of numerous adoption agencies that permit homosexual persons to adopt.

In considering appellants' argument, we must ask not whether the latest in social science research and professional opinion *support* the decision of the Florida legislature, but whether that evidence is so well established and so far beyond dispute that it would be irrational for the Florida legislature to believe that the interests of its children are best served by not permitting homosexual adoption. Also, we must credit any conceivable rational reason that the legislature might have for choosing not to alter its statutory scheme in response to this recent social science research. We must assume, for example, that the legislature might be aware of the critiques of the studies cited by appellants—critiques that have highlighted significant flaws in the studies' methodologies and conclusions, such as the use of small, self-selected samples; reliance on self-report instruments; politically driven hypotheses; and the use of unrepresentative study populations consisting of disproportionately affluent, educated parents. Alternatively, the legislature might consider and credit other studies that have found that children raised in homosexual households fare differently on a number of measures, doing worse on some of them, than children raised in similarly situated heterosexual households.[25] Or the legislature might consider, and even credit, the research cited by appellants, but find it premature to rely on a very recent and still developing

---

25. See, e.g., K. Cameron & P. Cameron, Homosexual Parents, 31 Adolescence 757, 770–774 (1996) (reporting study findings that children raised by homosexual parents suffer from disproportionately high incidence of emotional disturbance and sexual victimization); J. Stacey & T. Biblarz, (How) Does the Sexual Orientation of Parents Matter, 66 Am. Soc. Rev. 159, 170 (2001) (concluding, based on study results, that "parental sexual orientation is positively associated with the possibility that children will attain a similar orientation, and theory and common sense also support such a view").

body of research, particularly in light of the absence of longitudinal studies following child subjects into adulthood and of studies of adopted, rather than natural, children of homosexual parents.

[The Court distinguished *Romer v. Evans* (Casebook, pp. 259–71).] Unlike Colorado's Amendment 2 [struck down in *Romer*], Florida's statute is not so "sweeping and comprehensive" as to render Florida's rationales for the statute "inexplicable by anything but animus" toward its homosexual residents. Amendment 2 deprived homosexual persons of "protections against exclusion from an almost limitless number of transactions and endeavors that constitute ordinary civic life in a free society." In contrast to this "broad and undifferentiated disability," the Florida classification is limited to the narrow and discrete context of access to the statutory privilege of adoption and, more importantly, has a plausible connection with the state's asserted interest. Moreover, not only is the effect of Florida's classification dramatically smaller, but the classification itself is narrower. Whereas Amendment 2's classification encompassed both conduct *and* status, Florida's adoption prohibition is limited to conduct. Thus, we conclude that *Romer's* unique factual situation and narrow holding are inapposite to this case.

On Petition for Rehearing En Banc, 377 F.3d 1275

[Upon petition for rehearing en banc, six judges (Anderson, Barkett, Dubina, Marcus, Tjoflat, Wilson) of the full Eleventh Circuit voted to rehear the case en banc; six did not vote for rehearing. Because there was no *majority*, the rehearing was denied. Judge Barkett wrote a full-fledged critique of the panel opinion; Judge Birch responded.]

■ Judge Barkett, dissenting from the denial of rehearing en banc.

[*Equal Protection*] [T]he classification at issue in this case burdens personal relationships and exudes animus against a politically unpopular group. Under these circumstances, statutes have consistently failed rational basis review. Summarizing these cases, Justice O'Connor observed in her concurrence in *Lawrence* that

> laws such as economic or tax legislation that are scrutinized under rational basis review normally pass constitutional muster, since the Constitution presumes that even improvident decisions will eventually be rectified by the democratic processes. We have consistently held, however, that some objectives, such as a bare ... desire to harm a politically unpopular group, are not legitimate state interests. When a law exhibits such a desire to harm a politically unpopular group, we have applied a more searching form of rational basis review to strike down such laws under the Equal Protection Clause.

Lawrence (O'Connor, J., concurring). Justice O'Connor went on to explain how this principle has been applied by the Court in prior equal protection cases. [Justice O'Connor gave as examples of more searching review *Moreno, Cleburne, Eisenstadt,* and *Romer.*]

All four of these precedents involved legislation targeting politically unpopular groups to varying degrees: "hippies" (*Moreno*), unmarried users of birth control (*Eisenstadt*), the mentally disabled (*Cleburne*), and homosexuals (*Romer*). Moreover, in each case, the Court invalidated a law that had the effect of inhibiting personal relationships of one sort or another: among mentally disabled or unrelated persons who wished to share a common living space (*Cleburne* and *Moreno*); among unmarried individuals who wished to engage in intimate relations (*Eisenstadt*); and among individuals who wished to live without fear of state-sanctioned discrimination prompted solely by their attachment to persons of the same sex (*Romer*). * * *

* * * Florida prohibits homosexuals from being considered as adoptive parents because it wishes to place children with married couples. It wishes to do so for two alleged reasons: (1) to provide "stability" in the home, which the panel apparently believes can only be provided by married couples representing the "nuclear" family model; and (2) to properly shape heterosexual "sexual and gender identity," which the panel asserts should be accomplished by married couples.

Like the proffered reasons in *Eisenstadt*, which were "so riddled with exceptions" that the state's asserted goal could not "reasonably be regarded as its aim," the state's proffered rational basis for the statute here (providing adopted children with married couples as parents) cannot be legitimately credited because it fails the equal protection requirement that "all persons similarly situated should be treated alike." *Cleburne*. As noted at the beginning of this dissent, it is plainly false that Florida has established a preference for "married mothers and fathers" as adoptive parents. The 1977 statute prohibiting homosexual adoption expresses no preference whatsoever for married couples, expressly permitting an "unmarried adult" to adopt. Fla. Stat. § 63.042(2)(b) (2003). Moreover, the DCF administrative regulations that are inextricably tied to Florida's adoption statutes do not prefer married over single candidates for adoption. In short, the Florida legislature never did, and the Florida executive no longer does, express a preference for married over unmarried couples or singles in the area of adoption. The fact that Florida places children for adoption with single parents directly and explicitly contradicts Florida's post hoc assertion that the ban is justified by the state's wish to place children for adoption only with "families with married mothers and fathers." This contradiction alone is enough to prove that the state's alleged reasons are "illogical to the point of irrationality." *Eisenstadt*.

However, instead of acknowledging this glaring gap between the ban on homosexual adoption and the state's purported justification, as did the Supreme Court in invalidating the statutes in *Eisenstadt*, *Moreno*, *Cleburne*, and *Romer*, the *Lofton* panel stretches mightily to construct a hypothetical to bridge this gap. "It is not irrational," the panel opines, "to think that heterosexual singles have a markedly greater probability of eventually establishing a married household and, thus, providing their adopted children with a stable, dual-gender parenting environment." The panel's contrived hypothetical offering blatantly ignores not only the absence of any preference in Florida's statute for married couples but also the realities of the adoption process. Evaluations of prospective parents are based on present, not "eventual," status and conditions. Florida does not ask for a commitment of plans to marry someday in the future and permits single adults to adopt without making inquiry into whether they have immediate, or even long-range, marriage plans or prospects. Indeed, that many individuals choose to adopt outside of marriage is an indication that adoption and commitment to a permanent adult relationship are completely separate decisions. Moreover, experience leads one to believe that single heterosexuals who adopt are less likely to marry in the future, not more likely.

Finally, this speculative hypothesis also fails to take account of "non-practicing homosexuals" who are not likely to marry but can adopt under Florida law. The Supreme Court found the state's arguments in *Eisenstadt* to be a futile and transparent move to escape the reach of the Court's decision in *Griswold*. The hypothetical posited by the Lofton panel demonstrates a comparable and equally transparent attempt to ignore the equal protection cases applicable here. * * *

In addition to its failure to meaningfully distinguish homosexuals from single heterosexuals, the panel never explains why it is rational to believe that homosexuals, as a class, are unable to provide stable homes and appropriate role models for children. With respect to the first of these arguments, there is absolutely no record evidence to show that homosexuals are incapable of providing the permanent family life sought by Florida. To the contrary, as the facts in this case suggest, many children throughout the country are lovingly and successfully cared for by homosexuals in their capacity as biological parents, foster parents, or legal guardians. Furthermore, it is not marriage that guarantees a stable, caring environment for children but the character of the individual caregiver. Indeed, given the reality of foster care in Florida, the statute actually operates to impede, rather than promote, the placement of a child into a permanent family. Florida's statute expresses a clear intent "to protect and promote the well-being of persons being adopted ... and to provide to all children who can benefit by it a permanent family life." Fla. Stat. § 63.022(3) (2003). Yet, Florida's foster care system has a backlog of more than 3,400 children in it, far more than the number of married couples eligible to adopt. Given this backlog, the state's ban on gay adoption does nothing to increase the number of children being adopted, whether by married couples or anyone else. The state is evidently willing to allow children to live with the potential uncertainties of several foster-care placements rather than enjoy the security and certainty of an adoptive home with one or two caring parents who are also homosexual. * * *

Nor does the panel offer a reason for why it is rational to credit the state's second argument: that homosexuals are incapable of providing good role models. The panel claims that "[heterosexual] children will need education and guidance after puberty concerning relationships with the opposite sex.... It is in the best interests of a child if his or her parents can personally relate to the child's problems and assist the child in the difficult transition to heterosexual adulthood." Is the panel suggesting that heterosexual parents are necessary in order to tell children about their own dating experiences after puberty? For anyone who has been a parent, this will no doubt seem a very strange, even faintly comical, claim. There is certainly no evidence that the ability to share one's adolescent dating experiences (or lack thereof) is an important, much less essential, facet of parenting. The difficult transition to adulthood is a common human experience, not an experience unique to human beings of a particular race, gender, or sexual orientation. It is downright silly to argue that parents must have experienced everything that a child will experience in order to guide them. Indeed, that will generally not be the case. For example, immigrant parents help their children adjust to a world and culture they have not known. It cannot be suggested that such individuals are unfit to parent any more than it could be suggested that a mother is unfit to parent a son or that a white person is unfit to parent an African–American child. Furthermore, the panel's argument completely neglects to consider the situation of gay children of heterosexual parents. Children simply need parents who will love and support them. * * *

* * * Here, irrational prejudice can be inferred as the basis for this classification because there is no difference in relevant respects between single heterosexual persons and single homosexual persons with reference to the state's purported justification for the ban in the statute. Moreover, when all the proffered rationales for a law are clearly and manifestly implausible, a reviewing court may infer that animus is the only explicable basis. *Romer*. Since Florida's rationale is not plausible given that single persons may adopt, the inference is obvious that Florida's decision to single out homosexuals is based solely on anti-gay animus. Unsurprisingly, animus is just what the legislative history of Florida's ban confirms.

The Florida statute was enacted after an organized and relentless anti-homosexual campaign led by Anita Bryant, a pop singer who sought to repeal a January 1977 ordinance of the Dade County Metropolitan Commission prohibiting discrimination against homosexuals in the areas of housing, public accommodations, and employment. Bryant organized a drive that collected the 10,000 signatures needed to force a public referendum on the ordinance. In the course of her campaign, which the Miami Herald described as creating a "witch-hunting hysteria more appropriate to the 17th century than the 20th," Bryant referred to homosexuals as "human garbage." She also promoted the insidious myth that schoolchildren were vulnerable to molestation at the hands of homosexual schoolteachers who would rely on the ordinance to avoid being dismissed from their positions.

In response to Bryant's efforts, Senator Curtis Peterson introduced legislation in the Florida Senate banning both adoptions by and marriage between homosexuals. The legislative history reveals the very close and utterly transparent connection between Bryant's campaign and the Peterson bills. At the May 3, 1977 hearings of the Senate Judiciary Civil Committee, for example, Senator Peterson observed that "it is a possible problem, constantly in the news." Senator George Firestone commented that "this [gay rights controversy] has totally polarized [my] community unnecessarily." And Senator Don Chamberlin explicitly tied the Bryant campaign to the proposed ban on homosexual adoption, arguing that the latter would never have arisen without the ruckus over the Dade County anti-discrimination ordinance. The impetus for Florida's adoption ban exactly parallels the impetus for the state constitutional amendment struck down in *Romer.* * * *

As the House and Senate gave their final approval to the Peterson bills on May 31, Senator Peterson stated that his bills were a message to homosexuals that "we're really tired of you. We wish you would go back into the closet." On June 8, 1977, exactly one day after Dade County voters repealed the anti-discrimination ordinance, the Governor of Florida signed the Peterson bills into law, in what can only be seen as a deliberate acknowledgment of the orchestration between Bryant's campaign and the legislature's actions. In short, the legislative history shows that anti-gay animus was the major factor—indeed the sole factor—behind the law's promulgation, thereby confirming that the standard of review in this case is controlled by *Eisenstadt, Cleburne, Romer,* and *Moreno.* * * *

Whereas the Texas sodomy statute struck down in *Lawrence* treated homosexuals as criminals, Florida's ban on gay adoption treats criminals with more dignity than homosexuals. Nothing more clearly raises the "inevitable inference that the disadvantage imposed is born of animosity toward the class of persons affected," *Romer,* than this disparity of treatment.

[*Burden on Due Process Right of Sexual Intimacy*] *Lawrence* held that consenting adults have a right under the Due Process Clause to engage in private sexual conduct, including homosexual conduct. Because Florida's law punishes the exercise of this right by denying all active homosexuals the ability to be considered as adoptive parents, we are required to subject Florida's law to heightened scrutiny—not the cursory, attempted rational-basis analysis the panel employs. In addition to its failure to apply heightened scrutiny, the panel makes further errors of law in attempting to evade the application of *Lawrence.* It makes erroneous statements about the proper use of history and tradition in a substantive due process analysis, and mistakenly claims that *Lawrence* does not apply here because adoption is a privilege and not a right, and because Florida's statute is a civil rather than criminal law. These reasons are not only unsupported by, but are directly contrary to, Supreme Court precedent.

[Judge Barkett argued that, by overruling *Bowers* and extending *Griswold*'s privacy right to consensual sodomy, *Lawrence* necessarily recognized a fundamental right to engage in private homosexual intimacy. Florida is penalizing Lofton and Croteau for exercising their fundamental right, a burden which must be justified by a compelling state interest, and not just the rational basis found by the panel.]

■ JUDGE BIRCH, specially concurring in the denial of rehearing en banc.

* * * The real point of disagreement between the *Lofton* panel and the dissent is whether rational-basis review should always uphold a law as long as there exists some "conceivable" rational basis—or whether there are certain instances that call for a "more searching" form of rational-basis review that examines the actual motivations underlying the law. Accordingly, I offer the counter-argument to the dissent's "heightened rational-basis review" theory.

Aside from Justice O'Connor's *Lawrence* concurrence, I have found in the Supreme Court's language no explicit support for the theory that rational-basis review should examine the actual motivation behind legislation (assuming that such a thing can be divined with any accuracy). I also note the Supreme Court's own observation that "it is entirely irrelevant for constitutional purposes whether the conceived reason for the challenged distinction actually motivated the legislature." *F.C.C. v. Beach Communications, Inc.,* 508 U.S. 307, 315 (1993). * * *

The *Romer* Court found Colorado's Amendment 2—a "sweeping and comprehensive" measure that imposed a "broad and undifferentiated disability" on the state's homosexual residents—to be "inexplicable by anything but animus" because the breadth of the Amendment so exceeded its proffered rationales. As I understand it, the fatal defect in Amendment 2 was not that the Court determined that *actual* animus motivated passage of the Amendment. Indeed, in contrast to the dissent's scrutiny of the legislative history of the Florida statute, the *Romer* Court never examined the actual history of the plebiscite vote that led to passage of Amendment 2, nor the accompanying campaign rhetoric or the "intent" of the electorate. Instead, the Court found the proffered rationales so implausible that the Court *inferred* that animus was the only conceivable (as opposed to actual) rationale. * * *

[Judge Birch noted that the Supreme Court itself read *Cleburne* more narrowly than Judge Barkett did. In *Board of Trustees of the Univ. of Alabama v. Garrett*, 531 U.S. 356, 367 (2001),

> Justice Breyer [in dissent] suggests that *Cleburne* stands for the broad proposition that state decisionmaking reflecting "negative attitudes" or "fear" necessarily runs afoul of the Fourteenth Amendment. Although such biases may often accompany irrational (and therefore unconstitutional) discrimination, their presence alone does not a constitutional violation make. As we noted in *Cleburne*: "Mere negative

attitudes, or fear, *unsubstantiated by factors which are properly cognizable* in a zoning proceeding, are not permissible bases for treating a home for the mentally retarded differently...."

[Likewise, Judge Birch maintained that the Supreme Court itself announced no fundamental right in *Lawrence*.] An important point bears noting here. To say that *Lawrence* overruled *Bowers* is not to say that every question *Bowers* answered in the negative should now be answered in the affirmative (or vice versa). For example, although the *Lawrence* Court specifically noted that *Bowers* misframed the issue as one of whether there is a right to engage in sodomy, the Court never identified how *Bowers* should in fact have framed the inquiry—much less what the precise answer to that inquiry should have been. We see this pattern throughout the *Lawrence* opinion. * * *

The dissent translates [*Lawrence*'s] general references to "liberty" under the Due Process Clause into a specific due process right to engage in private sexual conduct. The dissent appears to be: (multiple references to Due Process liberty) + (decision finding Texas sodomy statute unconstitutional) = (holding that there is a substantive due process right to sexual intimacy). But even if I were persuaded that *Lawrence* announced, or "reaffirmed," a substantive due process right to sexual intimacy, I still am not convinced that burdens on this right necessarily would require strict scrutiny. First, as the *Lofton* panel observed, the *Lawrence* Court itself never applied, nor used any of the language of, strict scrutiny. Second, with all due respect, as cryptic as some of the Supreme Court's substantive due process precedents are, my recent review of them convinces me of this much: the mere presence of a substantive liberty interest does not automatically trigger strict scrutiny, as the dissent seems to suggest. [E.g., *City of Chicago v. Morales*, 527 U.S. 41 (1999).] * * *

I will conclude on a purely personal note. If I were a legislator, rather than a judge, I would vote in favor of considering otherwise eligible homosexuals for adoptive parenthood. In reviewing the record in this case one can only be impressed by the courage, tenacity and devotion of Messrs. Lofton [et al.] for the children placed in their care. For these children, these men are the only parents they have ever known. Thus, I consider the policy decision of the Florida legislature to be misguided and trust that over time attitudes will change and it will see the best interest of these children in a different light. Nevertheless, as compelling as this perspective is to me, I will not allow my personal views to conflict with my judicial duty— conduct that apparently fewer and fewer citizens, commentators and Senators seem to understand or appreciate. And, I hasten to add, the vast majority of federal judges, including each and every judge of the Eleventh Circuit, are similarly sensitive to separate their personal preferences from their duty to follow precedent as they understand it.

NOTE ON THE FLORIDA HOMOSEXUAL ADOPTION CASE

Lofton is a useful case, because it requires the judge (and the law student) to figure out how the holdings of *Romer* (on the equal protection issue) and *Lawrence* (on the substantive due process issue) should apply to a statutory policy excluding all practicing lesbians, gay men, and bisexuals from adopting children in Florida. Both Supreme Court decisions can be read narrowly (as Birch does) or broadly (as Barkett does)—so the key inquiry becomes: How broadly *should* we read *Romer* or *Lawrence*?

Arguments for Reading the Precedents Broadly include: (1) The Florida statute has the same outlier look as the Colorado initiative. No other state (as of 2007) has such a focused anti-gay exclusion. (2) The Bryant "Save Our Children" campaign demonized homosexuals as disgusting and subhuman, and it was the backdrop of the statute. Can that be entirely ignored? Isn't this the kind of prejudice-based discourse the Court ought to be discouraging? (3) *Romer/Lawrence* end the regime where homosexuals were second-class citizens. The Florida statute is a result of the old regime's ideology. Lose it for the same reasons important race- and sex-discriminations were swept away after *Brown* and *Craig*.

Arguments for Reading the Precedents Narrowly include: (1) The new norm to replace *Bowers* might be, tolerate homosexuality and don't make sodomy a crime, but the state still has a lot of room to promote and encourage heterosexuality. The adoption law is an example. (2) Adoption is a special creature of the state, and not some fundamental right, so the state ought to have leeway in defining its nature and terms. (3) A lower court should not make the move Barkett advocates; the Supreme Court is better situated to accomplish such a norm shift, but should not do so immediately. Let the issue percolate for a while. If other states do not follow Florida, then perhaps the Court should settle the issue for challenges like Lofton's.

Page 297. Insert the following Cases and Notes at the end of Section 2:

In re Marriage Cases

California Supreme Court, 2008.
43 Cal.4th 757, 183 P.3d 384, 76 Cal.Rptr.3d 683.

■ CHIEF JUSTICE GEORGE delivered the opinion for the Court. * * *

[These appeals consolidated six cases where lesbian and gay couples sought recognition of their committed relationships as *marriages*. Since statehood in 1850, California's family law had implicitly limited civil marriage to different-sex relationships. A 1977 statute limited marriage to unions between one man and one woman, and a 2000 initiative reaffirmed the limitation of marriage to different-sex couples and provided that the state would not recognize out-of-state same-sex marriages. Plaintiffs argued that the discrimination against their relationships violated the equality guarantee of the California Constitution. They argued that the discrimination was subject to strict scrutiny for three independent reasons: the exclusion of same-sex couples from state marriage law rested upon two "suspect" classifications, namely, (1) sex and (2) sexual orientation and, moreover, (3) denied those couples a "fundamental" interest in marriage. Under California's constitutional jurisprudence, the Court would apply strict scrutiny if *either* the classification were suspect *or* the excluded group were denied a fundamental right.]

[**Part IV** of the Chief Justice's opinion held that the plaintiff lesbian and gay couples have a "fundamental right to marry." Unlike the U.S. Constitution, the California Constitution mentions privacy rights, in Article I, section 1, which provides: "All people are by nature free and independent and have inalienable rights. Among these are enjoying and defending life and *liberty*, acquiring, possessing, and protecting property, and pursuing and obtaining safety, happiness, and *privacy*." (Added 1972, emphasis added.) Like the U.S. Constitution, however, the California Constitution does not explicitly protect a fundamental right to marry, but the state supreme court has inferred such a right from the 1972 amendment, which was meant to codify *Griswold v. Connecticut* in the state constitution.

[The lower court had rejected plaintiffs' claim on the ground that lesbian and gay couples enjoyed no "fundamental right to marriage," because marriage had traditionally not included them. Although all other state appeals courts had accepted or acquiesced in a similar argument, Chief Justice George rejected it as circular.] In *Perez v. Sharp*, this court's 1948 decision holding that the California statutory provisions prohibiting interracial marriage were unconstitutional—the court did not characterize the constitutional right that the plaintiffs in that case sought to obtain as "a right to interracial marriage" and did not dismiss the plaintiffs' constitutional challenge on the ground that such marriages never had been permitted in California. Instead, the *Perez* decision focused on the *substance* of the constitutional right at issue—that is, the importance to an individual of the freedom "to join in marriage *with the person of one's choice*"—in determining whether the statute impinged upon the plaintiffs' fundamental constitutional right. * * * And, in addressing a somewhat analogous point, the United States Supreme Court in *Lawrence v. Texas* concluded that its prior decision in *Bowers v. Hardwick* had erred in narrowly characterizing the constitutional right sought to be invoked in that case as the right to engage in intimate *homosexual* conduct, determining instead that the constitutional right there at issue properly should be understood in a broader and more neutral fashion so as to focus upon the substance of the interests that the constitutional right is intended to protect.

[When understood at the proper level of generality, the question becomes, what is the point of the important constitutional interest in marriage? *Perez* and other cases established a] linkage between marriage, establishing a home, and raising children in identifying civil marriage as the means available to an individual to establish, with a loved one of his or her choice, an officially recognized family relationship. In *De Burgh v. De Burgh* (1952) 39 Cal.2d 858, for example, in explaining "the public interest in the institution of marriage," this court stated: "The family is the basic unit of our society, the center of the personal affections that ennoble and enrich human life. It channels biological drives that might otherwise become socially destructive; it ensures the care and education of children in a stable environment; it establishes continuity from one generation to another; it nurtures and develops the individual initiative that distinguishes a free people. Since the family is the core of our society, the law seeks to foster and preserve marriage."

[The Chief Justice emphasized the social utility of marriage as a broadly available institution. *De Burgh* and other cases described marriage as the "building block" of society, by providing a good structure for rearing children as well as channeling adult behaviors in productive ways. And of course many cases recognized marriage as the most important individual right, for marriage is typically "the most socially productive and individually fulfilling relationship that one can enjoy in the course of a lifetime." These values of marriage, and its critical role as an enforceable individual right, are recognized in Article 16 of the U.N. Universal Declaration of Human Rights; Article 23 of the International Covenant of Civil and Political Rights; Article 12 of the European Convention for the Protection of Human Rights and Fundamental Freedoms; Article 17 of the American Convention on Human Rights; and the constitutions of many other countries. See Lynn Wardle, *Federal Constitutional Protection for Marriage: Why and How*, 20 BYU J. Pub. L. 439, 453–61 (2006).]

[In response to the argument that marriage had traditionally been reserved for different-sex couples only, the Chief Justice noted that precisely that argument had been rejected in *Perez*. The point of constitutional review is to subject tradition to normative scrutiny.] There can be no question but that, in recent decades, there has been a fundamental and dramatic transformation in this state's understanding and legal treatment of gay individuals and gay couples. California has repudiated past practices and policies that were based on a once common viewpoint that denigrated the general character and morals of gay individuals, and at one time even characterized homosexuality as a mental illness rather than as simply one of the numerous variables of our common and diverse humanity. This state's current policies and conduct regarding homosexuality recognize that gay individuals are entitled to the same legal rights and the same respect and dignity afforded all other individuals and are protected from discrimination on the basis of their sexual orientation, and, more specifically, recognize that gay individuals are fully capable of entering into the kind of loving and enduring committed relationships that may serve as the foundation of a family and of responsibly caring for and raising children.

[*Amici* argued that the main point of marriage is procreation, and that the valid state interest in channeling reproductive activity into marriage justified the omission of same-sex couples, who could not produce children through their sexual activities. The Chief Justice was unpersuaded, in part because as many as 70,000 children were being raised in California by same-sex couples (citing study that found that 28.4 percent of California lesbian and gay couples were raising children). Some of these children were adopted, others came through surrogates and artificial insemination, but the fact remained, for the Court, that even this traditional value of marriage was not served by excluding so many families from the state marriage law.]

Furthermore, although promoting and facilitating a stable environment for the procreation and raising of children is unquestionably one of the vitally important purposes underlying the institution of marriage and the constitutional right to marry, past cases make clear that this right is not confined to, or restrictively defined by, that purpose alone. As noted above, our past cases have recognized that the right to marry is the right to enter into a relationship that is "the center of the personal affections that ennoble and enrich human life" (*De Burgh*)—a relationship that is "at once the most socially productive and individually fulfilling relationship that one can enjoy in the course of a lifetime." (*Marvin v. Marvin.*) The personal enrichment afforded by the right to marry may be obtained by a couple whether or not they choose to have children, and the right to marry never has been limited to those who plan or desire to have children. Indeed, in *Griswold v. Connecticut*—one of the seminal federal cases striking down a state law as violative of the federal constitutional right of privacy—the high court upheld a married couple's right to use contraception *to prevent procreation*, demonstrating quite clearly that the promotion of procreation is not the sole or defining purpose of marriage. Similarly, in *Turner v. Safley*, the court held that the constitutional right to marry extends to an individual confined in state prison—even a prisoner who has no right to conjugal visits with his would-be spouse—emphasizing that "[m]any important attributes of marriage remain ... after taking into account the limitations imposed by prison life ... [including the] expressions of emotional support and public commitment [that] are an important and significant aspect of the marital relationship." Although *Griswold* and *Turner* relate to the right to marry under the federal Constitution, they accurately reflect the scope of the state constitutional right to marry as well. Accordingly, this right cannot properly be defined by or limited to the state's interest in fostering a favorable environment for the procreation and raising of children.

The Proposition 22 Legal Defense Fund and the Campaign also rely upon several academic commentators who maintain that the constitutional right to marry should be viewed as inapplicable to same-sex couples because a contrary interpretation assertedly would sever the link that marriage provides between procreation and child rearing and would "send a message" to the public that it is immaterial to the state whether children are raised by their biological mother and father. (See, e.g., Blankenhorn, The Future of Marriage (2007); Wardle, *"Multiply and Replenish:" Considering Same–Sex Marriage in Light of State Interests in Marital Procreation* (2001) 24 HARV. J.L. & PUB. POL'Y 771, 797–799; Gallagher, *What Is Marriage For? The Public Purposes of Marriage Law* (2002) 62 La. L.Rev. 773, 779–780, 790–791.) Although we appreciate the genuine concern for the well-being of children underlying that position, we conclude this claim lacks merit. Our recognition that the core substantive rights encompassed by the constitutional right to marry apply to same-sex as well as opposite-sex couples does not imply in any way that it is unimportant or immaterial to the state whether a child is raised by his or her biological mother and father. By recognizing this circumstance we do not alter or diminish either the legal responsibilities that biological parents owe to their children or the substantial incentives that the state provides to a child's biological parents to enter into and raise their child in a stable, long-term committed relationship. Instead, such an interpretation of the constitutional right to marry simply confirms that a stable two-parent family relationship, supported by the state's official recognition and protection, is equally as important for the numerous children in California who are being raised by same-sex couples as for those children being raised by opposite-sex couples (whether they are biological parents or adoptive parents). This interpretation also guarantees individuals who are in a same-sex relationship, and who are raising children, the opportunity to obtain from the state the official recognition and support accorded a family by agreeing to take on the substantial and long-term mutual obligations and responsibilities that are an essential and inseparable part of a family relationship.

[Finally, the Chief Justice rejected the Attorney General's argument that the Domestic Partnership Act, as amended to provide virtually all the legal benefits and duties of marriage for same-sex couples, satisfied the constitutional marriage right.] Whether or not the name "marriage," in the abstract, is considered a core element of the state constitutional right to marry, one of the core elements of this fundamental right is the right of same-sex couples to have their official family relationship accorded the same dignity, respect, and stature as that accorded to all other officially recognized family relationships. The current statutes—by drawing a distinction between the name assigned to the family relationship available to opposite-sex couples and the name assigned to the family relationship available to same-sex couples, and by reserving the historic and highly respected designation of marriage exclusively to opposite-sex couples while offering same-sex couples only the new and unfamiliar designation of domestic partnership—pose a serious risk of denying the official family relationship of same-sex couples the equal dignity and respect that is a core element of the constitutional right to marry. As observed by the City [and County] of San Francisco at oral argument, this court's conclusion in *Perez* that the statutory provision barring interracial marriage was unconstitutional, undoubtedly would have been the same even if alternative nomenclature, such as "transracial union," had been made available to interracial couples

[Sex-based classifications have long been subject to strict scrutiny under the California Constitution, see *Sail'er Inn, Inc. v. Kirby,* 5 Cal.3d 1 (1971). In **Part V.A.** of his opinion (excerpted below, in Section 3 of this chapter of the Supplement), the Chief Justice dismissed plaintiffs' argument that the marriage exclusion was subject to strict scrutiny as a *sex* discrimination. The California Supreme Court had not decided what level of scrutiny to apply to *sexual orientation* classifications. In **Part V.B.,** the Chief Justice answered that question.]

In arguing that the marriage statutes do not discriminate on the basis of sexual orientation, defendants rely upon the circumstance that these statutes, on their face, do not refer explicitly to sexual orientation and do not prohibit gay individuals from marrying a person of the opposite sex. Defendants contend that under these circumstances, the marriage statutes should not be viewed as directly classifying or discriminating on the basis of sexual orientation but at most should be viewed as having a "disparate impact" on gay persons.

In our view, the statutory provisions restricting marriage to a man and a woman cannot be understood as having merely a disparate impact on gay persons, but instead properly must be viewed as directly classifying and prescribing distinct treatment on the basis of sexual orientation. By limiting marriage to opposite-sex couples, the marriage statutes, realistically viewed, operate clearly and directly to impose different treatment on gay individuals because of their sexual orientation. By definition, gay individuals are persons who are sexually attracted to persons of the same sex and thus, if inclined to enter into a marriage relationship, would choose to marry a person of their own sex or gender.[59] A statute that limits marriage to a union of persons of opposite sexes, thereby placing marriage outside

---

59. As explained in the amicus curiae brief filed by a number of leading mental health organizations, including the American Psychological Association and the American Psychiatric Association: "Sexual orientation is commonly discussed as a characteristic of the *individual*, like biological sex, gender identity, or age. This perspective is incomplete because sexual orientation is always defined in relational terms and necessarily involves relationships with other individuals. Sexual acts and romantic attractions are categorized as homosexual or heterosexual according to the biological sex of the individuals involved in them, relative to each other. Indeed, it is by acting—or desiring to act—with another person that individuals express their heterosexuality, homosexuality, or bisexuality.... Thus, sexual orientation is integrally linked to the intimate personal relationships that human beings form with others to meet their deeply felt needs for love, attachment, and intimacy. In addition to sexual behavior, these bonds encompass nonsexual physical affection between partners, shared goals and values, mutual support, and ongoing commitment. [¶] Consequently, sexual orientation is not merely a personal characteristic that can be defined in isolation. Rather, one's sexual orientation defines the universe of persons with whom one is likely to find the satisfying and fulfilling relationships that, for many individuals, comprise an essential component of personal identity."

the reach of couples of the same sex, unquestionably imposes different treatment on the basis of sexual orientation. In our view, it is sophistic to suggest that this conclusion is avoidable by reason of the circumstance that the marriage statutes permit a gay man or a lesbian to marry someone of the opposite sex, because making such a choice would require the negation of the person's sexual orientation. * * *

Having concluded that the California marriage statutes treat persons differently on the basis of sexual orientation, we must determine whether sexual orientation should be considered a "suspect classification" under the California equal protection clause, so that statutes drawing a distinction on this basis are subject to strict scrutiny. * * *

In addressing this issue, the majority in the Court of Appeal stated: "For a statutory classification to be considered 'suspect' for equal protection purposes, generally three requirements must be met. The defining characteristic must (1) be based upon an 'immutable trait'; (2) 'bear[] no relation to [a person's] ability to perform or contribute to society'; and (3) be associated with a 'stigma of inferiority and second class citizenship,' manifested by the group's history of legal and social disabilities. (*Sail'er Inn.*) While the latter two requirements would seem to be readily satisfied in the case of gays and lesbians, the first is more controversial." Concluding that "whether sexual orientation is immutable presents a factual question" as to which an adequate record had not been presented in the trial court, the Court of Appeal ultimately held that "[l]acking guidance from our Supreme Court or decisions from our sister Courts of Appeal," the court would review the marriage statutes under the rational basis, rather than the strict scrutiny, standard.

Past California cases fully support the Court of Appeal's conclusion that sexual orientation is a characteristic (1) that bears no relation to a person's ability to perform or contribute to society, and (2) that is associated with a stigma of inferiority and second-class citizenship, manifested by the group's history of legal and social disabilities. [See *People v. Garcia* (2000) 77 Cal.App.4th 1269, treating lesbians and gay men as a social group like blacks and women that prosecutors could not exclude from juries through peremptory challenges.]

We disagree, however, with the Court of Appeal's conclusion that it is appropriate to reject sexual orientation as a suspect classification, in applying the California Constitution's equal protection clause, on the ground that there is a question as to whether this characteristic is or is not "immutable." Although we noted in *Sail'er Inn* that generally a person's gender is viewed as an immutable trait, immutability is not invariably required in order for a characteristic to be considered a suspect classification for equal protection purposes. California cases establish that a person's religion is a suspect classification for equal protection purposes, and one's religion, of course, is not immutable but is a matter over which an individual has control. (See also *Raffaelli v. Committee of Bar Examiners*

(1972) 7 Cal.3d 288, 292 [alienage treated as a suspect classification notwithstanding circumstance that alien can become a citizen].) Because a person's sexual orientation is so integral an aspect of one's identity, it is not appropriate to require a person to repudiate or change his or her sexual orientation in order to avoid discriminatory treatment.

In his briefing before this court, the Attorney General does not maintain that sexual orientation fails to satisfy the three requirements for a suspect classification discussed by the Court of Appeal, but instead argues that a *fourth* requirement should be imposed before a characteristic is considered a constitutionally suspect basis for classification for equal protection purposes—namely, that "a 'suspect' classification is appropriately recognized only for minorities who are unable to use the political process to address their needs." The Attorney General's brief asserts that "[s]ince the gay and lesbian community in California is obviously able to wield political power in defense of its interests, this Court should not hold that sexual orientation constitutes a suspect classification."

Although some California decisions in discussing suspect classifications have referred to a group's "political powerlessness" (see, e.g., *Raffaelli*), our cases have not identified a group's *current* political powerlessness as a necessary *prerequisite* for treatment as a suspect class. Indeed, if a group's *current* political powerlessness were a prerequisite to a characteristic's being considered a constitutionally suspect basis for differential treatment, it would be impossible to justify the numerous decisions that continue to treat sex, race, and religion as suspect classifications. Instead, our decisions make clear that the most important factors in deciding whether a characteristic should be considered a constitutionally suspect basis for classification are whether the class of persons who exhibit a certain characteristic historically has been subjected to invidious and prejudicial treatment, and whether society now recognizes that the characteristic in question generally bears no relationship to the individual's ability to perform or contribute to society. Thus, "courts must look closely at classifications based on that characteristic lest *outdated* social stereotypes result in invidious laws or practices." (*Sail'er Inn.*) This rationale clearly applies to statutory classifications that mandate differential treatment on the basis of sexual orientation. In sum, we conclude that statutes imposing differential treatment on the basis of sexual orientation should be viewed as constitutionally suspect under the California Constitution's equal protection clause. * * *

There is no persuasive basis for applying to statutes that classify persons on the basis of the suspect classification of sexual orientation a standard less rigorous than that applied to statutes that classify on the basis of the suspect classifications of gender, race, or religion. Because sexual orientation, like gender, race, or religion, is a characteristic that frequently has been the basis for biased and improperly stereotypical treatment and that generally bears no relation to an individual's ability to perform or contribute to society, it is appropriate for courts to evaluate with great care and with considerable skepticism any statute that embodies such a classification. The strict scrutiny standard therefore is applicable to statutes that impose differential treatment on the basis of sexual orientation. * * *

[**Part V.D.**] [I]n circumstances, as here, in which the strict scrutiny standard of review applies, the state bears a heavy burden of justification. In order to satisfy that standard, the state must demonstrate not simply that there is a rational, constitutionally legitimate interest that supports the differential treatment at issue, but instead that the state interest is a *constitutionally compelling* one that justifies the disparate treatment prescribed by the statute in question. Furthermore, unlike instances in which the rational basis test applies, the state does not meet its burden of justification under the strict scrutiny standard merely by showing that the classification established by the statute is rationally or reasonably related to such a compelling state interest. Instead, the state must demonstrate that the distinctions drawn by the statute (or statutory scheme) are *necessary* to further that interest.

[The Chief Justice summarily rejected the argument made by the Proposition 22 Legal Defense Fund that the California Constitution required the Legislature to follow the traditional definition of "marriage" as one man, one woman, as well as the Attorney General's argument that constitutional separation of powers precluded the judiciary from second-guessing legislative policy judgments. The Court gave greater attention to the argument that it ought to defer to the popular judgment, reflected in the Knight Initiative approved by a large majority in 2000, that the state ought to preserve the traditional definition of marriage.]

Although defendants maintain that this court has an obligation to defer to the statutory definition of marriage contained in section 308.5 because that statute—having been adopted through the initiative process—represents the expression of the "people's will," this argument fails to take into account the very basic point that the provisions of the California Constitution itself constitute the ultimate expression of the people's will, and that the fundamental rights embodied within that Constitution for the protection of all persons represent restraints that the people themselves have imposed upon the statutory enactments that may be adopted either by their elected representatives or by the voters through the initiative process. As the United States Supreme Court explained in *West Virginia State Board of Education v. Barnette* (1943) 319 U.S. 624, 638: "The very purpose of a Bill of Rights was to withdraw certain subjects from the vicissitudes of political controversy, to place them beyond the reach of majorities and officials and to establish them as legal principles to be applied by the courts. One's right to life, liberty, and property, to free speech, a free press, freedom of worship and assembly, and other fundamental rights may not be submitted to vote; they depend on the outcome of no elections."

[The Chief Justice then treated the Attorney General's argument that the state had a compelling interest in following the definition of marriage followed almost everywhere else in the United States, and indeed in the world.] Although the understanding of marriage as limited to a union of a man and a woman is undeniably the predominant one, if we have learned anything from the significant evolution in the prevailing societal views and official policies toward members of minority races and toward women over the past half-century, it is that even the most familiar and generally accepted of social practices and traditions often mask an unfairness and inequality that frequently is not recognized or appreciated by those not directly harmed by those practices or traditions. It is instructive to recall in this regard that the traditional, well-established legal rules and practices of our not-so-distant past (1) barred interracial marriage, (2) upheld the routine exclusion of women from many occupations and official duties, and (3) considered the relegation of racial minorities to separate and assertedly equivalent public facilities and institutions as constitutionally equal treatment. As the United States Supreme Court observed in its decision in *Lawrence v. Texas*, the expansive and protective provisions of our constitutions, such as the due process clause, were drafted with the knowledge that "times can blind us to certain truths and later generations can see that laws once thought necessary and proper in fact serve only to oppress." For this reason, the interest in retaining a tradition that excludes an historically disfavored minority group from a status that is extended to all others—even when the tradition is long-standing and widely shared—does not necessarily represent a compelling state interest for purposes of equal protection analysis.

After carefully evaluating the pertinent considerations in the present case, we conclude that the state interest in limiting the designation of marriage exclusively to opposite-sex couples, and in excluding same-sex couples from access to that designation, cannot properly be considered a compelling state interest for equal protection purposes. To begin with, the limitation clearly is not necessary to preserve the rights and benefits of marriage currently enjoyed by opposite-sex couples. Extending access to the designation of marriage to same-sex couples will not deprive any opposite-sex couple or their children of any of the rights and benefits conferred by the marriage statutes, but simply will make the benefit of the marriage designation available to same-sex couples and their children. As Chief Judge Kaye of the New York Court of Appeals succinctly observed in her dissenting opinion in *Hernandez v. Robles*: "There are enough marriage licenses to go around for everyone." Further, permitting same-sex couples access to the designation of marriage will not alter the substantive nature of the legal institution of marriage; same-sex couples who choose to enter into the relationship with that designation will be subject to the same duties and obligations to each other, to their children, and to third parties that the law currently imposes upon opposite-sex couples who marry. Finally, affording same-sex couples the opportunity to obtain the designation of marriage will not impinge upon the religious freedom of any religious organization, official, or any other person; no religion will be required to change its religious policies or practices with regard to same-sex couples, and no religious officiant will be required to solemnize a marriage in contravention of his or her religious beliefs.

While retention of the limitation of marriage to opposite-sex couples is not needed to preserve the rights and benefits of opposite-sex couples, the exclusion of same-sex couples from the designation of marriage works a real and appreciable harm upon same-sex couples and their children. As discussed above, because of the long and celebrated history of the term "marriage" and the widespread understanding that this word describes a family relationship unreservedly sanctioned by the community, the statutory provisions that continue to limit access to this designation exclusively to opposite-sex couples—while providing only a novel, alternative institution for same-sex couples—likely will be viewed as an official statement that the family relationship of same-sex couples is not of comparable stature or equal dignity to the family relationship of opposite-sex couples. Furthermore, because of the historic disparagement of gay persons, the retention of a distinction in nomenclature by which the term "marriage" is withheld only from the family relationship of same-sex couples is all the more likely to cause the new parallel institution that has been established for same-sex couples to be considered a mark of second-class citizenship. Finally, in addition to the potential harm flowing from the lesser stature that is likely to be afforded to the family relationships of same-sex couples by designating them domestic partnerships, there exists a substantial risk that a judicial decision upholding the differential treatment of opposite-sex and same-sex couples would be understood as *validating* a more general proposition that our state by now has repudiated: that it is permissible, under the law, for society to treat gay individuals and same-sex couples differently from, and less favorably than, heterosexual individuals and opposite-sex couples. * * *

[We omit the concurring opinion of JUSTICE KENNARD as well as the concurring and dissenting opinions of JUSTICE BAXTER and JUSTICE CORRIGAN. Four Justices joined the opinion for the Court; three dissented.]

NOTES ON THE CALIFORNIA SAME–SEX MARRIAGE CASES

1. *The Right to Marry Argument.* Lesbian and gay couples have been arguing for their "fundamental right to marry" since 1971, see William N. Eskridge, Jr., *The Case for Same–Sex Marriage* 42–62 (1996) (history of right to marry litigation), but no appellate court in the United States had ever ruled that lesbian and gay couples qualified for such a right. *E.g.*, *Baehr v. Lewin*, 852 P.2d 44 (Haw. 1993) (requiring that the marriage exclusion be subjected to strict scrutiny on suspect classification grounds but explicitly rejecting the argument that strict scrutiny was also required on fundamental right grounds). This uniformity was especially frustrating in light of the Rehnquist Court's ruling, with no dissent, that the right to marry extended to convicted rapists, murderers, and other felons. *Turner v. Safley*, 482 U.S. 78 (1987).

Why did it take so long for a court to accept that argument, even as some courts were striking down the marriage exclusion for other equal protection reasons?

One reason was apparently the fear of the slippery slope: if all Americans have a "fundamental right to marry" the person(s) of their choice, then judges would strictly examine not only the state's refusal to give marriage licenses to lesbian and gay couples, but also to couples who are underage or closely related, as well as polyamorous sets. (A number of pundits made further analogies that probably cross the line between provocative and insulting, such as the argument that if a woman can marry a woman, Richard Posner can marry his cat.) The slippery slope argument has always been an implausible one, in part because the state does have important interests in refusing to issue marriage licenses to underage and polyamorous couples. See Eskridge, *Case for Same–Sex Marriage*, 144–52.

Perhaps a deeper concern was judicial reluctance to say that something so novel—gay marriage—was "fundamental," a term that the United States Supreme Court and most state high courts have reserved for rights or privileges that have a traditional roots in American society. (Even different-race marriages, long barred in the southern states, were allowed in other parts of the country.) Linguistically, many judges could not bring themselves to put "gay" and "marriage" in the same sentence, and the judges who were supple enough to put the terms together usually bracketed them with quote marks and the like (same-sex "marriages" or so-called "gay marriages"). See Mae Kuykendall, "Resistance to Same–Sex Marriage as a Story About Language: Linguistic Failure and the Priority of a Living Language," 34 *Harv. C.R.-C.L. L. Rev.* 385 (1999).

As lesbian and gay *couples* (especially those with children) have come out of the closet since the 1990s, more and more people (including judges) are capable of saying and thinking same-sex marriage without the quote marks. Kuykendall, *supra*. Once Denmark legalized same-sex partnerships in 1989, and The Netherlands same-sex marriages in 2001 (followed by Belgium, Massachusetts, Canada, Spain, and South Africa in short order), not only did more people become comfortable with putting same-sex together with marriage, but in many circles it came to look like "prejudice" *not* to do so. Hence, the Chief Justice's remarkable Part IV. Are there other reasons why judicial practice may have shifted?

2. *State Constitutional Marriage Cases and the Level of Scrutiny for Sexual Orientation.* In the pre–2008 marriage cases, courts (with the exception of the Hawaii Supreme Court) evaluated the sexual orientation discrimination along *Romer v. Evans* rational-basis-with-bite lines. See *Baker v. State*, 744 A.2d 864 (Vt. 1999) (unanimously striking down the discrimination, divided 4–1 against requiring marriage); *Goodridge v. Department of Pub. Health*, 798 N.E.2d 941 (Mass. 2003) (split court requiring same-sex marriage); *Hernandez v. Robles*, 855 N.E.2d 1 (N.Y.2006) (split court upholding the discrimination as rational); *Lewis v. Harris*, 908 A.2d 196 (N.J. 2006) (unanimously striking down the discrimination, divided 4–3 against requiring marriage). The California Supreme Court's opinion disrupted this pattern—and essentially followed Judge Norris's reasoning in *Watkins* to hold that sexual orientation classifications require strict scrutiny.* Courts since the *California Marriage Cases* have tended to apply some form of heightened scrutiny.

Shortly after the California decision, the Connecticut Supreme Court (divided 4–3) struck down its marriage exclusion in *Kerrigan v. Commissioner of Pub. Health*, 957 A.2d 407, 425–61 (Conn. 2008), and the Iowa Supreme Court unanimously (7–0) invalidated its discriminatory marriage law in *Varnum v. Brien*, 763 N.W.2d 862, 885–96 (Iowa 2009). In both *Kerrigan* and *Varnum*, the state essentially conceded (1) the history of discrimination against lesbian and gay citizens and (2) the relationship between sexual orientation and one's ability to contribute to society, but disputed (3) and the relative immutability of sexual orientation and argued that there was a fourth criterion, namely political powerlessness, that was a prerequisite for heightened scrutiny. The Connecticut and Iowa courts ruled that sexual orientation met all these requirements; *Kerrigan* also discussed constitutional text, decisions from other states, and public policy advantages, all supporting heightened scrutiny.

Both courts ruled that sexual orientation was subject to heightened but not necessarily strict scrutiny. *Kerrigan*'s verbal formulation of "intermediate" scrutiny accorded quasi-suspect classifications borrowed language from the U.S. Supreme Court's VMI Case evaluating sex discriminations under the U.S. Constitution (quotation marks omitted):

> Focusing on the differential treatment or denial of opportunity for which relief is sought, the reviewing court must determine whether the proffered justification is exceedingly persuasive. The burden of justification is demanding and it rests entirely on the [s]tate . . . . . The [s]tate must show at least that the [challenged] classification serves important governmental objectives and that the discriminatory means employed are substantially related to the achievement of those objectives. . . . The justification must be genuine, not hypothesized or invented post hoc in response to [the] litigation. And it must not rely on

---

* California was not the first state to say that sexual orientation is a suspect classification. In *Baehr v. Miike*, 994 P.2d 566 (Haw. 1999) (summary disposition), the Hawaii Supreme Court ruled that a state constitutional amendment required dismissal of same-sex marriage claims but said, in dictum, that sexual orientation classifications were "suspect" ones triggering strict scrutiny. In *Commonwealth v. Wasson*, 842 S.W.2d 487, 499–500 (Ky. 1992), a sodomy case, the Kentucky Supreme Court reasoned in dictum, that sexual orientation discriminations should be treated as suspect.

overbroad generalizations about the different talents, capacities, or preferences of [the groups being classified].

How is this different from strict scrutiny? (In the VMI Case, Chief Justice Rehnquist and dissenting Justice Scalia worried that the majority was applying strict scrutiny under the aegis of intermediate scrutiny.)

3. *Strict/Heightened Scrutiny for Sexual Orientation Classifications: The Immutability Argument.* The Casebook's notes following *Tanner* critically discuss the immutability "requirement" for strict scrutiny. Many academics agree with Judge Landau's argument that immutability can be neither necessary nor sufficient for strict scrutiny, but judges tend to treat immutability as a requirement, or at least a big plus, in the level-of-scrutiny inquiry. State judges are following the approach to immutability taken by Judge Norris in *Watkins*, that is, viewing it through the prism of identity: a trait is "effectively immutable if changing it would involve great difficulty, such as requiring a major physical change or a traumatic change of identity." The *California Marriage Cases* follow this approach, as do *Kerrigan* and *Varnum*.

Under an identity-based view of immutability, is this criterion doing any real "work" in the level-of-scrutiny inquiry? Judge Norris's approach seems to be saying: look, this group has been subjected to pervasive state discrimination and private prejudices that are not rational; under these circumstances, who should be accommodated by state policy, the citizen who finds other people's (or his own) homosexuality creepy? Or productive lesbian and gay citizens, as well as anyone else who is attracted to persons of the same sex?

Should the immutability criterion be retired? If so, why are judges clinging to it?

4. *Strict Scrutiny for Sexual Orientation Classifications: The Political Powerlessness Argument.* In the *California Marriage Cases*, Attorney General Jerry Brown argued that sexual orientation could not be a suspect classification because lesbians and gay men are no longer "politically powerless"; the Legislature had adopted one statute after another granting this minority rights and repealing discriminations (including two bills recognizing same-sex marriages that were successfully vetoed by the state Governator). The Chief Justice responded that the Attorney General's theory would negate the suspectness of "race, sex, and religion." Not so clear. When the California Supreme Court overruled the state different-race marriage bar in 1948, racial minorities were politically powerless in the state. Sex was rendered suspect in California by a constitutional amendment, albeit one codifying the California Supreme Court's holding in *Sail'er Inn*. While mainstream religion is hardly powerless, a reason religion is a suspect classification is that *minority religions* like the Jehovah's Witnesses have been and probably remain politically marginalized.

As Justice Baxter's dissent emphasized, the utility of a "political powerlessness" criterion is that it restrains judges from interfering in the political process *unless* that process is working inadequately. See John Hart Ely, *Democracy and Distrust: A Theory of Judicial Review* (1980) (making this point in some detail). Judges were best situated to resist apartheid, because African and Latino Americans were literally excluded from political participation in the apartheid states. Lesbians and gay men, in contrast, have not been excluded from participation and, in California, have had many political successes. Does the Chief Justice have a persuasive answer to this concern?

Justice Palmer's opinion for the Connecticut Supreme Court in *Kerrigan* was a more sophisticated response to the "political powerlessness" argument. He recharacterized the relevant inquiry as "whether the group lacks sufficient political strength to bring a prompt end to the prejudice and discrimination through traditional political means." *Kerrigan*, 957 A.2d at 444. The inquiry then becomes who should bear the *burden of inertia* as regards discriminatory laws: Should the minority subjected to prejudice and persecution bear the burden? Or should the mainstream majority bear the burden? Whichever way the Court ruled in Connecticut and Iowa, it appears that the losing side was unable to bear the high burden of imposing its viewpoint against opposition in the political process—so Justice Palmer's approach leaves courts in a powerful position on this issue.

5. *Is a Same–Sex Marriage Bar a "Discrimination" against Sexual Orientation Minorities?* In dissent, Justice Baxter argued that there was actually no "discrimination" against lesbian and gay couples when the Legislature and the voters limited civil marriage to one man, one woman, because the gay couple is not "similarly situated" to the straight couple. This kind of argument is circular in the sense that it assumes the answer to the legal issue presented. That is, Justice Baxter believes that marriage is inherently one man, one woman; anything else is not "marriage." Being excluded from an institution that you cannot be a part of by definition is not "discrimination" in the Aristotelian sense (treat like things alike). Indeed, it is "discrimination" to provide similar treatment to dissimilar things, as Justice Baxter believes gay and straight unions to be.

Justice Baxter further argued that the marriage law does not even technically discriminate against gay people: the lesbian is free to marry a man! This kind of argument has an off-the-wall quality to it, especially in light of *Loving v. Virginia* (rejecting Virginia's argument that its anti-miscegenation law does not discriminate against people of color, because its bar applies to white people as well). But a lot of intelligent Americans literally cannot see this as discrimination (a term stuffed with normative significance), and this is the kind of argument that pops up under such circumstances. Cf. *Lawrence v. Texas* (Scalia, J., dissenting) (arguing that Texas's "Homosexual Conduct Law" does not discriminate based on homosexuality, because it prohibits "homosexual conduct" by straight people as well as by gay people).

6. *Popular Constitutionalism.* Justice Baxter's dissenting opinion objected that the Court's result not only ran against the state's traditional understanding of the definition of marriage and repeated affirmations of that traditional understanding in legislative enactments, but also against the will of the people. In 2000, voters by a wide margin passed the Knight Initiative, which added this language to the California Family Code: "Only marriage between a man and a woman is valid or recognized in California." Under the California Constitution, the Legislature could not retract any part of this Knight Initiative without putting the matter to another vote of the people. Justice Baxter suggested that this deepens the countermajoritarian difficulty with the majority's activism. The Chief Justice responded that the Constitution itself is a supermajoritarian expression of the people's will and trumps the Knight Initiative as well as legislated portions of the Family Code.

An *amicus* brief one of us filed in the *Marriage Cases* suggested another response to the countermajoritarian difficulty. The brief recounted the history of state regulation of sexual and gender minorities in California, demonstrating that the Legislature was responsible for decades of oppressive anti-gay measures that reinforced social beliefs that gay people were predatory and anti-family. The only relief came from California court decisions overturning or narrowly construing measures criminalizing homosexual solicitation, cross-dressing, etc. and excluding gay people from teaching positions, as well as decisions affirmatively prohibiting anti-gay discrimination:

> The California Legislature would not have enacted laws accomplishing what this Court * * * did in that period. By protecting sexual minorities, this Court * * * *reversed the burden of inertia*: Did the Legislature or the People really believe gay people were such immediate threats that majorities in both chambers were willing to override the Court? Reversing the burden of inertia also created *conditions for disproving stereotypes*. Popular fears, long fanned by the State, that homosexuals prey on schoolchildren proved unfounded in the wake of [court decisions protecting gay schoolteachers]; myths that homosexuals disrupted workplaces, accepted by the federal as well as state governments, also failed to materialize after [court decisions and an executive order protecting them from job discrimination]. By creating a tolerant space for gay people within the State itself, this Court and the Governor gave gay people opportunities to contribute to public projects, sometimes as openly gay people. That was educational for all concerned.**

** Brief of Professor William N. Eskridge, Jr., as *Amicus Curiae*, in *The Marriage Cases* (California Supreme Court, Case No. S147999).

Less than six months after *The Marriage Cases* were decided, California voters had an opportunity to amend the state constitution to override the Court through a constitutional initiative, Proposition 8, on the November 2008 ballot. Prop 8 stated: "Only marriage between a man and a woman is valid or recognized in California." Unlike the Knight Initiative, however, voters were be able to consider the 2008 initiative in light of some experience with same-sex marriage in their state. On June 17, the state issued the first official marriage licenses to lesbian and gay couples, and no catastrophe occurred. How could Justice Baxter respond to this argument, that popular opinion is shaped by the state, and the Court was right to give gay marriage a chance?

In any event, to the surprise of many observers (but not to Justice Baxter), the California voters passed Prop 8 by a 52.3–47.7% margin. Supporters of marriage equality were disappointed in this result, and some complained that the margin of victory was due to Prop 8 supporters' appeals to anti-gay prejudices and stereotypes. However, the Prop 8 arguments were much more civil and respectful of gay people than had been the case in earlier anti-gay initiative campaigns, especially the Briggs Initiative defeated in 1978 and even the Knight Initiative adopted in 2000. Probably the main argument for Prop 8 was that the Court (or "four Justices from San Francisco," as the official Prop 8 website inaccurately put it) was not only forcing gay marriage onto citizens, but were forcing it on schoolchildren, who would be taught that gay marriage was just as good as straight marriage, even if parents objected.*** The argument misstated the law of California and exploited concerns that "impressionable" youth would be seduced by gay marriage, but this was not the kind of open appeal to prejudice traditionally made in popular initiative campaigns. On the other hand, some of the commercials and ads run by some supporters were more open appeals to anti-gay prejudice. Should they be "attributed" to the official supporters? Could they have made a difference in such a close vote?

Karen L. Strauss v. Mark B. Horton

California Supreme Court, 2009.
46 Cal.4th 364, 207 P.3d 48.

■ CHIEF JUSTICE GEORGE delivered the opinion for the Court. * * *

The federal Constitution provides that an amendment to that Constitution *may be proposed* either *by two-thirds of both houses of Congress* or by a convention called on the application *of two-thirds of the state legislatures*,

---

*** www.ProtectMarriage.com (primary website for Prop 8 supporters, with a pop-up cartoon making the protect-schoolchildren-from-being-forced-to-like-homosexual-marriage argument and inaccurately charging "four Justices from San Francisco" with foisting this upon the citizenry). The campaign is discussed in William N. Eskridge, Jr., "The Supreme Court, 2007 Term—Foreword: The Marriage Cases, Reversing the Burden of Inertia in a Pluralist Democracy," *Calif. L. Rev.* (forthcoming, 2009).

and requires, in either instance, that any proposed amendment *be ratified by the legislatures of (or by conventions held in) three-fourths of the states.* (U.S. Const., art. V.) In contrast, the California Constitution provides that an amendment to that Constitution *may be proposed* either *by two-thirds of the membership of each house of the Legislature* (Cal. Const., art. XVIII, § 1) or *by an initiative petition signed by voters numbering at least 8 percent of the total votes cast for all candidates for Governor in the last gubernatorial election* (Cal. Const., art. II, § 8, subd. (b); *id.*, art. XVIII, § 3), and further specifies that, once an amendment is proposed by either means, the amendment becomes part of the state Constitution *if it is approved by a simple majority of the voters who cast votes on the measure at a statewide election.* (*Id.*, art. XVIII, § 4.)

As is evident from the foregoing description, the process for amending our state Constitution is considerably less arduous and restrictive than the amendment process embodied in the federal Constitution, a difference dramatically demonstrated by the circumstance that only 27 amendments to the United States Constitution have been adopted since the federal Constitution was ratified in 1788, whereas more than 500 amendments to the California Constitution have been adopted since ratification of California's current Constitution in 1879. (See Council of State Governments, *The Book of the States* (2008 ed.) p. 10.)

At the same time, as numerous decisions of this court have explained, although the initiative process may be used to propose and adopt *amendments* to the California Constitution, under its governing provisions that process may not be used to *revise* the state Constitution. (See, e.g., *McFadden v. Jordan* (1948) 32 Cal.2d 330; *Amador Valley Joint Union High Sch. Dist. v. State Bd. of Equalization* (1978) 22 Cal.3d 208; *Raven v. Deukmejian* (1990) 52 Cal.3d 336.) Petitioners' principal argument rests on the claim that Proposition 8 should be viewed as *a constitutional revision* rather than as *a constitutional amendment*, and that this change in the state Constitution therefore could not lawfully be adopted through the initiative process.

* * * [I]n determining whether Proposition 8 constitutes a constitutional amendment or, instead, a constitutional revision, we by no means write on a clean slate. Although the issue arises in this case in the context of an initiative measure, the distinction drawn in the California Constitution between constitutional amendments and constitutional revisions long predates the adoption in 1911 of the initiative process as part of the California Constitution. The origin and history in the pre-initiative era of this distinction between an amendment and a revision shed considerable light upon the contemplated scope of the two categories. [O]ur state's original 1849 California Constitution provided that *the Legislature* could propose *constitutional amendments*, but * * * a *constitutional revision* could be proposed only by means of *a constitutional convention*, the method used in 1849 to draft the initial constitution in anticipation of California's

statehood the following year. Thus, as originally adopted, the constitutional amendment/revision dichotomy in California—which mirrored the framework set forth in many other state constitutions of the same vintage—indicates that the category of *constitutional revision* referred to the kind of wholesale or fundamental alteration of the constitutional structure that appropriately could be undertaken only by a constitutional convention, in contrast to the category of *constitutional amendment*, which included any and all of the more discrete changes to the Constitution that thereafter might be proposed. ([I]t was not until the state Constitution was changed *in 1962*—through *a constitutional amendment*—that *the Legislature* obtained the authority to propose revisions to all or part of the Constitution.)

Furthermore, in addition to the historical background of the amendment/revision language that appears in the California Constitution itself, over the past three decades numerous decisions of this court have considered whether a variety of proposed changes to the California Constitution represented constitutional amendments or instead constitutional revisions. Those decisions establish both the analytical framework and the legal standard that govern our decision in this case, and further apply the governing standard to a wide array of measures that added new provisions and substantially altered existing provisions of the state Constitution. Those decisions explain that in resolving the amendment/revision question, a court carefully must assess (1) the meaning and scope of the constitutional change at issue, and (2) the effect—both quantitative and qualitative—that the constitutional change will have on *the basic governmental plan or framework* embodied in the preexisting provisions of the California Constitution.

In analyzing the constitutional challenges presently before us, we first explain that the provision added to the California Constitution by Proposition 8, when considered in light of the majority opinion in the *Marriage Cases* (which preceded the adoption of Proposition 8), properly must be understood as having a considerably narrower scope and more limited effect than suggested by petitioners in the cases before us. Contrary to petitioners' assertion, Proposition 8 does not *entirely repeal* or *abrogate* the aspect of a same-sex couple's state constitutional right of privacy and due process that was analyzed in the majority opinion in the *Marriage Cases*— that is, the constitutional right of same-sex couples to "choose one's life partner and enter with that person into a committed, officially recognized, and protected family relationship that enjoys all of the constitutionally based incidents of marriage" (*Marriage Cases*). Nor does Proposition 8 *fundamentally alter* the meaning and substance of state constitutional equal protection principles as articulated in that opinion. Instead, the measure carves out a narrow and limited exception to these state constitutional rights, reserving the official *designation* of the term "marriage" for the union of opposite-sex couples as a matter of state constitutional law, but leaving undisturbed all of the other extremely significant substantive aspects of a same-sex couple's state constitutional right to establish an officially recognized and protected family relationship and the guarantee of equal protection of the laws.

By clarifying this essential point, we by no means diminish or minimize the significance that the official designation of "marriage" holds for both the proponents and opponents of Proposition 8; indeed, the importance of the marriage designation was a vital factor in the majority opinion's ultimate holding in the *Marriage Cases*. Nonetheless, it is crucial that we accurately identify the actual effect of Proposition 8 on same-sex couples' state constitutional rights, as those rights existed prior to adoption of the proposition, in order to be able to assess properly the constitutional challenges to the proposition advanced in the present proceeding. We emphasize only that among the various constitutional protections recognized in the *Marriage Cases* as available to same-sex couples, it is only the designation of marriage—albeit significant—that has been removed by this initiative measure.

Taking into consideration the actual limited effect of Proposition 8 upon the preexisting state constitutional right of privacy and due process and upon the guarantee of equal protection of the laws, and after comparing this initiative measure to the many other constitutional changes that have been reviewed and evaluated in numerous prior decisions of this court, we conclude Proposition 8 constitutes a constitutional amendment rather than a constitutional revision. As a quantitative matter, petitioners concede that Proposition 8—which adds but a single, simple section to the Constitution—does not constitute a revision. As a qualitative matter, the act of limiting access to the designation of marriage to opposite-sex couples does not have a substantial or, indeed, even a minimal effect on *the governmental plan or framework of California* that existed prior to the amendment. Contrary to petitioners' claim in this regard, the measure does not transform or undermine the judicial function; this court will continue to exercise its traditional responsibility to faithfully enforce *all* of the provisions of the California Constitution, which now include the new section added through the voters' approval of Proposition 8. Furthermore, the judiciary's authority in applying the state Constitution always has been limited by the content of the provisions set forth in our Constitution, and that limitation remains unchanged.

Petitioners contend, however, that even if Proposition 8 does not affect the *governmental plan* or *framework* established by the state Constitution, the measure nonetheless should be considered to be a revision because it conflicts with an assertedly fundamental constitutional principle that protects a minority group from having its constitutional rights diminished *in any respect* by majority vote. Petitioners, however, cannot point to any authority supporting their claim that under the California Constitution, a constitutional amendment—proposed and adopted by a majority of voters through the initiative process—cannot diminish in any respect the content of a state constitutional right as that right has been interpreted in a judicial decision. [T]here have been many amendments to the California Constitution, adopted by the people through the initiative process in response to court decisions interpreting various provisions of the California Constitution, that have had just such an effect.

We agree with petitioners that the state constitutional right to equal protection of the laws unquestionably represents a long-standing and fundamental constitutional principle (a constitutional principle that, as we already have explained, has *not generally* been repealed or eliminated by Proposition 8). There are many other constitutional rights that have been amended in the past through the initiative process, however, that also are embodied in the state Constitution's Declaration of Rights and reflect equally long-standing and fundamental constitutional principles whose purpose is to protect often unpopular individuals and groups from overzealous or abusive treatment that at times may be condoned by a transient majority. Neither the language of the relevant constitutional provisions, nor our past cases, support the proposition that any of these rights is totally exempt from modification by a constitutional amendment adopted by a majority of the voters through the initiative process.

The constitutions of a number of other states contain express provisions precluding the use of the initiative power to amend portions or specified provisions of those states' constitutions (see, e.g., Mass. Const., amend. art. XLVIII, pt. II, § 2 ["No proposition inconsistent with any one of the following rights of the individual, as at present declared in the declaration of rights, shall be the subject of an initiative ... petition: [listing a number of rights, including the rights to just compensation, jury trial, and protection from unreasonable search, and the freedoms of speech, assembly, and of the press"]; Miss. Const., art. 15, § 273, subd. (5) ["The initiative process shall not be used: [¶] (a) For the proposal, modification or repeal of any portion of the Bill of Rights of this Constitution"].) In contrast, the California Constitution contains no comparable limitation. In the absence of such an express restriction on the initiative power, and in light of past California authorities, we conclude that the California Constitution cannot be interpreted as restricting the scope of the people's right to amend their Constitution in the manner proposed by petitioners. * * *

The Attorney General, in his briefing before this court, has advanced an alternative theory—not raised by petitioners in their initial petitions— under which he claims that even if Proposition 8 constitutes a constitutional amendment rather than a constitutional revision, that initiative measure nonetheless should be found invalid under the California Constitution on the ground that the "inalienable rights" embodied in article I, section 1 of that Constitution are not subject to "abrogation" by constitutional amendment without a compelling state interest. The Attorney General's contention is flawed, however, in part because, like petitioners' claims, it rests inaccurately upon an overstatement of the effect of Proposition 8 on both the fundamental constitutional right of privacy guaranteed by article I, section 1, and on the due process and equal protection guarantees of article I, section 7. As explained below, Proposition 8 does not abrogate any of these state constitutional rights, but instead carves out a narrow exception applicable only to access to the *designation* of the term "marriage," but not to any other of "the core set of basic *substantive* legal rights and attributes traditionally associated with marriage ..." (*Marriage Cases*), such as the right to establish an officially recognized and protected family relationship with the person of one's choice and to raise children within that family.

In addition, no authority supports the Attorney General's claim that a constitutional amendment adopted through the constitutionally prescribed procedure is invalid simply because the amendment affects a prior judicial interpretation of a right that the Constitution denominates "inalienable." The natural-law jurisprudence reflected in passages from the few early judicial opinions relied upon by the Attorney General has been discredited for many years, and, in any event, *no* decision suggests that when a constitution has been explicitly amended to modify a constitutional right (including a right identified in the Constitution as "inalienable"), the amendment may be found unconstitutional on the ground that it conflicts with some *implicit or extraconstitutional* limitation that is to be framed and enforced by the judiciary. Although the amending provisions of a constitution can *expressly* place some subjects or portions of the constitution off-limits to the amending process—as already noted, some state constitutions contain just such explicit limits—the California Constitution contains no such restraints. This court would radically depart from the well-established limits of the judicial function were it to engraft such a restriction onto the Constitution in the absence of an explicit constitutional provision limiting the amendment power.

Accordingly, we conclude that each of the state constitutional challenges to Proposition 8 advanced by petitioners and the Attorney General lacks merit. Having been approved by a majority of the voters at the November 4, 2008 election, the initiative measure lawfully amends the California Constitution to include the new provision as article I, section 7.5.

In a sense, petitioners' and the Attorney General's complaint is that it is just too easy to amend the California Constitution through the initiative process. But it is not a proper function of this court to curtail that process; we are constitutionally bound to uphold it. If the process for amending the Constitution is to be restricted—perhaps in the manner it was explicitly limited in an earlier version of our state Constitution, or as limited in the present-day constitutions of some of our sister states—this is an effort that the people themselves may undertake through the process of amending their Constitution in order to impose further limitations upon their own power of initiative.

Finally, we consider whether Proposition 8 affects the validity of the marriages of same-sex couples that were performed prior to the adoption of Proposition 8. Applying well-established legal principles pertinent to the question whether a constitutional provision should be interpreted to apply prospectively or retroactively, we conclude that the new section cannot properly be interpreted to apply retroactively. Accordingly, the marriages of same-sex couples performed prior to the effective date of Proposition 8 remain valid and must continue to be recognized in this state. * * *

[JUSTICES KENNARD, CHIN, BAXTER, CORRIGAN joined the Chief Justice's opinion. We omit the concurring opinion of JUSTICE KENNARD.]

■ JUSTICE WERDEGAR, concurring [in the judgment].

[Justice Werdegar rejected the majority's ruling that only changes in the fundamental nature of governmental organs would qualify as revisions requiring legislative involvement in changing the California Constitution.] The history of our California Constitution belies any suggestion that the drafters envisioned or would have approved a rule, such as that announced today, that affords governmental structure and organization more protection from casual amendment than civil liberties. The delegates to the 1849 constitutional convention recognized that "government was instituted for the protection of minorities," and that "[t]he majority of any community is the party to be governed; the restrictions of law are interposed between them and the weaker party; they are to be restrained from infringing upon the rights of the minority." (Browne, Rep. of the Debates in Convention of Cal. on Formation of State Const. (1850) p. 22 [remarks of delegate William Gwin].) Similarly, the delegates to the second constitutional convention in 1878–1879 well understood the charter they were drafting would provide the only effective protection for civil liberties. The initial draft of the 1879 Constitution, in a provision ultimately rejected, would expressly have looked to the federal Constitution for this purpose by declaring "that the U.S. Constitution was 'the great charter of our liberties.' Not so, cried delegate [Horace] Rolfe, for 'we had State charters before there was any Constitution of the United States.' Even the conservative delegates conceded that reliance on the federal Constitution as the principal author of liberties was 'a mistake historically, a mistake in law, and it is a blunder all around.' Thus, the convention's refusal to label the federal Constitution 'the great charter of our liberties' provided a clear indicator 'that the idea of rights rooted in the state's own constitution was a robust one'. . . ." (Grodin et al., *The Cal State Constitution: A Reference Guide* (1993) p. 15.) The delegates, moreover, were suspicious of government to a degree that scholars have described as "generalized distrust." (Grodin et al., *supra*, at pp. 14–15.) The task on which these delegates embarked was to create a legal structure for a *society*, not just for a *government*. To conclude they intended to protect individual liberties less jealously, and to give them less permanence, than the forms of governmental organization and structure is unsupportable.

The Constitution does not define the terms "revision" and "amendment" (Cal. Const., art. XVIII, §§ 1, 4), but we found these plain English words clear enough when we first considered them in 1894, within the memory of living delegates to the 1878–1879 constitutional convention. (*Livermore v. Waite* (1894) 102 Cal. 113.) We wrote then that "[t]he very term 'constitution' implies an instrument of a permanent and abiding nature, and the provisions contained therein for its revision indicate the will of the people that the underlying principles upon which it rests, as well as the substantial entirety of the instrument, shall be of a like permanent and abiding nature. On the other hand, the significance of the term 'amendment' implies such an addition or change within the lines of the original instrument as will effect an improvement, or better carry out the purpose for which it was framed." (*Id.*, at pp. 118–119.) In other words, a revision is a more substantial or extensive change, an amendment a less substantial or extensive one. In the years following *Livermore v. Waite*, experience with the initiative process led us to recognize that a single, concise change proposed as an amendment could have an extensive, revisional effect on the Constitution. (*McFadden v. Jordan* (1948) 32 Cal.2d 330, 345–346.) Thus we speak today of both "qualitative" and "quantitative" revisions. Yet it remains true that the scope of the change, and not its subject matter, is the point of distinction.

[Justice Werdegar did not, however, believe that Proposition 8 effected a broad change in the constitutional principle of equal protection and so concurred in the Court's judgment that Proposition 8 was not a revision.] Equal protection's continuing vitality in the present context is shown by this court's unanimous reaffirmation of its conclusions in the *Marriage Cases* that laws discriminating on the basis of sexual orientation are subject to strict scrutiny, and that—excepting the name—same-sex couples are entitled to enjoy all of the rights of marriage. Accordingly, all three branches of state government continue to have the duty, within their respective spheres of operation, today as before the passage of Proposition 8, to eliminate the remaining important differences between marriage and domestic partnership, both in substance and perception. The measure puts one solution beyond reach by prohibiting the state from naming future same-sex unions "marriages," but it does not otherwise affect the state's obligation to enforce the equal protection clause by protecting the "fundamental right . . . of same-sex couples to have their official family relationship accorded the same dignity, respect, and stature as that accorded to all other official recognized family relationships." (*Marriage Cases*) For the state to meet its obligations under the equal protection clause will now be more difficult, but the obligation remains.

■ Concurring and Dissenting Opinion of JUSTICE MORENO.

[Justice Moreno concurred with the Court and Justice Werdegar, that Proposition 8 did not abrogate the 18,000 lesbian and gay marriages celebrated between June and November 2008 but dissented from the unanimous view of his colleagues that Proposition 8 was not an unconstitutional revision.] I conclude that requiring discrimination against a minority group on the basis of a suspect classification strikes at the core of the promise of equality that underlies our California Constitution and thus "represents such a drastic and far-reaching change in the nature and operation of our governmental structure that it must be considered a 'revision' of the state Constitution rather than a mere 'amendment' thereof." (*Amador Valley.*) The rule the majority crafts today not only allows same-sex couples to be stripped of the right to marry that this court recognized in the *Marriage Cases*, it places at risk the state constitutional rights of all disfavored minorities. It weakens the status of our state Constitution as a bulwark of fundamental rights for minorities protected from the will of the majority. * * *

NOTES ON THE PROPOSITION 8 CHALLENGE: WHAT IS A CONSTITUTION FOR?

1. *Direct Democracy and Hyper–Amendability of State Constitutions.* Bruce Cain and other political scientists have warned that state constitutions that can be changed through a process of simple majority votes through popular initiatives are subject to the phenomenon of *hyper-amendability.* See Bruce Cain et al., "Constitutional Change: Is It Too Easy to Amend Our State Constitution?," in Bruce Cain & Roger Noll, eds., *Constitutional Reform in California: Making State Government More Effective and Responsive* (1995). It is now too easy to amend state constitutions (there were 689 amendments in the period from 1994 to 2001), and much of the normal lawmaking process has been hijacked by constitutional initiatives. A large chunk of those initiative-based state constitutional amendments have been aimed at sexual and gender minorities—not only the anti-gay-marriage initiatives that have been adopted in California and twenty-nine other states but also initiatives depriving sexual and gender minorities rights to adopt children and to the protections of anti-discrimination laws. In contrast, the pace of state constitutional revision or replacement has slowed to a dead stop.

   Amici argued that the California Supreme Court ought to regulate the hyper-amendability phenomenon by setting limits on constitutional initiatives, and that the Prop 8 Case was an appropriate case for setting those limits. The Court clearly disagreed with the second point, but the first may be up for grabs still. Is this a phenomenon we should be concerned with? If so, what limits (if any) should the Court apply?

2. *What Is a Constitution For?* Whether or how much one is concerned about hyper-amendability and anti-gay initiatives depends in large part on what you think the Constitution is for. Two different theories were reflected in the briefs, and a third was suggested in Justice Werdegar's concurring opinion. See William N. Eskridge, Jr., "The California Proposition 8 Case: What Is a Constitution For?," *Calif. L. Rev.* (forthcoming 2009).

(A) *Aristotle: The Constitution as the Soul of the City.* Representing the interveners in the Proposition 8 Case, groups favoring traditional marriage who were the official proponents of the initiative, former Judge (now Dean) Kenneth W. Starr reminded the Court at every turn that We the People had decisively rejected the Court's earlier requirement of same-sex marriage. However unjust the petitioners and some of the justices might consider Proposition 8, they were obliged to defer to the considered judgment of the people, under both the positive terms of the California Constitution, which allows amendment by direct vote, and the popular sovereignty announced in its preamble. The petitioners objected that Judge Starr's brief was inconsistent with the concept of "constitutionalism," but Judge Starr's argument has deep roots in constitutional theory itself.

In his landmark work of constitutional theory, *The Politics*, Aristotle considered a constitution to be the soul of a city: more than territory or the inhabitants, a city's constitution accounted for its civic identity across time. "This community *is* the constitution," according to the *Politics* (Book III, § 4). "[T]he constitution is so to speak the life of the city." (Book IV, § 11.) It is the institutions and practices by which a people were governed. "A constitution is the organization of offices in a state, and determines what is to be the governing body, and what is the end of each community." (Book IV, § 1.) Thus, Aristotle described Sparta's constitution as one that tilted strongly toward aristocracy because its base of citizenship was narrow and the exercise of political authority was more tightly controlled. In contrast, the Athenian constitution was more democratic, for included Solon's fundamental laws which abolished serfdom, specified legal rights and duties for all citizens, and guaranteed every adult male Athenian the right to vote in the *ekklesia,* to serve on juries, and to act as magistrates.

Aristotle's constitutionalism was more than just a description of the institutions and values of the polity; it was a description with normative power. The *Politics* did not assume that the unwritten Athenian constitution trumped ordinary statutes, as a matter of legal hierarchy. But the constitution was nevertheless superior, as a matter of political morality, to everyday decrees and legal rules. According to Aristotle, "the laws are, and ought to be, framed with a view to the constitution, and not the constitution to the laws." (Book IV, § 1.) The normative force of a constitution derives from the coherence it gives the city's identity; in modern terminology, the constitution's power comes from its network effects rather than (or more than) from an appeal to legal hierarchy. This is more or less the same way that the British have traditionally thought about their constitution. Under the British system, the "constitution" has traditionally been understood to be the fundamental laws of the land, including landmark statutes, foundational precedents, and established customs. (Great Britain has recently adopted written constitutional protections for individual rights, so this old model is evolving toward a documentary constitution.)

This deeper constitutional vision helps explain how the proponents of Proposition 8 distanced themselves from the reductio argument that popular sovereignty could justify any kind of tyranny. Proposition 8's constitutional theory was a wedding of popular sovereignty and tradition, each having a legitimating force. Under an Aristotelian constitutionalism, marriage between one man and one woman is deeply constitutive of the polity: it provides a legal means by which romantic relationships and lifetime commitments can be formalized and a normative structure for families. That normative structure has been awesomely powerful because the commands and exhortations of the law have interacted with social norms deeply embedded in centuries of practice and reinforced by religious teachings. From this point of view, the *California Marriage Cases* were a constitutional rupture: even though the Court's requirement that civil marriage be opened up to lesbian and gay couples carried the full force of law, for a few months at least, it was inconsistent with the social and religious norms that were powerfully connected to the state by the traditional definition and practice of marriage. From this deeper Aristotelian perspective, it was a constitutional atrocity for the petitioners to argue that Proposition 8, rather than same-sex marriage, was constitutionally infirm.

Without going as far as Dean Starr, Chief Justice George's opinion seems responsive to the Aristotelian perspective, updated through the lens of modern democratic theory.

(B) *Locke: The Constitution as Social Contract, with Inalienable Rights.* Article I, Section 1 of the California Constitution says that all people retain "inalienable rights, among which are those of enjoying and defending life and liberty; acquiring, possessing, and protecting property; and pursuing and obtaining safety, happiness, and privacy." In the *California Marriage Cases*, the Court had ruled that civil marriage is one of the basic, inalienable civil rights that lesbian and gay citizens are guaranteed on the same terms as straight citizens. Because Proposition 8 took away this inalienable constitutional right and because inalienable means that a right cannot be taken away, Attorney General Jerry Brown argued that Proposition 8 was an unconstitutional constitutional amendment. (The petitioners made much the same point in support of their argument that only legislature-sponsored revisions could take away "fundamental" rights.) The concept of inalienable rights reflects a different understanding of constitutionalism than Aristotle's theory does.

In *Leviathan* (1651), Thomas Hobbes argued that government is justified, and earns our consent, by allowing us to escape the "state of nature." The civil state created by the social contract exists so that citizens can pursue their lives without fear that other citizens, or outside invaders, will interfere with their lives and their ability to operate in the world (chaps. XIII–XVIII). To protect citizens thus, the civil state needs legislatures to enact laws serving the public interest, police to enforce those laws, and courts to adjudicate controversies without resort to private feuds. These protections, moreover, need to be made available to *everyone*. The state's failure to protect all of us so that we can live our lives secure from fear, is for Hobbes the failure of the state to do its job. If the state protects only some, or provides protection ineptly, this is a justification—and according to Hobbes the *only* justification—for civil disobedience (Review and Conclusion). John Locke expanded upon Hobbes' analysis in his *Second Treatise of Government* (1689). Locke argued that the civil state not only saves people from risks to life and limb, but also provides citizens with the ability to add to their liberties and possessions, and enrich their lives beyond what they could possibly enjoy in the state of nature. Like Hobbes, Locke maintained that arbitrary governmental treatment denying some citizens their fundamental "lives, liberties, and estates" is justification for dissolving the social contract (¶ ¶ 222–43). This is how social contract theory supports certain "inalienable" rights: they are pre-political guarantees made to all of us as a condition of the social contract.

Locke's theory of pre-political rights was an important justification for the American Revolution: the colonists believed that they were treated arbitrarily by a distant government, which violated Locke's first maxim of governance: "They [legislators] are to govern by promulgated established laws, not to be varied in particular cases, but to have one rule for the rich and poor, for the favorite at court and the countryman at plough." (¶ 142.) Locke's notion of inalienable rights, including the equal treatment principle, was a central feature of early American state and federal constitutional law, starting with the Declaration of Independence (1775), which memorably said that "all men are created equal" and have "certain inalienable rights." From the earliest days of the American republic, state as well as federal judges invalidated discriminatory measures they deemed to be "class legislation," singling out one group for special advantages or disabilities. See Melissa Lamb Saunders, "Equal Protection, Class Legislation, and Color–Blindness," 96 *Mich. L. Rev.* 245 (1996).

Although not following the Attorney General, Justice Moreno' s dissenting opinion and Justice Werdegar's concurring opinion understand constitutionalism from this point of view.

(C) *Bentham: The Constitution as a Restraint on Excessive Costs.* Most of the *amicus* briefs focused on the costs and benefits of different dispositions in the Prop 8 Case—and those briefs suggested a third way of thinking about what a Constitution is for. Constitutions provide governance rules and structures, and constitutionalism is the ongoing conversation about what the more precise rules might be and what the structures might look like. Philosophically, such an understanding might rest upon the greatest-good-for-the-greatest-number philosophy of Jeremy Bentham, as updated by modern utilitarian institutionalists such as Richard Posner (*The Problems of Jurisprudence* (1990)) and Neil Komesar (*Imperfect Alternatives* (1994)).

In the Proposition 8 Case, a utilitarian constitutionalism would ask what are the costs and benefits of (1) same-sex marriage, (2) judicial trumping the popular referendum on that issue, and (3) the limits on popular initiatives suggested by the Court's disposition of the case. Admittedly, these are very hard questions to answer in the Proposition 8 Case, but given the open-texture of the legal sources as regards the amendment-revision distinction it is likely that the Justices's votes in the Proposition 8 Case boiled down to such a rough calculus. Specifically, a Benthamite calculus would reveal three different groupings on the Court:

- *The Marriage Equality Dissenters* (Justices Baxter, Chin, Corrigan), who felt that the marginal benefits (beyond domestic partnership already on the books) of same-sex marriage were low, that the vote on Prop 8 confirmed their view that there were significant symbolic costs of gay marriage for many citizens, and that the judiciary had already gone too far in pushing for gay marriage.

- *The Marriage Equality Pro–Initiative Center* (Chief Justice George and probably Justice Kennard), who felt there were benefits for same-sex marriage but that there would be high costs to the judiciary and to democratic values if the Court trumped Prop 8 and, in the process, invited other challenges to future initiatives.

- *The Marriage Equality Critics of Initiatives* (Justices Werdegar and Moreno), who felt there were strong benefits for same-sex marriage and that judges ought to be second-guessing constitutional initiatives to protect fundamental constitutional principles; these justices differed as to the constitutional cost of denying full marriage to lesbian and gay couples.

Part of the institutional calculus may have been a desire by the Chief Justice and perhaps other members of the Court to give something to each side: traditionalists had the satisfaction of seeing Prop 8 upheld, while marriage equality advocates won on the issue of retroactivity. This Solomonic resolution had the additional feature of providing 18,000 lesbian and gay marriages as a small social experiment that could be discussed in a future initiative. Did these unions end up being a net benefit for society? Or a source of trouble and turmoil?

3. *Social Movements Theory, Incrementalism, and Gay Rights.* Put together the *California Marriage Cases* and the Proposition 8 Case. They might be read to support an incrementalist model for social movement influence on public law.**** An incrementalist model assumes that traditional attitudes or prejudices do not change easily, or perhaps at all, except genera-

---

**** The account in text is taken from William N. Eskridge, Jr., *Equality Practice: Civil Unions and the Future of Gay Rights* (2002); Kees Waaldijk, *Small Change: How the Road to Same–Sex Marriage Got Paved in* *The Netherlands*, in *Legal Recognition of Same–Sex Partnerships: A Study of National, European and International Law* (Robert Wintemute & Mads Andenaes eds. 2001).

tionally, but that legal reform can have traction if it proceeds in little steps that are buttressed by social and economic reinforcements. This step-by-step process has three features. First, start with the easiest issue, in this instance sodomy reform; some conservative libertarians as well as liberal humanitarians were able to go along with this reform, and there were strong constitutional arguments for it. See *Lawrence v. Texas* (2003), in Chapter 1 of the Casebook. Be opportunistic: if judges are unreceptive, turn to legislators or prosecutors for relief. Once sodomy reform is procured, move on to the harder issues entailing affirmative state support, namely, hate crime laws, statutes barring employment and other forms of discrimination, and protection for lesbian and gay families. Even if one victory is preceded by ten defeats, a victory that is reinforced by positive social and economic feedback advances the cause. Success creates both momentum and a feeling of political efficacy, and wins over new political allies.

Second, success also brings more people out of their closets, either as openly gay people or as straight allies. Sodomy reform might embolden more gays to come out of the closet, because they have fewer fears of being arrested; more come out of the closet once anti-discrimination laws protect them against job discrimination. Once more people are openly lesbian or gay, stereotypes can be undermined; officials are more reluctant to demonize gays if they work with openly gay people, or even count them as friends, neighbors, or relatives. State recognition of relationships and child-rearing is most important, for that helps gays come out as families.

Third, each success can discredit opposition, which tends to rely on the same, now-falsifiable stereotyping to oppose each pro-gay move. So a gay-fearful parent who opposes sodomy reform because he or she believes that it will "promote homosexuality" and child abuse may be surprised when there appear to be no malignant effects of sodomy reform. When similar end-of-morality arguments are raised against anti-discrimination laws, some previous skeptics are more persuadable—and even more join them if anti-discrimination laws, too, fail to have the bad effects traditionalists predict. The "Defense of Marriage Act" rested upon the silly, and now falsified, assertion that gay marriage was a "threat" to different-sex marriages.

This "equality practice" model explains why it was safer for judges to require gay marriage in Canada, Massachusetts, and California than in Florida, Ohio, or even New York. Equality practice also suggests that compromises, such as civil unions and statewide domestic partnership, can powerfully advance the rights of LGBT persons. Finally, this model argues that reforms such as same-sex marriage ought to be debated at the state level before the U.S. Supreme Court takes a firm position. Indeed, the Supreme Court's decision in *Loving v. Virginia* (1967) was preceded by widespread state abandonment of anti-miscegenation laws. Between *Brown,* when 30 states had such laws, and *Loving,* when only 16 did, equality practice paved the way for the Court to invalidate the remaining southern laws, without significant backlash. See Randall Kennedy, "Marriage and the Struggle for Gay, Lesbian, and Black Liberation," 2005 *Utah L. Rev.* 781.

Page 320. Insert the following Case and Note at the end of Section 3:

In re Marriage Cases

California Supreme Court, 2008.
43 Cal.4th 757, 183 P.3d 384, 76 Cal.Rptr.3d 683.

■ CHIEF JUSTICE GEORGE delivered the opinion for the Court.

[Our earlier excerpt from the Chief Justice's opinion omitted his discussion of the appellants' argument that the state's exclusion of same-sex couples from marriage was subject to strict scrutiny because it was a "sex discrimination." **Part V.A.** of the Chief Justice's opinion for the Court discusses this issue.]

* * * In drawing a distinction between opposite-sex couples and same-sex couples, the challenged marriage statutes do not treat men and women differently. Persons of either gender are treated equally and are permitted to marry only a person of the opposite gender. In light of the equality of treatment between genders, the distinction prescribed by the relevant statutes plainly does not constitute discrimination on the basis of sex as that concept is commonly understood.

Plaintiffs contend, however, that the statutory distinction nonetheless should be viewed as sex or gender discrimination because the statutory limitation upon marriage in a particular case is dependent upon an individual person's sex or gender. Plaintiffs argue that because a woman who wishes to marry another woman would be permitted to do so if she were a man rather than a woman, and a man who wishes to marry another man would be permitted to do so if he were a woman rather than a man, the statutes must be seen as embodying discrimination on the basis of sex. Plaintiffs rely on the decisions in [*Perez v. Sharp*, 32 Cal.2d 711 (1948)], and *Loving v. Virginia*, in which this court and subsequently the United States Supreme Court found that the antimiscegenation statutes at issue in those cases discriminated on the basis of race, even though the statutes prohibited White persons from marrying Black persons and Black persons from marrying White persons.

The decisions in *Perez* and *Loving v. Virginia*, however, are clearly distinguishable from this case, because the antimiscegenation statutes at issue in those cases plainly treated members of minority races differently from White persons, prohibiting only intermarriage that involved White persons in order to prevent (in the undisguised words of the defenders of the statute in *Perez*) "the Caucasian race from being contaminated by races whose members are by nature physically and mentally inferior to Caucasians." (*Perez*; see also *Loving*.) Under these circumstances, there can be no doubt that the reference to race in the statutes at issue in *Perez* and *Loving* unquestionably reflected the kind of racial discrimination that always has been recognized as calling for strict scrutiny under equal protection analysis.

In *Perez, Loving*, and a number of other decisions (see, e.g., *McLaughlin v. Florida* (1964) 379 U.S. 184, 192), courts have recognized that a statute that treats a couple differently based upon whether the couple consists of persons of the same race or of different races generally reflects a policy disapproving of the integration or close relationship of individuals of different races in the setting in question, and as such properly is viewed as embodying an instance of *racial discrimination* with respect to the interracial couple and both of its members. By contrast, past judicial decisions, in California and elsewhere, virtually uniformly hold that a statute or policy that treats men and women equally but that accords differential treatment either to a couple based upon whether it consists of persons of the same sex rather than opposite sexes, or to an individual based upon whether he or she generally is sexually attracted to persons of the same gender rather than the opposite gender, is more accurately characterized as involving differential treatment on the basis of *sexual orientation* rather than an instance of *sex discrimination*, and properly should be analyzed on the *former* ground. These cases recognize that, in realistic terms, a statute or policy that treats same-sex couples differently from opposite-sex couples, or that treats individuals who are sexually attracted to persons of the same gender differently from individuals who are sexually attracted to persons of the opposite gender, does not treat an individual man or an individual woman differently *because of* his or her *gender* but rather accords differential treatment *because of* the individual's *sexual orientation*. * * *

Although plaintiffs further contend that the difference in treatment prescribed by the relevant statutes should be treated as sex discrimination for equal protection purposes because the differential treatment reflects illegitimate gender-related stereotyping based on the view that men are attracted to women and women are attracted to men, this argument again improperly conflates two concepts—discrimination on the basis of sex, and discrimination on the basis of sexual orientation—that traditionally have been viewed as distinct phenomena. Under plaintiffs' argument, discrimination on the basis of sexual orientation always would constitute a subset of discrimination on the basis of sex. * * *

Accordingly, we conclude that in the context of California's equal protection clause, the differential treatment prescribed by the relevant statutes cannot properly be found to constitute discrimination on the basis of sex, and thus that the statutory classification embodied in the marriage statutes is not subject to strict scrutiny on that ground.

[There was no dissent from this portion of the Chief Justice's opinion.]

NOTE ON THE CURRENT STATUS OF THE SEX DISCRIMINATION ARGUMENT FOR GAY RIGHTS

Are the *Marriage Cases* the Waterloo for the sex discrimination argument for gay rights that was given a judicial push in *Baehr v. Lewin* (1993)?

One might dispute much of the Chief Justice's logic. His attempt to distinguish *Perez* and *Loving* is questionable. The Chief Justice found those race discriminations motivated by an ideology of racism—but he did not deny that California's exclusion of same-sex couples from marriage was explicitly motivated by a sexist ideology. The Bill Digest for the 1977 statutory amendment, that explicitly excluded same-sex couples from marriage, said that the "special benefits" of marriage were "designed to meet situations where one spouse, typically the female, could not adequately provide for herself because she was engaged in raising children. . . . Why extend the same windfall to homosexual couples except in those rare situations (perhaps not so rare among females) where they function as parents with at least one of the partners devoting a significant period of his or her life to staying home and raising children?" Isn't this confirmation of the core argument, namely, that gender stereotyping through sex-based classifications is intimately related to homophobia and anti-gay policies?

The Chief Justice's apparent aversion to "conflating" different forms of discrimination is at odds with the rich literature on "intersectionality" (excerpted in Chapter 4): many Americans are subject to discrimination for more than one reason. An observant Jew might be discriminated against *either* because of his religion *or* because of his ethnicity. Shouldn't *both* forms of discrimination be recognized? Or is that "conflating" two different forms of discrimination?

Whatever the logical objections to the Chief Justice's opinion, it represented the considered judgment of all seven Justices (themselves representing a variety of perspectives). Its message was clear: LGBT advocates need to focus on their argument that sexual orientation is a (quasi-) suspect classification; the sex discrimination argument is a diversion. Is that right? Is there still value in making the sex discrimination argument for gay rights?

CHAPTER 3

IDENTITY SPEECH IN THE BODY POLITIC

SECTION 2

IDENTITY AND VIEWPOINT

Page 418.   Insert the following Case and Note at the end of Section 2:

Donald H. Rumsfeld v. Forum for Academic and Institutional Rights, Inc., et al.

United States Supreme Court, 2006.
547 U.S. 47, 126 S.Ct. 1297, 164 L.Ed.2d 156.

■ CHIEF JUSTICE ROBERTS delivered the opinion for the Court.

[The Forum for Academic & Institutional Rights (FAIR), an association of law schools formed to protect academic freedom, challenged the Defense Department's enforcement of the Solomon Amendment, 10 U.S.C. § 983. As amended by Congress in 2004, § 983 provides that if any part of an institution of higher education denies military recruiters access equal to that provided other recruiters, the entire institution would lose certain federal funds. The lower court ruled that the Solomon Amendment violated the First Amendment rights of FAIR's members and remanded to the trial court to enter an injunction against terminating federal funds to universities with noncomplying law schools. The Supreme Court reversed.]

III. * * * Although Congress has broad authority to legislate on matters of military recruiting, it nonetheless chose to secure campus access for military recruiters indirectly, through its Spending Clause power. The Solomon Amendment gives universities a choice: Either allow military recruiters the same access to students afforded any other recruiter or forgo certain federal funds. Congress' decision to proceed indirectly does not reduce the deference given to Congress in the area of military affairs. Congress' choice to promote its goal by creating a funding condition deserves at least as deferential treatment as if Congress had imposed a mandate on universities.

Congress' power to regulate military recruiting under the Solomon Amendment is arguably greater because universities are free to decline the federal funds. In *Grove City College v. Bell*, 465 U.S. 555, 575–575 (1984), we rejected a private college's claim that conditioning federal funds on its compliance with Title IX of the Education Amendments of 1972 violated the First Amendment. We thought this argument "warrant[ed] only brief consideration" because "Congress is free to attach reasonable and unambiguous conditions to federal financial assistance that educational institutions are not obligated to accept." We concluded that no First Amendment violation had occurred—without reviewing the substance of the First Amendment claims—because Grove City could decline the Government's funds.

Other decisions, however, recognize a limit on Congress' ability to place conditions on the receipt of funds. We recently held that " 'the government may not deny a benefit to a person on a basis that infringes his constitutionally protected ... freedom of speech even if he has no entitlement to that benefit.' " *United States v. Am. Library Ass'n*, 539 U.S. 194, 210 (2003). Under this principle, known as the unconstitutional conditions doctrine, the Solomon Amendment would be unconstitutional if Congress could not directly require universities to provide military recruiters equal access to their students.

This case does not require us to determine when a condition placed on university funding goes beyond the "reasonable" choice offered in *Grove City* and becomes an unconstitutional condition. It is clear that a funding condition cannot be unconstitutional if it could be constitutionally imposed directly. Because the First Amendment would not prevent Congress from directly imposing the Solomon Amendment's access requirement, the statute does not place an unconstitutional condition on the receipt of federal funds.

A. The Solomon Amendment neither limits what law schools may say nor requires them to say anything. Law schools remain free under the statute to express whatever views they may have on the military's congressionally mandated employment policy, all the while retaining eligibility for federal funds. See Tr. of Oral Arg. 25 (Solicitor General acknowledging that law schools "could put signs on the bulletin board next to the door, they could engage in speech, they could help organize student protests"). As a general matter, the Solomon Amendment regulates conduct, not speech. It affects what law schools must *do*—afford equal access to military recruiters—not what they may or may not *say*.

Nevertheless, the Third Circuit concluded that the Solomon Amendment violates law schools' freedom of speech in a number of ways. First, in assisting military recruiters, law schools provide some services, such as sending e-mails and distributing flyers, that clearly involve speech. The Court of Appeals held that in supplying these services law schools are unconstitutionally compelled to speak the Government's message. Second, military recruiters are, to some extent, speaking while they are on campus. The Court of Appeals held that, by forcing law schools to permit the military on campus to express its message, the Solomon Amendment unconstitutionally requires law schools to host or accommodate the military's speech. Third, although the Court of Appeals thought that the Solomon Amendment regulated speech, it held in the alternative that, if the statute regulates conduct, this conduct is expressive and regulating it unconstitutionally infringes law schools' right to engage in expressive conduct. We consider each issue in turn.

Some of this Court's leading First Amendment precedents have established the principle that freedom of speech prohibits the government from telling people what they must say. In *West Virginia Bd. of Ed. v. Barnette*, 319 U.S. 624. 642 (1943), we held unconstitutional a state law requiring schoolchildren to recite the Pledge of Allegiance and to salute the flag. And in *Wooley v. Maynard*, 430 U.S. 705, 717 (1977), we held unconstitutional another that required New Hampshire motorists to display the state motto—"Live Free or Die"—on their license plates.

The Solomon Amendment does not require any similar expression by law schools. Nonetheless, recruiting assistance provided by the schools often includes elements of speech. For example, schools may send e-mails or post notices on bulletin boards on an employer's behalf. Law schools offering such services to other recruiters must also send e-mails and post notices on behalf of the military to comply with the Solomon Amendment. As FAIR points out, these compelled statements of fact ("The U. S. Army recruiter will meet interested students in Room 123 at 11 a.m."), like compelled statements of opinion, are subject to First Amendment scrutiny.

This sort of recruiting assistance, however, is a far cry from the compelled speech in *Barnette* and *Wooley*. The Solomon Amendment, unlike the laws at issue in those cases, does not dictate the content of the speech at all, which is only "compelled" if, and to the extent, the school provides such speech for other recruiters. There is nothing in this case approaching a Government-mandated pledge or motto that the school must endorse.

The compelled speech to which the law schools point is plainly incidental to the Solomon Amendment's regulation of conduct, and "it has never been deemed an abridgment of freedom of speech or press to make a course of conduct illegal merely because the conduct was in part initiated, evidenced, or carried out by means of language, either spoken, written, or printed." Congress, for example, can prohibit employers from discriminating in hiring on the basis of race. The fact that this will require an employer to take down a sign reading "White Applicants Only" hardly means that the law should be analyzed as one regulating the employer's speech rather than conduct. Compelling a law school that sends scheduling e-mails for other recruiters to send one for a military recruiter is simply not the same as forcing a student to pledge allegiance, or forcing a Jehovah's Witness to display the motto "Live Free or Die" and it trivializes the freedom protected in *Barnette* and *Wooley* to suggest that it is.

Our compelled-speech cases are not limited to the situation in which an individual must personally speak the government's message. We have also in a number of instances limited the government's ability to force one speaker to host or accommodate another speaker's message. See *Hurley* (state law cannot require a parade to include a group whose message the parade's organizer does not wish to send); *Pacific Gas & Elec. Co. v. Public Util. Comm'n of Cal.,* 475 U.S. 1, 20–21 (1986) (plurality opinion); accord, *id.,* at 25 (Marshall, J., concurring in judgment) (state agency cannot require a utility company to include a third-party newsletter in its billing envelope); *Miami Herald Publishing Co. v. Tornillo,* 418 U.S. 241 (1974) (right-of-reply statute violates editors' right to determine the content of their newspapers). Relying on these precedents, the Third Circuit concluded that the Solomon Amendment unconstitutionally compels law schools to accommodate the military's message "[b]y requiring schools to include military recruiters in the interviews and recruiting receptions the schools arrange."

The compelled-speech violation in each of our prior cases, however, resulted from the fact that the complaining speaker's own message was affected by the speech it was forced to accommodate. The expressive nature of a parade was central to our holding in *Hurley* ("Parades are . . . a form of expression, not just motion, and the inherent expressiveness of marching to make a point explains our cases involving protest marches"). We concluded that because "every participating unit affects the message conveyed by the [parade's] private organizers," a law dictating that a particular group must be included in the parade "alter[s] the expressive content of th[e] parade." As a result, we held that the State's public accommodation law, as applied to a private parade, "violates the fundamental rule of protection under the First Amendment, that a speaker has the autonomy to choose the content of his own message." * * *

In this case, accommodating the military's message does not affect the law schools' speech, because the schools are not speaking when they host interviews and recruiting receptions. Unlike a parade organizer's choice of parade contingents, a law school's decision to allow recruiters on campus is not inherently expressive. Law schools facilitate recruiting to assist their students in obtaining jobs. A law school's recruiting services lack the expressive quality of a parade, a newsletter, or the editorial page of a newspaper; its accommodation of a military recruiter's message is not compelled speech because the accommodation does not sufficiently interfere with any message of the school.

The schools respond that if they treat military and nonmilitary recruiters alike in order to comply with the Solomon Amendment, they could be viewed as sending the message that they see nothing wrong with the military's policies, when they do. We rejected a similar argument in *PruneYard Shopping Center v. Robins*, 447 U.S. 74 (1980). In that case, we upheld a state law requiring a shopping center owner to allow certain expressive activities by others on its property. We explained that there was little likelihood that the views of those engaging in the expressive activities would be identified with the owner, who remained free to disassociate himself from those views and who was "not ... being compelled to affirm [a] belief in any governmentally prescribed position or view."

The same is true here. Nothing about recruiting suggests that law schools agree with any speech by recruiters, and nothing in the Solomon Amendment restricts what the law schools may say about the military's policies. We have held that high school students can appreciate the difference between speech a school sponsors and speech the school permits because legally required to do so, pursuant to an equal access policy. Surely students have not lost that ability by the time they get to law school.

Having rejected the view that the Solomon Amendment impermissibly regulates *speech*, we must still consider whether the expressive nature of the *conduct* regulated by the statute brings that conduct within the First Amendment's protection. In *O'Brien*, we recognized that some forms of " 'symbolic speech' " were deserving of First Amendment protection. But we rejected the view that "conduct can be labeled 'speech' whenever the person engaging in the conduct intends thereby to express an idea." Instead, we have extended First Amendment protection only to conduct that is inherently expressive. In *Texas v. Johnson*, for example, we applied *O'Brien* and held that burning the American flag was sufficiently expressive to warrant First Amendment protection.

Unlike flag burning, the conduct regulated by the Solomon Amendment is not inherently expressive. Prior to the adoption of the Solomon Amendment's equal-access requirement, law schools "expressed" their disagreement with the military by treating military recruiters differently from other recruiters. But these actions were expressive only because the law schools accompanied their conduct with speech explaining it. For example, the point of requiring military interviews to be conducted on the undergraduate campus is not "overwhelmingly apparent." *Johnson*. An observer who sees military recruiters interviewing away from the law school has no way of knowing whether the law school is expressing its disapproval of the military, all the law school's interview rooms are full, or the military recruiters decided for reasons of their own that they would rather interview someplace else.

The expressive component of a law school's actions is not created by the conduct itself but by the speech that accompanies it. The fact that such explanatory speech is necessary is strong evidence that the conduct at issue here is not so inherently expressive that it warrants protection under *O'Brien*. If combining speech and conduct were enough to create expressive conduct, a regulated party could always transform conduct into "speech" simply by talking about it. For instance, if an individual announces that he intends to express his disapproval of the Internal Revenue Service by refusing to pay his income taxes, we would have to apply *O'Brien* to determine whether the Tax Code violates the First Amendment. Neither *O'Brien* nor its progeny supports such a result. * * *

B.   The Solomon Amendment does not violate law schools' freedom of speech, but the First Amendment's protection extends beyond the right to speak. We have recognized a First Amendment right to associate for the purpose of speaking, which we have termed a "right of expressive association." See, *e.g.*, *Dale*. The reason we have extended First Amendment protection in this way is clear: The right to speak is often exercised most effectively by combining one's voice with the voices of others. If the government were free to restrict individuals' ability to join together and speak, it could essentially silence views that the First Amendment is intended to protect.

FAIR argues that the Solomon Amendment violates law schools' freedom of expressive association. According to FAIR, law schools' ability to express their message that discrimination on the basis of sexual orientation is wrong is significantly affected by the presence of military recruiters on campus and the schools' obligation to assist them. Relying heavily on our decision in *Dale*, the Court of Appeals agreed.

In *Dale*, we held that the Boy Scouts' freedom of expressive association was violated by New Jersey's public accommodations law, which required the organization to accept a homosexual as a scoutmaster. After determining that the Boy Scouts was an expressive association, that "the forced inclusion of Dale would significantly affect its expression," and that the State's interests did not justify this intrusion, we concluded that the Boy Scouts' First Amendment rights were violated.

The Solomon Amendment, however, does not similarly affect a law school's associational rights. To comply with the statute, law schools must allow military recruiters on campus and assist them in whatever way the school chooses to assist other employers. Law schools therefore "associate" with military recruiters in the sense that they interact with them. But recruiters are not part of the law school. Recruiters are, by definition, outsiders who come onto campus for the limited purpose of trying to hire students—not to become members of the school's expressive association. This distinction is critical. Unlike the public accommodations law in *Dale*, the Solomon Amendment does not force a law school " 'to accept members it does not desire.' " [*Dale*, quoting *Roberts*.] The law schools *say* that allowing military recruiters equal access impairs their own expression by requiring them to associate with the recruiters, but just as saying conduct is undertaken for expressive purposes cannot make it symbolic speech, so too a speaker cannot "erect a shield" against laws requiring access "simply by asserting" that mere association "would impair its message." [*Dale*.]

FAIR correctly notes that the freedom of expressive association protects more than just a group's membership decisions. For example, we have held laws unconstitutional that require disclosure of membership lists for groups seeking anonymity, or impose penalties or withhold benefits based on membership in a disfavored group. Although these laws did not directly interfere with an organization's composition, they made group membership less attractive, raising the same *First Amendment* concerns about affecting the group's ability to express its message.

The Solomon Amendment has no similar effect on a law school's associational rights. Students and faculty are free to associate to voice their disapproval of the military's message; nothing about the statute affects the composition of the group by making group membership less desirable. The Solomon Amendment therefore does not violate a law school's First Amendment rights. A military recruiter's mere presence on campus does not violate a law school's right to associate, regardless of how repugnant the law school considers the recruiter's message.

* * *

In this case, FAIR has attempted to stretch a number of First Amendment doctrines well beyond the sort of activities these doctrines protect. The law schools object to having to treat military recruiters like other recruiters, but that regulation of conduct does not violate the First Amendment. To the extent that the Solomon Amendment incidentally affects expression, the law schools' effort to cast themselves as just like the schoolchildren in *Barnette*, the parade organizers in *Hurley*, and the Boy Scouts in *Dale* plainly overstates the expressive nature of their activity and the impact of the Solomon Amendment on it, while exaggerating the reach of our First Amendment precedents. * * *

■ JUSTICE ALITO took no part in the deliberation or decision of this case.

NOTE ON THE *FAIR* CASE AND THE LIMITS OF *HURLEY* AND *DALE*

The Forum for Academic & Institutional Rights (FAIR) sought to apply the principles of *Hurley* and *Dale* to protect law schools' expressive conduct (*Hurley*) and expressive association (*Dale*) critical of the Department of Defense's exclusion of openly lesbian and gay service personnel. Could decisions protecting anti-gay speech and association against state regulation *also* protect pro-gay speech and association? Not in this particular case. The Court's analysis of *Hurley* and *Dale* may be significant, however.

As FAIR and the lower court had argued, the Chief Justice's opinion characterized *Hurley* as a case where the state had "sought to force one speaker to host or accommodate another speaker's message." But the Court found *Hurley* different, because "the complaining speaker's own message was affected by the speech it was forced to accommodate." The law schools' career service offices were not, the Court found, engaged in expressive activities when they arranged and publicized employer interviews with their law students. In short, a job fair does not have the expressive qualities of a parade. Is that true of all job fairs and all parades?

Recall that the parade in *Hurley* had no expressive content (beyond "Irish Are Great") *until* openly gay people tried to crash it; in order to exclude homosexuals, the parade organizers came up with different explanations at different times, finally settling on the idea that theirs was a traditional family values parade. In contrast, the law school job fairs were politicized *before* Don't Ask, Don't Tell. NYU and Yale banned gay-discriminating employers since the late 1970s, and almost all other AALS-member schools followed in the 1980s and 1990s. The Department of Defense got caught in these politicized job fairs—but doesn't that make the FAIR case *more* rather than *less* expressive than the anything-goes-except-for-homosexuals Boston parade?

The Chief Justice's opinion characterized *Dale* as a case where the state sought to control the *membership* of an expressive association, an intrusion much deeper than the Solomon Amendment's effort to regulate law schools' interaction with *outsiders* (the recruiters who come to campus). The Court concluded: "A military recruiter's mere presence on campus does not violate a law school's freedom to associate, regardless of how repugnant the law school considers the recruiter's message." What if the recruiter repeated General Peter Pace's observation that homosexuals are excluded because their conduct is immoral? This would be covered by the Chief Justice's holding. Now consider: Is this so much less an intrusion into law schools' expressive association than the state intrusion in *Dale*?

Consider this variation of *FAIR*: For most of the twentieth century, the armed forces segregated African Americans, on the ground that their presence would disrupt unit cohesion (Chapter 4, Section 1 of the Casebook). Assume that Progressive Law School took the position that segregation reflected an ideology of racism and did not permit discriminatory employers to interview through its career services office. PLS took the position that the mere presence of a military interviewer sent a message that the school "cooperated" with racist employers. Would the Chief Justice allow the Department of Defense to force its way into the PLS process?

At oral argument in *FAIR*, Justice Breyer was concerned that a broad reading of *Dale* and *Hurley* would undermine federal statutes that prohibited employers, public accommodations, and federally-funded institutions from engaging in race discrimination. The Chief Justice's opinion provides an easy justification for regulating public accommodations: the state is not affecting their message by requiring them to deal with outsiders on a fair and equal basis. But the opinion may invite challenges to Title VII, which regulates the composition of an employer's workforce. For example, if the KKK, an openly racist organization, has an office falling under Title VII, the KKK might argue that *Dale* bars application of Title VII to require it to consider hiring people of color. As in *Dale*, the KKK could argue that a racially *integrated* workforce would be inconsistent with its philosophy of racial *segregation*. Would *FAIR* bolster such an argument?

At oral argument, and in its brief, FAIR had a response to Justice Breyer's concern and a possible limiting principle for the First Amendment rights it was pressing. FAIR argued that the Solomon Amendment was enacted as a response to law schools' criticism and resistance to the statutory exclusion of gay people from the armed forces; that the intent of Congress was to discipline dissent; and that the Defense Department enforced the statute in a punitive manner that was aimed at suppressing the law schools' expressed belief that the armed forces were dishonorable in their exclusion of a class of Americans for bad reasons. Indeed, the Solomon Amendment on its face was viewpoint-discriminatory: schools excluding military recruiters because of their objection to its anti-gay discrimination were subject to funding cutoffs, but schools excluding military recruiters because they had a religious or philosophical commitment to peace were not subject to those cutoffs. Nor were schools that devoted no space to outside recruiters of any sort.

The Chief Justice's opinion does not mention this argument. Construct the Chief Justice's best answer to this argument. Does Congress have the authority to use funding cutoffs to discipline institutions that criticize government policies? When would this be appropriate—and when not?

Christian Legal Soc. Chapter of University of California v. Kane

U.S. District Court for the Northern District of California, 2006.
2006 WL 997217.

. . . This case concerns whether a religious student organization may compel a public university law school to fund its activities and to allow the group to use the school's name and facilities even though the organization admittedly discriminates in the selection of its members and officers on the basis of religion and sexual orientation.

CLS is an unincorporated student organization comprised of students attending University of California, Hastings College of the Law (the "Law School"). The mission of CLS is "to maintain a vibrant Christian Law Fellowship on the School's campus which enables its members, individually and as a group, to love the Lord with their whole beings-hearts, souls, and minds-and to love their neighbors as themselves." In the beginning of the 2004–2005 academic year, CLS applied for, but was denied the privilege of becoming a recognized student organization at the Law School.

University of California, Hastings College of the Law is a public law school located in San Francisco and is part of the University of California school system. ... The Hastings Defendants permit student organizations to register with the Office of Student Services. Student organizations must be registered in order to gain access to [various] benefits....

As a condition of becoming a "registered student organization," the Hastings Defendants require a student organization to comply with the Law School's Policies and Regulations Applying to College Activities, Organizations and Students, which requires, *inter alia,* registered student organizations to abide by the Policy on Nondiscrimination ("Nondiscrimination Policy.") The Nondiscrimination Policy provides:

> The College is committed to a policy against legally impermissible, arbitrary or unreasonable discriminatory practices. All groups, including administration, faculty, student governments, College-owned student residence facilities and programs sponsored by the College, are governed by this policy of nondiscrimination....

> The University of California, Hastings College of the Law shall not discriminate unlawfully on the basis of race, color, religion, national origin, ancestry, disability, age, sex or sexual orientation. This nondiscrimination policy covers admission, access and treatment in Hastings-sponsored programs and activities.

Hastings requires registered student organizations to allow any student to participate, become a member, or seek leadership positions, regardless of their status or beliefs.

[Different groups, using different names, organized Christian student organizations at Hastings starting in the 1994–1995 academic year. For most of that time, there was no conflict between the group's bylaws and the school's non-discrimination policy. At the end of the 2003–2004 academic year, the group's leaders decided to affiliate their student organization officially with a national organization known as the Christian Legal Society ("CLS–National").] CLS–National requires its formally-associated student chapters to use a specific set of bylaws. The bylaws require any student who wants to become a member to sign a "Statement of Faith"....

CLS will not permit students who do not sign the Statement of Faith [professing belief in God as embodied in the trinity, as father, son and holy ghost] to become members or officers. CLS also bars individuals who engage in "unrepentant homosexual conduct" or are members of religions that have tenets which differ from those set forth in the Statement of Faith from becoming members or officers. The bylaws also pronounce a "code of conduct" for officers which provides that officers "must exemplify the highest standards of morality as set forth in Scripture.'' While only actual members of CLS may vote for or remove officers, stand for election to become an officer, or vote to amend the organization's constitution, CLS's meetings and activities are open to all students, regardless of their religion or sexual orientation.

. . . On September 17, 2004, CLS submitted its registration form and set of bylaws to the Office of Student Services. Hastings informed CLS that its bylaws did not appear to be compliant with the Nondiscrimination Policy, in particular the religion and sexual orientation provisions, and invited CLS to discuss changing them. Hastings further advised CLS that to become a recognized student organization, CLS would have to open its membership to all students irrespective of their religion or sexual orientation. . . .

CLS contends that Hastings' enforcement of its Nondiscrimination Policy, and its refusal to grant CLS an exception to exclude students on the basis of religion and sexual orientation, infringes its members' rights to free speech, free association, free exercise, and equal protection. As set forth below, the Court finds that Hastings' uniform enforcement of its Nondiscrimination Policy infringes none of these constitutional rights.

1.   First Amendment: Free Speech.

a.   Regulation of Conduct.

i.   Hastings' Nondiscrimination Policy Regulates Conduct.

The parties dispute whether Hastings' Nondiscrimination Policy regulates speech or conduct. The Nondiscrimination Policy prohibits discrimination on the basis of religion and sexual orientation, among other categories. Courts have consistently held that regulations prohibiting discrimination, similar to Hastings' Nondiscrimination Policy, regulate conduct, not speech. . . . [The court analyzes *Hurley v. Irish–American Gay, Lesbian and Bisexual Group of Boston* and *Roberts v. United States Jaycees.* The court concluded that when civil rights laws regulated conduct rather than speech, they had survived a First Amendment challenge.]

The Supreme Court recently reiterated the distinction between regulating speech and conduct in *Rumsfeld v. Forum for Academic and Institutional Rights, Inc.,* when it affirmed the enforcement of the Solomon Amendment against law schools with policies that prohibit discrimination on the basis of, among other things, sexual orientation. The Solomon Amendment provides that "if any part of an institution of higher education denies military recruiters access equal to that provided other recruiters, the entire institution will lose certain federal funds." The Supreme Court rejected the argument by an association of laws schools and law faculties that requiring law schools with anti-discrimination policies to provide the same level of access to the military recruiters as employers who do not discriminate on the basis of sexual orientation infringed the association's members' First Amendment rights. The Court held that:

> [t]he Solomon Amendment neither limits what law schools may say nor requires them to say anything. Law schools remain free under the statute to express whatever views they may have on the military's congressionally mandated employment policy, all the while retaining eligibility for federal funds.... As a general matter, the Solomon Amendment regulates conduct, not speech. It affects what law schools must *do*-afford equal access to military recruiters-not what they may or may not *say*.

[T]he Court finds that on its face, Hastings' Nondiscrimination Policy targets conduct, *i.e.* discrimination, not speech. As in *Rumsfeld*, the Court finds that the Nondiscrimination Policy regulates conduct, not speech because it affects what CLS must *do* if it wants to become a registered student organization-not engage in discrimination-not what CLS may or may not *say* regarding its beliefs on non-orthodox Christianity or homosexuality.

In *Hurley*, even though the [Supreme] Court found that the anti-discrimination statute did not target speech on its face, the Court focused on the "peculiar" application of the statute to require a private entity organizing a parade to admit a group seeking to march behind a particular banner. Significantly, the private group expressly disclaimed any intent to exclude all openly gay, lesbian, or bisexual individuals from participating in other approved parade contingents. In contrast to *Hurley*, CLS is not excluding certain students who wish to make a particular statement, but rather, CLS is excluding all students who are lesbian, gay, bisexual, or not orthodox Christian....

At the hearing on these motions, CLS argued that Hastings' enforcement of its Nondiscrimination Policy suppressed CLS's speech that "homosexuality is not Christian." First, as discussed above, the evidence does not show that CLS has been precluded from expressing any particular idea or viewpoint. Rather, to become a recognized student group, Hastings requires that CLS merely refrain from excluding students on the basis of their religion or sexual orientation. Second, even if the record could be construed to support CLS's position that its speech regarding homosexuality has been suppressed, CLS has not shown that the Nondiscrimination Policy targets "speech" as opposed to conduct....

Therefore, the Court concludes that on its face and in its application to CLS, the Nondiscrimination Policy regulates conduct, not speech.

ii. Analysis Pursuant to *United States v. O'Brien.*

Because the Court finds that the Nondiscrimination Policy regulates conduct, the Court will analyze whether CLS's free speech rights have been infringed pursuant to the standard from *United States v. O'Brien.* Under

O'Brien, governmental regulation of conduct is valid, even if it incidentally restricts speech, so long as: (1) the regulation is within the constitutional power of the government; (2) it furthers an important or substantial government interest; (3) the government interest is unrelated to the suppression of free expression; and (4) the incidental restriction on the alleged First Amendment freedoms is no greater than is essential to the furtherance of that interest.

States have the constitutional authority and a substantial, indeed compelling, interest in prohibiting discrimination on the basis of religion and sexual orientation. The interest in prohibiting discrimination is particularly critical in the context of education.

Moreover, "[t]he governmental interest in prohibiting such discrimination . . . is not directed at or related to suppression expression." Therefore, the Court concludes that the Policy prohibiting discrimination on the basis of religion and sexual orientation, among other categories, is within the Hastings' constitutional authority as a state institution, and that the Nondiscrimination Policy furthers a governmental interest unrelated to the suppression of free expression-protecting students from discrimination. Furthermore, as discussed above, . . . Hastings' Nondiscrimination Policy is directed at conduct unrelated to the suppression of expression. Thus, the first three prongs of the *O'Brien* test have been satisfied.

With respect to the last prong of the *O'Brien* test, courts have found that the incidental restrictions on free speech rights when a government enforces an anti-discrimination statute against an organization seeking to exclude individuals were no greater than essential to the furtherance of the state's interest in prohibiting discrimination. "[A]n incidental burden on speech is no greater than essential, and therefore permissible under *O'Brien,* so long as the neutral regulation promotes a substantial government interest that would be achieved less effectively absent the regulation." *Rumsfeld.* The Hastings' Nondiscrimination Policy easily meets this standard. Hastings' interest in eradicating discrimination would certainly be achieved less effectively without a policy which prohibits the harmful conduct. Moreover, the Court notes that the Nondiscrimination Policy only targets the conduct of discrimination. As long as student groups do not exclude students based on the prohibited categories, the groups are free to express any beliefs or perspectives they choose. Thus, the Court finds Hastings' implementation of its Nondiscrimination Policy the most direct method of achieving Hastings' goal of eradicating harmful discrimination. . . .

2.   First Amendment: Expressive Association.

. . . CLS argues that its right to expressive association has been infringed. It is undisputed that CLS is being denied the right to official recognition by Hastings and that it is being denied access to particular areas of the campus and some avenues of communicating with its members and other students. What is disputed is the legal and practical effect of these limitations.

First, it is important to note what this case is not about. Although CLS relies heavily on *Dale* and *Roberts,* these cases are inapplicable. *Dale* stands for the proposition that "forced inclusion of an unwanted person in a group infringes on the group's freedom of expressive association if the presence of that person affects in a significant way the group's ability to advocate public or private viewpoints.". Similarly, the Court in *Roberts* addressed the validity of forcing a group to accept members it did not desire. Here, CLS is not being forced, as a private entity, to include certain members or officers. . . .

. . . Rather, Hastings has merely placed conditions on using aspects of its campus as a forum and providing subsidies to organizations. If CLS wishes to participate in the forum and be eligible to receive funds, it must comply with Hastings' Nondiscrimination Policy. If not, CLS is "free to terminate its participation . . . and thus avoid the requirement of the nondiscrimination provision." CLS may continue to meet as the group of its choice on campus, excluding any students they wish, and may continue to communicate its beliefs as it did all through the 2004–2005 academic year. Therefore, *Dale* and *Roberts* are inapplicable here. . . .

The broad class of students CLS seeks to exclude significantly differs from the Boy Scouts' conduct in *Dale*. CLS does not confine its desired discrimination to students who are open and honest about being gay, lesbian, or non-orthodox Christian, let alone leaders on campus advocating for gay rights or non-Christian faiths. Rather, CLS seeks to exclude *all* lesbian, gay, bisexual or non-orthodox Christian students.

Moreover, CLS does not demonstrate how admitting lesbian, gay, bisexual or non-orthodox Christian students would impair its mission. Significantly, unlike the Boy Scouts in *Dale,* CLS has not submitted any evidence demonstrating that teaching certain values to other students is part of the organization's mission or purpose, or that it seeks to do so by example, such that the mere presence of someone who does not fully comply with the prescribed code of conduct would force CLS to send a message contrary to its mission. . . .

CLS also argues that if it complied with the Nondiscrimination Policy, it would be stripped of its Christian beliefs and cease to exist. Because officers and members have the authority to elect officers, and to amend the group's bylaws and constitution, and officers lead bible studies, CLS argues that opening up these functions to all students would lead CLS to cease being a vibrant Christian organization. However, the evidence in the record does not support CLS's argument. For the previous ten years, a predecessor organization to CLS was on campus as a recognized student organization. The predecessor organization did not exclude openly gay and lesbian students or non-Orthodox Christians. In fact, during the 2003–2004 academic year, one student who was openly lesbian and at least two students who held beliefs inconsistent with what CLS considers to be orthodox

Christianity participated in the group's meetings. Yet, there is no indication that the participation of such students made the organization any less Christian or hampered the organization's ability to express any particular message or belief. Nor is there any evidence that during those ten years students hostile to CLS's beliefs tried to overtake the organization or alter its views....

3.   First Amendment: Free Exercise.

     ... [T]he Nondiscrimination Policy does not target or single out religious beliefs, but rather, is a policy that is neutral and of general applicability. The Policy prohibits discrimination on the basis of protected categories, including religion and sexual orientation, irrespective of the motivation for such discrimination. Contrary to CLS's contention, regulating the conduct of discrimination on the basis, *inter alia,* of religion is not equivalent to regulating religious beliefs. CLS may be motivated by its religious beliefs to exclude students based on their religion or sexual orientation, but that does not convert the reason for Hastings' policy prohibiting the discrimination to be one that is religiously-based....

4.   Equal Protection Clause.

     ... CLS has not presented any evidence demonstrating that Hastings exempts other registered student organizations from complying with the Nondiscrimination Policy. CLS also argues that the treatment of CLS was intentional and argues that CLS may rely on evidence of the circumstances surrounding the passage of the policy to demonstrate intentional discrimination against it. Yet, CLS does not submit any evidence with respect to the passage of the Nondiscrimination Policy. Nor does CLS present any other evidence demonstrating any discriminatory intent by Hastings. Accordingly, CLS's equal protection claim fails as a matter of law....

NOTES ON THE CHRISTIAN LEGAL SOCIETY LITIGATION CAMPAIGN

Kane is one in a series of cases brought by the Christian Legal Society seeking to expand the principles of *Dale* and *FAIR* to gain an exemption from university anti-discrimination policies. See, e.g., *Christian Legal Society v. Walker*, 453 F.3d 853 (7th Cir. 2006) (finding evidence that school's anti-discrimination policy had not been uniformly applied and granting injunction to CLS); *Christian Legal Society v. Eck*, ___ F.Supp.2d ___, 2009 WL 1439709 (D.Mont. 2009) (granting summary judgment to defendant). The decision that you just read was summarily affirmed by the Ninth Circuit, 2009 WL 693391 (9th Cir. 2009). As this Supplement goes to press, a petition for certiorari filed by CLS is pending before the Supreme Court.

     Most universities require that recognized student groups allow all students to participate. Should an exception to that rule be required when voting rights or organizational leadership positions are at stake? Can *Kane* be squared with *Dale*?

                              *

CHAPTER 5

U.S. MILITARY EXCLUSIONS AND THE CONSTRUCTION OF MANHOOD

SECTION 3

THE MILITARY'S EXCLUSION OF LESBIANS, GAY MEN, AND BISEXUALS

Page 753.   Add the following Case and Notes immediately after the Notes to *X. v. Commonwealth***:**

United States v. Eric P. Marcum, Technical Sergeant for the U.S. Air Force

United States Court of Appeals for the Armed Forces, 2004.
60 M.J. 198.

■ JUDGE BAKER delivered the opinion of the Court.

[Eric P. Marcum, the appellant], a cryptologic linguist, technical sergeant (E–6), and the supervising noncommissioned officer in a flight of Persian–Farsi speaking intelligence analysts, was stationed at Offutt Air Force Base, Nebraska. His duties included training and supervising airmen newly assigned to the Operations Training Flight.

While off-duty Appellant socialized with airmen from his flight at parties. According to the testimony of multiple members of his unit, airmen "often" spent the night at Appellant's off-base home following these parties. The charges in this case resulted from allegations by some of these subordinate airmen that Appellant engaged in consensual and nonconsensual sexual activity with them.

Among other offenses, Appellant was charged with the forcible sodomy of Senior Airman (SrA) Harrison (E–4). Specifically, Specification 1 of Charge II alleged that Appellant "did, at or near Omaha, Nebraska, between on or about 1 September 1998 and on or about 16 October 1998, commit sodomy with Senior Airman Robert O. Harrison by force and without consent of the said Senior Airman Robert O. Harrison."

With regard to the charged offense, SrA Harrison testified that after a night of drinking with Appellant he stayed at Appellant's apartment and slept on the couch. SrA Harrison further testified that at some point he woke up to find Appellant orally sodomizing him. Although Appellant testified that he "did not perform oral sex on [SrA Harrison] at all," he testified to "kissing [SrA Harrison's] penis twice." When asked "did you, at any time, use any force, coercion, pressure, intimidation or violence?" Appellant responded, "No, sir, I did not and neither did Airman Harrison." Moreover, Appellant testified that the activity that occurred between Appellant and SrA Harrison was "equally participatory."

According to SrA Harrison's testimony, he did not say anything to Appellant at the time of the charged incident, but grabbed the covers, pulled them up over his torso, and turned away from Appellant into the couch. SrA Harrison left the apartment soon after this incident took place. SrA Harrison testified that he didn't protest at the time because he didn't know how Appellant would react. SrA Harrison also testified that Appellant's actions made him scared, angry, and uncomfortable.

According to SrA Harrison, he later confronted Appellant about this incident. He told Appellant, "I just want to make it clear between us that this sort of thing doesn't ever happen again." Nevertheless, SrA Harrison forgave Appellant and continued their friendship. SrA Harrison testified that he considered his relationship with Appellant like that of "a father type son relationship or big brother, little brother type relationship[.]" Subsequent to this incident, SrA Harrison explained how he and Appellant salsa danced together and kissed each other in the "European custom of men." SrA Harrison also told Appellant that he loved him, bought him a t-shirt as a souvenir, and sent numerous e-mails to Appellant expressing his continued friendship.

Appellant and SrA Harrison also provided testimony regarding an incident that occurred prior to the charged offense. SrA Harrison testified that during the incident he woke up in the morning and he was on top of Appellant with his face near Appellant's stomach. Appellant testified, "I was laying on my side, actually almost on top of the couch, with my belly on the couch but turned a little bit like this towards, with my face towards the rest of the living room. Airman Harrison was [on] top of me with, facing me. Airman Harrison was moving his pelvis area against my butt which is what woke me up. He had an erection, he had his arm around me, around the part that was actually touching the couch."

At the time of the charged conduct in question, Appellant and SrA Harrison were both subject to Dep't of the Air Force, Instruction 36–2909 (May 1, 1996). This instruction addresses professional and unprofessional relationships within the Air Force. Dep't of the Air Force, Instruction 36–2909 is subject to criminal sanction through operation of *Article 92* (Failure to obey order or regulation). Although this instruction was not admitted into evidence at trial, Appellant admitted during cross-examination that he was "aware of an Air Force policy" and that through his actions he had "broken more than an Air Force policy."

A panel of officers and enlisted members found Appellant "not guilty of forcible sodomy but guilty of non-forcible sodomy" in violation of Article 125. [Article 125 states:

(a) Any person subject to this chapter who engages in unnatural carnal copulation with another person of the same or opposite sex or with an animal is guilty of sodomy. Penetration, however slight, is sufficient to complete the offense.

(b) Any person found guilty of sodomy shall be punished as a court-martial may direct.

The Court of Appeals has interpreted Article 125 to prohibit "every kind of unnatural carnal intercourse, whether accomplished by force or fraud, or with consent. Similarly, the article does not distinguish between an act committed in the privacy of one's home, with no person present other than the sexual partner, and the same act committed in a public place in front of a group of strangers, who fully apprehend in the nature of the act." *United States v. Scoby*, 5 M.J. 160, 163 (C.M.A. 1978). Appellant Marcum challenged the application of Article 125 to him as a violation of the Due Process Clause as construed in *Lawrence v. Texas*, Casebook, pp. 78–91.]

The Supreme Court and this Court have long recognized that "men and women in the Armed Forces do not leave constitutional safeguards and judicial protection behind when they enter military service." *United States v. Mitchell*, 39 M.J. 131, 135 (C.M.A. 1994) (quoting *Weiss v. United States*, 510 U.S. 163, 194 (1994) (Ginsburg, J., concurring)). "Our citizens in uniform may not be stripped of basic rights simply because they have doffed their civilian clothes." *Goldman v. Weinberger*, 475 U.S. 503, 507 (1986). As a result, this Court has consistently applied the Bill of Rights to members of the Armed Forces, except in cases where the express terms of the Constitution make such application inapposite.

At the same time, these constitutional rights may apply differently to members of the armed forces than they do to civilians. "The military is, by necessity, a specialized society." [*Parker v. Levy*, 417 U.S. 733, 743 (1974).] Thus, when considering how the First Amendment and Fourth Amendment apply in the military context, this Court has relied on Supreme Court civilian precedent, but has also specifically addressed contextual factors involving military life. In light of the military mission, it is clear that servicemembers, as a general matter, do not share the same autonomy as civilians. See *Parker*.

While the Government does not contest the general proposition that the Constitution applies to members of the Armed Forces, it argues that *Lawrence* only applies to civilian conduct. Moreover, with respect to the military, the Government contends that Congress definitively addressed homosexual sodomy by enacting 10 U.S.C. § 654 (Casebook, p. 739–41). According to the Government, pursuant to Congress's Article I authority to make rules and regulations for the Armed Forces, Congress not only prohibited sodomy through Article 125, but with Article 125 as a backdrop, determined in 1993 through 10 U.S.C. § 654, that homosexuality, and, therefore, sodomy was incompatible with military service. In enacting § 654, Congress determined that "the presence in the armed forces of persons who demonstrate a propensity or intent to engage in homosexual acts would create an unacceptable risk to the high standards of morale, good order and discipline, and unit cohesion that are the essence of military capability." 10 U.S.C. § 654(a)(15). Thus, according to the Government, this Court should apply traditional principles of deference to Congress's exercise of its Article I authority and not apply *Lawrence* to the military.

The military landscape, however, is less certain than the Government suggests. The fog of constitutional law settles on separate and shared powers where neither Congress nor the Supreme Court has spoken authoritatively. Congress has indeed exercised its Article I authority to address homosexual sodomy in the Armed Forces, but this occurred prior to the Supreme Court's constitutional decision and analysis in *Lawrence* and at a time when *Bowers* served as the operative constitutional backdrop. Moreover, the Supreme Court did not accept the Government's present characterization of the right as one of homosexual sodomy. The Court stated, "To say that the issue in *Bowers* was simply the right to engage in certain sexual conduct demeans the claim the individual put forward[.]" *Lawrence*. "The State cannot demean their existence or control their destiny by making their private sexual conduct a crime." *Id*. Nor did the Supreme Court define the liberty interest in *Lawrence* in a manner that on its face would preclude its application to military members.

Constitutional rights identified by the Supreme Court generally apply to members of the military unless by text or scope they are plainly inapplicable. Therefore, we consider the application of *Lawrence* to Appellant's conduct. However, we conclude that its application must be addressed in context and not through a facial challenge to Article 125. This view is consistent with the principle that facial challenges to criminal statutes are "best when infrequent" and are "especially to be discouraged." *Sabri v. United States,* 541 U.S. 600 (2004). In the military setting, as this case demonstrates, an understanding of military culture and mission cautions against sweeping constitutional pronouncements that may not account for the nuance of military life. This conclusion is also supported by this Court's general practice of addressing constitutional questions on an as applied basis where national security and constitutional rights are both paramount interests. Further, because Article 125 addresses both forcible and non-forcible sodomy, a facial challenge reaches too far. Clearly, the *Lawrence* analysis is not at issue with respect to forcible sodomy. * * *

Appellant was charged with dereliction of duty, three specifications of forcible sodomy, three specifications of indecent assault, and two specifications of committing an indecent act. With regard to the charge addressed on appeal, the members found Appellant "not guilty of forcible sodomy, but guilty of non-forcible sodomy." As part of Appellant's contested trial, the following additional facts surrounding his conduct were elicited: The act of sodomy occurred in Appellant's off-base apartment during off-duty hours; no other members of the military were present at the time of the conduct; Appellant was an E–6 and the supervising noncommissioned officer in his flight. His duties included training and supervising airmen. SrA Harrison, an E–4, was one of the airmen Appellant supervised. As a result, SrA Harrison was subordinate to, and directly within, Appellant's chain of command.

The first question we ask is whether Appellant's conduct was of a nature to bring it within the *Lawrence* liberty interest. Namely, did Appellant's conduct involve private, consensual sexual activity between adults? In the present case, the members determined Appellant engaged in non-forcible sodomy. This sodomy occurred off-base in Appellant's apartment and it occurred in private. We will assume without deciding that the jury verdict of non-forcible sodomy in this case satisfies the first question of our as applied analysis.

The second question we ask is whether Appellant's conduct nonetheless encompassed any of the behavior or factors that were identified by the Supreme Court as not involved in *Lawrence*. For instance, did the conduct involve minors? Did it involve public conduct or prostitution? Did it involve persons who might be injured or coerced or who are situated in relationships where consent might not easily be refused?

When evaluating whether Appellant's conduct involved persons who might be injured or coerced or who were situated in relationships where consent might not easily be refused, the nuance of military life is significant. An Air Force instruction applicable to Appellant at the time of the offenses included the following proscriptions.

> Unduly familiar relationships between members in which one member exercises supervisory or command authority over the other can easily

be or become unprofessional. Similarly, as differences in grade increase, even in the absence of a command or supervisory relationship, there may be more risk that the relationship will be, or be perceived to be unprofessional because senior members in military organizations normally exercise authority or some direct or indirect organizational influence over more junior members.

Relationships are unprofessional, whether pursued on-or off-duty, when they detract from the authority of superiors or result in, or reasonably create the appearance of, favoritism, misuse of office or position, or the abandonment of organizational goals for personal interests.

Dep't. of the Air Force Instruction, 36–2909 Professional and Unprofessional Relationships, paras. 2.2, 3.1 (May 1, 1996).

For these reasons, the military has consistently regulated relationships between servicemembers based on certain differences in grade in an effort to avoid partiality, preferential treatment, and the improper use of one's rank. Indeed, Dep't of the Air Force Instruction 36–2909 is subject to criminal sanction through operation of Article 92, UCMJ. As both the Supreme Court and this Court have recognized elsewhere, "The fundamental necessity for obedience and the consequent necessity for imposition of discipline, may render permissible within the military that which would be constitutionally impermissible outside it." *Parker*. While servicemembers clearly retain a liberty interest to engage in certain intimate sexual conduct, "this right must be tempered in a military setting based on the mission of the military, the need for obedience of orders, and civilian supremacy." *United States v. Brown*, 45 M.J. 389, 397 (C.A.A.F. 1996).

In light of Air Force Instructions at the time, Appellant might have been charged with a violation of Article 92 for failure to follow a lawful order. However, the Government chose to proceed under Article 125. Nonetheless, the fact that Appellant's conduct might have violated Article 92 informs our analysis as to whether Appellant's conduct fell within the *Lawrence* zone of liberty.

As the supervising noncommissioned officer, Appellant was in a position of responsibility and command within his unit with respect to his fellow airmen. He supervised and rated SrA Harrison. Appellant also testified that he knew he should not engage in a sexual relationship with someone he supervised. Under such circumstances, which Appellant acknowledged was prohibited by Air Force policy, SrA Harrison, a subordinate airman within Appellant's chain of command, was a person "who might be coerced" or who was "situated in [a] relationship[] where consent might not easily be refused." *Lawrence*. Thus, based on this factor, Appellant's conduct fell outside the liberty interest identified by the Supreme Court. As a result, we need not consider the third step in our *Lawrence* analysis. Nor, given our determination that Appellant's conduct fell outside the liberty interest identified in *Lawrence*, need we decide what impact, if any, 10 U.S.C. § 654 would have on the constitutionality of Article 125 as applied in other settings.

[Judge Baker agreed with Marcum's challenge to the sentence he received, namely, that it was tainted by a statement that defense counsel released without Marcum's authorization. The statement was an account, taken from defense counsel's notes of interviews with Marcum, of the many other homosexual liaisons Marcum had with other service personnel. (Marcum was absent without leave (AWOL) at the time of sentencing, so he had waived his right to be present and heard at sentencing, but the Court found he had not waived his attorney-client privilege.) This statement was not only unauthorized, but was prejudicial, for the prosecuting attorney used it to argue for a higher sentence, on the ground that Marcum was a predatory homosexual corrupting the entire unit, man by man.]

[■ CHIEF JUDGE CRAWFORD dissented from this relief and concurred with the result reached by Judge Baker on the *Lawrence* issue. The Chief Judge would have found *Lawrence* completely inapplicable. "Clearly, Appellant's offense occurred in the context of a casual relationship with a subordinate airman who testified that he was too frightened to protest. This is a far cry from the consensual adult relationship, born of intimate and personal choice, which characterized the petitioners' behavior in *Lawrence*."]

NOTES ON *MARCUM* AND A NEW DEFENSE OF DON'T ASK, DON'T TELL

1. *The Reach of* Lawrence: *Thinking More Deeply About "Consent."* None of the judges in *Marcum* concluded that *Lawrence* is inapplicable to personnel in the armed forces, but all of them found that *Lawrence*'s articulation of the privacy right did not extend to Sergeant Marcum's conduct with Senior Airman Harrison. The Chief Judge objected that the conduct was not consensual because the Airman was too frightened to protest. Although Marcum was not actually convicted of forcible sodomy (under the criminal standard of proof), the Chief Judge reasoned that it was more likely than not that Harrison had been orally raped (under a civil standard of proof). The civil standard rendered *Lawrence* inapplicable in his view.

Judge Baker did not accept this argument but reasoned that *Lawrence* was inapplicable because Air Force regulations prohibited sexual fraternization between officers and those under his or her command. Hence, all the activities with Airman Harrison were off-limits and constitutionally unprotected by *Lawrence*. There is some ambiguity as to the basis of Judge Baker's judgment: Is he inferring lack of "consent" on the part of Harrison? Or is this a case of "constructive nonconsent" for policy reasons? Perhaps it is both: Harrison's failure to object may be a product of the officer-subordinate relationship *and* may be an example of why the Air Force needs an anti-fraternization policy.

Note the relevance of feminist theory to the *Marcum* opinions. As Chapter 10 develops in some detail, feminists have claimed that lack of consent can be deduced from the exercise of sexual authority by a superior (a boss as well as a commanding officer). Most states now make some of these situations a sexual assault. More controversial have been claims that sexual assault can occur when the victim is too afraid to protest. When the fear is the result of a knife to the throat or even an implicit physical threat, as in *State v. Rusk* (Casebook, pp. 1242–49), it is easier to conclude that sexual assault has occurred. But Marcum's oral sex upon Harrison was not in such a context. Unless sexual assault is defined to include any "unwelcome" sexual contact, as some reformers have argued, Chief Judge Crawford's point has less cogency.

Should it make a difference that the activities occurred between persons of the same sex?

2. *The Difficulty of Finding a Test Case for Consensual Sodomy Challenges in the Armed Forces.* Sergeant Marcum's case illustrates the difficulty of finding a case where *Lawrence* clearly applies. Remember, it took almost two decades for such an ideal case—two adults engaged in consensual sodomy in the privacy of the home (*Lawrence*)—in the civilian arena. Most of the military prosecutions involve charges of forcible sodomy, men sodomizing women as well as men without consent. Many of the cases involve sex between service personnel, and these cases often raise fraternization concerns not present in civilian cases. Finally, although not present in Marcum's case, some of the cases involve sexual activities on government property—barracks, storerooms, public toilets, etc. These, too, may not easily fall within *Lawrence*.

There may never be a suitable test case. Is that a matter of grave concern—especially if Article 125 proves to be an efficacious mechanism for prosecuting nonconsensual activities involving he-said/she-said (or he-said/he-said) scenarios? Perhaps one reason to lament is that the exclusion of gay people—Don't Ask, Don't Tell—is founded upon the rationale that homosexuals violate Article 125. That may have been one original justification, but it has been eclipsed by institutional justifications, including one for which *Marcum* is a possible citation.

3. *The New Justification for the Military Exclusion of Gay People: Fraternization Concerns.* In the Casebook, Chapter 5 demonstrates ways in which justifications for excluding people of color, women, and gay people evolved over time. Generally, the evolution was from natural law arguments (blacks are an inferior race, women are domestic, homosexuals are immoral sodomites) *toward* medical arguments (blacks are mentally inferior, women are weaker, homosexuals are degenerate) and then *finally toward* social republican or institutional arguments (troop morale and unit cohesion, in all three cases). Reva Siegel calls this process the *modernization of justification*. William Eskridge maintains that justifications are *sedimented*: the natural law and medical ones never disappear, as they lie beneath and shape the new social republican ones. (These theories are presented in Chapter 4, Casebook, pp. 542–45).

Notice how the social republican or institutional arguments against gays in the military have changed—and *are changing* as this Casebook moves toward a third edition. Originally, the social republican argument against gays in the military was premised upon the notion that homosexuals would prey on vulnerable young men, or that some of those young men would fear such predation. This justification was founded upon, essentially, zero evidence and reflected anti-homosexual prejudice.

Discerning that, the Clinton Administration defended Don't Ask, Don't Tell through a kinder, gentler version of the unit cohesion argument (Casebook, pp. 729–37): homosexuals are a credit to their sexual orientation, but red-blooded but homophobic young men would be upset by their open presence and would even harm them. So homosexuals had to be kept out (or kept in the closet) for their own protection! This argument has lost much of its force as country after country has successfully integrated lesbians, gay men, and bisexuals into its armed forces—including such military powerhouses as Israel and Great Britain. Also, young men's attitudes seem to have changed. In the new era of *Will and Grace* and *Brokeback Mountain*, it is no longer quite so cool for a young straight man to be homophobic. Like dozens of aesthetically-challenged straight men fawned over by gay fashionistas in *Queer Eye for the Straight Guy*, Airman Harrison may be a lonely heterosexual who likes attention and affection from his homosexual buddy, Eric Marcum. Or he might be bisexual or gay. Should Uncle Sam care?

Reflecting this new social reality, but strongly invested in defending the policy excluding homosexuals from the military, the Bush 43 Administration changed the argument yet again. In a fresh challenge filed in Massachusetts federal court, the challengers and their amici not only made equal protection claims, but argued that DADT violates the First Amendment as well. Most observers think that if federal judges applied any kind of heightened scrutiny, the policy would fail—but *Rostker* leads many observers to wonder whether any federal appeals court would dare apply heightened scrutiny to a military exclusion endorsed by a Democratic President and his GOP successor, and enacted by large bipartisan majorities in a Democratic Congress.

In any event, the newest "rational basis" for the exclusion is that open homosexuals would pose a risk of greater sexual fraternization among military personnel; such fraternization is not only contrary to military rules, but is a greater threat to unit cohesion and morale than homophobia! Fraternization creates sexual jealousies, beliefs that soldiers receive preferential or disfavored treatment for sexual reasons, and a breakdown of the unit. (This argument was a major focus of the government's brief on appeal in *Cook v. Gates*, 528 F.3d 42 (1st Cir.2008).) Notice how the federal government is now running away from open reliance on homophobia—

especially now that the opposite argument (gay people will be too attractive, not too threatening) can do the job of protecting a policy which disrespects and penalizes homosexuals, and authorizes episodic witch-hunts against them, as well as straight women.

How would you respond to this new argument if you were a lawyer attacking DADT? Is your argument likely to have any traction after *Rostker* and *FAIR*? Is the government's new argument a good response to the First Amendment claims made by the challenges? For the First Circuit's response, read the next case.

Thomas COOK v. Robert M. GATES, 528 F.3d 42 (1st Cir. 2008). In the wake of *Lawrence v. Texas* (2003), twelve service personnel challenged the 1993 Don't Ask, Don't Tell statute on three constitutional grounds: (1) substantive due process; (2) equal protection, and (3) freedom of expression. Although dismissing plaintiffs' constitutional claims, **Judge Howard**'s opinion for the court engaged in an interesting discussion of current law.

(1) Substantive Due Process. Rejecting the government's view, the First Circuit accepted the plaintiffs' view that *Lawrence* recognized a constitutionally protected liberty interest in "consensual sexual intimacy in the home." Some of the conduct justifying exclusion from the armed forces fell within this protected liberty interest. Although *Lawrence* did not apply strict scrutiny, it seemed to apply a level of scrutiny somewhere between rational basis and strict scrutiny. But the court also observed that its scrutiny should be deferential because the matter fell within Congress's plenary authority over military affairs (*Rostker*). After extensive hearings, public debate, and deliberation (including rejection of more moderate policies), Congress decided that a total exclusion was needed to preserve the military's effectiveness as a fighting force. Citing *Rostker*, Judge Howard concluded that "where Congress has articulated a substantial government interest for a law, and where the challenges in question implicate that interest, judicial intrusion is simply not warranted." Contrast the more searching review used by the Ninth Circuit in *Witt v. Dep't of Air Force*, excerpted in Chapter 1 of this Supplement.

(2) Equal Protection. Judge Howard applied the *Romer* rational basis review for sexual orientation classifications and summarily upheld the law. "Congress has put forward a non-animus based explanation for its decision to pass the Act. Given the substantial deference owed Congress' assessment of the need for the legislation, the Act survives rational basis review."

(3) Freedom of Expression. Plaintiffs argued that the statute directly censors identity speech, as the statement "I am a lesbian" triggers automatic discharge under the 1993 law. Under *Hurley*, that statement is protected by the First Amendment, "to some degree." Following and quoting the Supreme Court's opinion in *Goldman v. Weinberger*, 475 U.S. 503 (1986) (upholding military rule barring a rabbi from wearing a yarmulke), Judge Howard cautioned that "our review of military regulations challenged on First Amendment grounds is far more deferential than constitutional review of similar laws or regulations designed for civilian

society." This limitation is rooted in the recognition that free expression can sometimes conflict with the military's compelling need to "foster instinctive obedience, unity, commitment, and espirit de corps" and that "the essence of military service is the subordination of the desires and interests of the individual to the needs of service."

Moreover, "the Act's purpose is not to restrict this kind of speech. Its purpose is to identify those who have engaged or are likely to engage in a homosexual act as defined by the statute. The law is thus aimed at eliminating certain conduct or the possibility of certain conduct from occurring in the military environment, not at restricting speech. The Act relies on a member's speech only because a member's statement that he or she is homosexual will often correlate with a member who has a propensity to engage in a homosexual act." The Supreme Court has repeatedly upheld the use of statements otherwise protected by the First Amendment to be used as evidence that someone has committed an illegal act. E.g., *Wisconsin v. Mitchell*, 508 U.S. 476 (1993) (hate speech).

Judge Saris joined the majority's discussion of the due process and equal protection claims but dissented from its disposition of the First Amendment claim. Under the test of *Wayte v. United States*, 470 U.S. 598, 611 (1985), applicable to content-neutral speech restrictions, the government must show that the restriction is "substantially related" to an "important" state interest and that the restriction on speech is no greater than is "essential" to meet such an interest. Judge Saris found that the statute applied to service personnel who made statements about their sexual orientation but were willing to forego "homosexual sodomy" during their military service. As such, the statute as written amounted to an exclusion based upon mere status and not conduct, for at least some "homosexuals." The government claimed that there were cases where personnel had "rebutted" the case against them under the statute, but Judge Saris noted that its examples were all over 12 years old and that plaintiffs' as-applied challenge alleged that the presumption was in practice not rebuttable. (This allegation must be taken as true on motion to dismiss, as this appeal arose.)

In the context of a motion to dismiss, where plaintiffs' allegations must be treated as correct, Judge Saris also credited plaintiffs' argument that the policy had a chilling effect on protected speech. The statute apparently applies to statements made outside military settings and in private circumstances (such as doctor-patient contexts). See Tobias Barrington Wolff, "Political Representation and Accountability Under Don't Ask, Don't Tell," 89 *Iowa L. Rev.* 1633, 1644–50 (2004) (examples where the presumption was applied to conversations with family members, sessions with chaplains and psychotherapists, and public statements outside military confines). It is not clear from Judge Saris's opinion whether this was an independent basis for finding a First Amendment violation; it strikes us as more likely that this buttressed the conclusion that Don't Ask, Don't Tell's restriction on protected speech was potentially greater than that "essential" to preserve the government's interest in an efficient armed forces.

NOTE ON FIRST AMENDMENT ATTACKS ON DON'T ASK, DON'T TELL

1. *Is the Statute's Restriction on Speech Content Neutral?* The First Circuit unanimously (Judge Saris agreeing on this point) ruled that the regulation of speech is content neutral. Consider this objection. The statement "I am a gay man" is evidence that the man has a propensity to commit sodomy—but so is the statement "I am a straight man." See Edward O. Laumann, John H. Gagnon, Robert T. Michael & Stuart Michaels, *The Social Organization of Sexuality: Sexual Practices in the United States* 98–99 (1994) (79% of straight men have engaged in oral sex, which is illegal "sodomy" under the Uniform Code of Military Justice). Yet the statute censors only the former statement. The court's apparent assumption is that Congress can make "homosexual sodomy" a crime and hunt down offenders, but not "heterosexual sodomy." But Congress in fact made both crimes. And Justice O'Connor's opinion in *Lawrence* suggests that criminalizing *only* homosexual sodomy might violate *Romer*.

In short, the law does not appear to be content neutral. Under the Supreme Court's jurisprudence, the government must demonstrate that the censorship is narrowly tailored to serve a compelling government purpose other than suppressing its message. *R.A.V. v. City of St. Paul*, 505 U.S. 377 (1992). Can Don't Ask, Don't Tell satisfy such a test? (Hint: the majority would surely say yes. What would its reasoning be?)

2. *Does the Statute Violate the* O'Brien *Test? Is It Overbroad?* Judge Saris's objection is that the 1993 statute covers more protected expression than is needed to serve the important government interest. By going along with the majority on the due process and equal protection claims, however, Judge Saris seems to be agreeing that the exclusion of probable "homosexual sodomites" is rationally related to the efficient operation of the armed forces. A lot of the evidence Congress heard, and most of the evidence reproduced in the Casebook, was to the effect that open "homosexuals" would disrupt military efficiency. If that is the case, the statute seems to fit the goal better than Judge Saris admits. Why care about chilling effect if what you are trying to chill is disruptive speech?

Judge Saris flirts with the argument that the statute is "overbroad." The Supreme Court has applied the overbreadth doctrine cautiously. In *Broadrick v. Oklahoma*, 413 U.S. 601 (1973), the Court upheld a state law restricting political activities by public employees. Although the law seemed to reach core First Amendment activities that posed no danger to state policies (e.g., display of campaign buttons or bumper stickers), the Court declined to strike down the law. Justice White's opinion required that overbreadth "must not only be real, but substantial as well," to justify invalidation. Judge Saris's opinion did not discuss *Broadrick*, perhaps because it involved a facial challenge to the Oklahoma law; *Cook* involved an as-applied challenge as well. Still, *Broadrick* might be cited for the proposition that First Amendment chilling effect arguments must meet a high threshold.

3.   *Can Deference Save an Arguably Obsolete Statute?* Congressional deliberations in 1993 came perilously close to excluding a class of Americans because of their membership in a despised group. This was troubling feature of the statute under all three kinds of constitutional challenge. However troubling this concern was in 1993, it was heightened by 2009, when the Supreme Court declined to review the First Circuit's decision in *Cook v. Gates*.

On the one hand, however weak the Clinton Administration's justifications for Don't Ask, Don't Tell were in 1993, they were weaker by 2009— and the evidence is assembled in Nathaniel Frank, *Unfriendly Fire: How the Gay Ban Undermines the Military and Weakens America* (2009). Dr. Frank argues, from both data and detailed case histories, that the exclusion of gay people has been very costly to military efficiency, through forced retirements and expulsions of needed personnel, through expensive witch hunts and investigations, and through a regime of episodic terror that the policy empowers commanders and military investigators to visit upon service personnel. Is this cost worth it? Dr. Frank argues not. There is now a tremendous amount of evidence (from military powerhouses like Israel and Great Britain as well as dozens of other countries, and platoons within our own armed forces as well) about what happens when military forces allow openly gay personnel: the emerging consensus seems to be that there are not discernible bad effects. (This proposition is worth further study through student notes and projects, in coordination with the armed forces and other sources of information in other countries such as Israel etc.)

The drafters of the 1993 statute have renounced it; General John Shalikashvili, Chair of the Joint Chiefs of Staff, 1993–97, and an early implementer of the policy, has renounced it; dozens of leading generals, admirals, and military experts have renounced it. The statute still has many defenders, however. More than 1000 retired generals and admirals signed a letter urging retention of Don't Ask, Don't Tell. Thus, there remain plenty of military experts willing to defend the policy, and to whom the Court might defer.

On the other hand, is the Court's deference jurisprudence itself obsolete? Professor Diane Mazur argues in a forthcoming book that two intertwined developments—the all-volunteer armed forces and the near-absolute deference to military policies—have dramatically undermined our armed forces by creating a militarized ghetto that is not only unrepresentative of America (in contrast to the armed forces constituted by the draft), but also unresponsive to America and its public values. See Diane Mazur, *A More Perfect Military: How the Constitution Can Make Our Military Strong-*

er (Oxford, 2010). This is bad news not only for LGBT people, whom Mazur believes have gravitated away from military careers, but also for people of color and women.

As we await the publication of this important book, consider whether its evidence, if persuasive, would justify a major change in course for the Supreme Court. Are there benefits of the Court's deference jurisprudence that might justify its perseverance?

CHAPTER 6

SEXUALITY, GENDER, AND THE LAW IN THE WORKPLACE

SECTION 2C

SEXUAL HARASSMENT AND HOSTILE WORK ENVIRONMENT UNDER TITLE VII

Page 864. Add the following Case and Notes immediately after Problem 6–3:

Darlene Jespersen v. Harrah's Operating Co., Inc.

U.S. Court of Appeals for the Ninth Circuit, *en banc*, 2006.
444 F.3d 1104.

■ SCHROEDER, CHIEF JUDGE.

. . . The plaintiff, Darlene Jespersen, was terminated from her position as a bartender at the sports bar in Harrah's Reno casino not long after Harrah's began to enforce its comprehensive uniform, appearance and grooming standards for all bartenders. The standards required all bartenders, men and women, to wear the same uniform of black pants and white shirts, a bow tie, and comfortable black shoes. The standards also included grooming requirements that differed to some extent for men and women, requiring women to wear some facial makeup and not permitting men to wear any. Jespersen refused to comply with the makeup requirement and was effectively terminated for that reason.

The district court granted summary judgment to Harrah's on the ground that the appearance and grooming policies imposed equal burdens on both men and women bartenders because, while women were required to use makeup and men were forbidden to wear makeup, women were allowed to have long hair and men were required to have their hair cut to a length above the collar. *Jespersen v. Harrah's Operating Co.,* 280 F.Supp.2d 1189 (D.Nev.2002). The district court also held that the policy could not run afoul of Title VII because it did not discriminate against Jespersen on the basis of the immutable characteristics of her sex. The district court further observed that the Supreme Court's decision in *Price Waterhouse v. Hopkins,* 490 U.S. 228 (1989) (plurality opinion), prohibiting discrimination on the basis of sex stereotyping, did not apply to this case because in the district court's view, the Ninth Circuit had excluded grooming standards from the reach of Price Waterhouse [citing earlier cases].

The three-judge panel affirmed, but on somewhat different grounds. *Jespersen v. Harrah's Operating Co.,* 392 F.3d 1076 (9th Cir.2004). The panel majority held that Jespersen, on this record, failed to show that the appearance policy imposed a greater burden on women than on men. It pointed to the lack of any affidavit in this record to support a claim that the burdens of the policy fell unequally on men and women. Accordingly, the panel did not agree with the district court that grooming policies could never discriminate as a matter of law. . . .

We agree with the district court and the panel majority that on this record, Jespersen has failed to present evidence sufficient to survive summary judgment on her claim that the policy imposes an unequal burden on women. With respect to sex stereotyping, we hold that appearance standards, including makeup requirements, may well be the subject of a Title VII claim for sexual stereotyping, but that on this record Jespersen has failed to create any triable issue of fact that the challenged policy was part of a policy motivated by sex stereotyping. We therefore affirm.

I. BACKGROUND

Plaintiff Darlene Jespersen worked successfully as a bartender at Harrah's for twenty years and compiled what by all accounts was an exemplary record. During Jespersen's entire tenure with Harrah's, the company maintained a policy encouraging female beverage servers to wear makeup. The parties agree, however, that the policy was not enforced until 2000. In February 2000, Harrah's implemented a "Beverage Department Image Transformation" program at twenty Harrah's locations, including its casino in Reno. Part of the program consisted of new grooming and appearance standards, called the "Personal Best" program. The program contained certain appearance standards that applied equally to both sexes, including a standard uniform of black pants, white shirt, black vest, and black bow tie. Jespersen has never objected to any of these policies. The program also contained some sex-differentiated appearance requirements as to hair, nails, and makeup.

In April 2000, Harrah's amended that policy to require that women wear makeup. Jespersen's only objection here is to the makeup requirement. The amended policy provided in relevant part: . . .

- Males:
  - Hair must not extend below top of shirt collar. Ponytails are prohibited.
  - Hands and fingernails must be clean and nails neatly trimmed at all times. No colored polish is permitted.
  - Eye and facial makeup is not permitted.
  - Shoes will be solid black leather or leather type with rubber (non skid) soles.
- Females:
  - Hair must be teased, curled, or styled every day you work. Hair must be worn down at all times, no exceptions.
  - Stockings are to be of nude or natural color consistent with employee's skin tone. No runs.
  - Nail polish can be clear, white, pink or red color only. No exotic nail art or length.
  - Shoes will be solid black leather or leather type with rubber (non skid) soles.
  - *Make up (face powder, blush and mascara) must be worn and applied neatly in complimentary colors. Lip color must be worn at all times. (emphasis added).*

Jespersen did not wear makeup on or off the job, and in her deposition stated that wearing it would conflict with her self-image. It is not disputed that she found the makeup requirement offensive, and felt so uncomfortable wearing makeup that she found it interfered with her ability to perform as a bartender. Unwilling to wear the makeup, and not qualifying for any open positions at the casino with a similar compensation scale, Jespersen left her employment with Harrah's. . . .

In her deposition testimony, attached as a response to the motion for summary judgment, Jespersen described the personal indignity she felt as a result of attempting to comply with the makeup policy. Jespersen testified that when she wore the makeup she "felt very degraded and very demeaned." In addition, Jespersen testified that "it prohibited [her] from doing [her] job" because "[i]t affected [her] self-dignity . . . [and] took away

[her] credibility as an individual and as a person." Jespersen made no cross-motion for summary judgment, taking the position that the case should go to the jury. Her response to Harrah's motion for summary judgment relied solely on her own deposition testimony regarding her subjective reaction to the makeup policy, and on favorable customer feedback and employer evaluation forms regarding her work.

The record therefore does not contain any affidavit or other evidence to establish that complying with the "Personal Best" standards caused burdens to fall unequally on men or women, and there is no evidence to suggest Harrah's motivation was to stereotype the women bartenders. Jespersen relied solely on evidence that she had been a good bartender, and that she had personal objections to complying with the policy, in order to support her argument that Harrah's " 'sells' and exploits its women employees." . . .

. . . In this appeal, Jespersen maintains that the record before the district court was sufficient to create triable issues of material fact as to her unlawful discrimination claims of unequal burdens and sex stereotyping. We deal with each in turn.

II.   UNEQUAL BURDENS

. . . Harrah's "Personal Best" policy contains sex-differentiated requirements regarding each employee's hair, hands, and face. While those individual requirements differ according to gender, none on its face places a greater burden on one gender than the other. Grooming standards that appropriately differentiate between the genders are not facially discriminatory.

We have long recognized that companies may differentiate between men and women in appearance and grooming policies, and so have other circuits. [citations omitted] The material issue under our settled law is not whether the policies are different, but whether the policy imposed on the plaintiff creates an "unequal burden" for the plaintiff's gender.

Not every differentiation between the sexes in a grooming and appearance policy creates a "significantly greater burden of compliance[.]" *Gerdom v. Continental Airlines, Inc.*, [692 F.2d 602, 606 (9th Cir. 1982)] . . . Under established equal burdens analysis, when an employer's grooming and appearance policy does not unreasonably burden one gender more than the other, that policy will not violate Title VII.

Jespersen asks us to take judicial notice of the fact that it costs more money and takes more time for a woman to comply with the makeup requirement than it takes for a man to comply with the requirement that he keep his hair short, but these are not matters appropriate for judicial notice. Judicial notice is reserved for matters "generally known within the territorial jurisdiction of the trial court" or "capable of accurate and ready determination by resort to sources whose accuracy cannot reasonably be questioned." Fed.R.Evid. 201. The time and cost of makeup and haircuts is in neither category. . . .

Having failed to create a record establishing that the "Personal Best" policies are more burdensome for women than for men, Jespersen did not present any triable issue of fact. The district court correctly granted summary judgment on the record before it with respect to Jespersen's claim that the makeup policy created an unequal burden for women.

III. SEX STEREOTYPING

. . . Harrah's "Personal Best" policy is very different [from the stereotyping that occurred in *Price Waterhouse*]. The policy does not single out Jespersen. It applies to all of the bartenders, male and female. It requires all of the bartenders to wear exactly the same uniforms while interacting with the public in the context of the entertainment industry. It is for the most part unisex, from the black tie to the non-skid shoes. There is no evidence in this record to indicate that the policy was adopted to make women bartenders conform to a commonly-accepted stereotypical image of what women should wear. The record contains nothing to suggest the grooming standards would objectively inhibit a woman's ability to do the job. The only evidence in the record to support the stereotyping claim is Jespersen's own subjective reaction to the makeup requirement. . . .

We respect Jespersen's resolve to be true to herself and to the image that she wishes to project to the world. We cannot agree, however, that her objection to the makeup requirement, without more, can give rise to a claim of sex stereotyping under Title VII. If we were to do so, we would come perilously close to holding that every grooming, apparel, or appearance requirement that an individual finds personally offensive, or in conflict with his or her own self-image, can create a triable issue of sex discrimination. . . .

We emphasize that we do not preclude, as a matter of law, a claim of sex-stereotyping on the basis of dress or appearance codes. Others may well be filed, and any bases for such claims refined as law in this area evolves. This record, however, is devoid of any basis for permitting this particular claim to go forward, as it is limited to the subjective reaction of a single employee, and there is no evidence of a stereotypical motivation on the part of the employer. This case is essentially a challenge to one small part of what is an overall apparel, appearance, and grooming policy that applies largely the same requirements to both men and women. . . . [T]he touchstone is reasonableness. A makeup requirement must be seen in the context of the overall standards imposed on employees in a given workplace.

AFFIRMED.

■ Pregerson, Circuit Judge, with whom Judges Kozinski, Graber, and W. Fletcher join, dissenting:

... I part ways with the majority ... inasmuch as I believe that the "Personal Best" program was part of a policy motivated by sex stereotyping and that Jespersen's termination for failing to comply with the program's requirements was "because of" her sex. Accordingly, I dissent from Part III of the majority opinion and from the judgment of the court.

The majority contends that it is bound to reject Jespersen's sex stereotyping claim because she presented too little evidence—only her "own subjective reaction to the makeup requirement." I disagree. Jespersen's evidence showed that Harrah's fired her because she did not comply with a grooming policy that imposed a facial uniform (full makeup) on only female bartenders. Harrah's stringent "Personal Best" policy required female beverage servers to wear foundation, blush, mascara, and lip color, and to ensure that lip color was on at all times. Jespersen and her female colleagues were required to meet with professional image consultants who in turn created a facial template for each woman. Jespersen was required not simply to wear makeup; in addition, the consultants dictated where and how the makeup had to be applied.

Quite simply, her termination for failing to comply with a grooming policy that imposed a facial uniform on only female bartenders is discrimination "because of" sex. Such discrimination is clearly and unambiguously impermissible under Title VII, which requires that "gender must be *irrelevant* to employment decisions." *Price Waterhouse.*

Notwithstanding Jespersen's failure to present additional evidence, little is required to make out a sex-stereotyping—as distinct from an undue burden—claim in this situation....

... I believe that the fact that Harrah's designed and promoted a policy that required women to conform to a sex stereotype by wearing full makeup is sufficient "direct evidence" of discrimination.

The majority contends that Harrah's "Personal Best" appearance policy is very different from the policy at issue in *Price Waterhouse* in that it applies to both men and women. I disagree. As the majority concedes, "Harrah's 'Personal Best' policy contains sex-differentiated requirements regarding each employee's hair, hands, and face." The fact that a policy contains sex-differentiated requirements that affect people of both genders cannot excuse a particular requirement from scrutiny. By refusing to consider the makeup requirement separately, and instead stressing that the policy contained some gender-neutral requirements, such as color of clothing, as well as a variety of gender-differentiated requirements for "hair, hands, and face," the majority's approach would permit otherwise impermissible gender stereotypes to be neutralized by the presence of a stereotype or burden that affects people of the opposite gender, or by some separate non-discriminatory requirement that applies to both men and women. ... [T]he fact that employees of both genders are subjected to gender-specific requirements does not necessarily mean that particular requirements are not motivated by gender stereotyping....

... The inescapable message [of the make-up requirement] is that women's undoctored faces compare unfavorably to men's, not because of a physical difference between men's and women's faces, but because of a cultural assumption—and gender-based stereotype—that women's faces are incomplete, unattractive, or unprofessional without full makeup. We need not denounce all makeup as inherently offensive ... to conclude that *requiring* female bartenders to wear full makeup is an impermissible sex stereotype and is evidence of discrimination because of sex. Therefore, I strongly disagree with the majority's conclusion that there "is no evidence in this record to indicate that the policy was adopted to make women bartenders conform to a commonly-accepted stereotypical image of what women should wear." ...

■ Kozinski, Circuit Judge, with whom Judges Graber and W. Fletcher join, dissenting:

I agree with Judge Pregerson and join his dissent—subject to one caveat: I believe that Jespersen also presented a triable issue of fact on the question of disparate burden.

The majority is right that "[t]he [makeup] requirements must be viewed in the context of the overall policy." But I find it perfectly clear that Harrah's overall grooming policy is substantially more burdensome for women than for men. Every requirement that forces men to spend time or money on their appearance has a corresponding requirement that is as, or more, burdensome for women: short hair v. "teased, curled, or styled" hair; clean trimmed nails v. nail length and color requirements; black leather shoes v. black leather shoes. The requirement that women spend time and money applying full facial makeup has no corresponding requirement for men, making the "overall policy" more burdensome for the former than for the latter. The only question is how much.

It is true that Jespersen failed to present evidence about what it costs to buy makeup and how long it takes to apply it. But is there any doubt that putting on makeup costs money and takes time? Harrah's policy requires women to apply face powder, blush, mascara and lipstick. You don't need an expert witness to figure out that such items don't grow on trees.

Nor is there any rational doubt that application of makeup is an intricate and painstaking process that requires considerable time and care. Even those of us who don't wear makeup know how long it can take from the hundreds of hours we've spent over the years frantically tapping our toes and pointing to our wrists. It's hard to imagine that a woman could "put on her face," as they say, in the time it would take a man to shave—certainly not if she were to do the careful and thorough job Harrah's expects....

Alternatively, Jespersen did introduce evidence that she finds it burdensome to *wear* makeup because doing so is inconsistent with her self-image and interferes with her job performance. My colleagues dismiss this evidence, apparently on the ground that wearing makeup does not, as a matter of law, constitute a substantial burden. This presupposes that Jespersen is unreasonable or idiosyncratic in her discomfort. Why so? Whether to wear cosmetics—literally, the face one presents to the world—is an intensely personal choice. ... If you are used to wearing makeup—as most American women are—this may seem like no big deal. But those of us not used to wearing makeup would find a requirement that we do so highly intrusive. Imagine, for example, a rule that all judges wear face powder, blush, mascara and lipstick while on the bench. Like Jespersen, I would find such a regime burdensome and demeaning; it would interfere with my job performance. I suspect many of my colleagues would feel the same way.

Everyone accepts this as a reasonable reaction from a man, but why should it be different for a woman? It is not because of anatomical differences, such as a requirement that women wear bathing suits that cover their breasts. Women's faces, just like those of men, can be perfectly presentable without makeup; it is a cultural artifact that most women raised in the United States learn to put on—and presumably enjoy wearing—cosmetics. But cultural norms change; not so long ago a man wearing an earring was a gypsy, a pirate or an oddity. Today, a man wearing body piercing jewelry is hardly noticed. So, too, a large (and perhaps growing) number of women choose to present themselves to the world without makeup. I see no justification for forcing them to conform to Harrah's quaint notion of what a real woman looks like.

Nor do I think it appropriate for a court to dismiss a woman's testimony that she finds wearing makeup degrading and intrusive, as Jespersen clearly does. Not only do we have her sworn statement to that effect, but there can be no doubt about her sincerity or the intensity of her feelings: She quit her job—a job she performed well for two decades—rather than put on the makeup. That is a choice her male colleagues were not forced to make. To me, this states a case of disparate burden, and I would let a jury decide whether an employer can force a woman to make this choice.

Finally, I note with dismay the employer's decision to let go a valued, experienced employee who had gained accolades from her customers, over what, in the end, is a trivial matter. Quality employees are difficult to find in any industry and I would think an employer would long hesitate before forcing a loyal, long-time employee to quit over an honest and heartfelt difference of opinion about a matter of personal significance to her. Having won the legal battle, I hope that Harrah's will now do the generous and decent thing by offering Jespersen her job back, and letting her give it her personal best—without the makeup.

NOTES ON DISCRIMINATION AND GROOMING STANDARDS

Unfortunately, despite Judge Kozinski's effort in dissent, Harrah's did not relent and give Darlene Jespersen her job back. Instead, the decision has come to symbolize the deep connection between gender norms and "reasonableness," and the tension between anti-discrimination law and the perceived naturalness of gendered job requirements. The *Duke Journal of Gender Law and Policy* published a symposium issue devoted to analysis of the *Jespersen* case: volume 14, issue 1 (spring 2007).

In developing your own critique of the decision, the first challenge is to disaggregate the points at which the naturalization of gender occurs. Map the logic of the various opinions: where are the missteps? Should the Harrah's grooming code be treated as a BFOQ? Would it pass muster under that standard? (See discussion in *Chambers*, pp. 813–14 of the Casebook.) What are the strongest arguments for Harrah's position? Are Jespersen's arguments too subjective?

*

CHAPTER 7

Sexuality, Gender, and Education

SECTION 2A

Academic Freedom: Teachers, Schools and the State

Page 943. Add the following Case and Notes immediately after Problem 7–3:

Parker v. Hurley

U.S. Court of Appeals for the First Circuit, 2008.
514 F.3d 87.

■ Lynch, Circuit Judge.

Two sets of parents, whose religious beliefs are offended by gay marriage and homosexuality, sued the Lexington, Massachusetts school district in which their young children are enrolled. They assert that they must be given prior notice by the school and the opportunity to exempt their young children from exposure to books they find religiously repugnant. Plaintiffs assert violations of their own and their children's rights under the Free Exercise Clause and their substantive parental and privacy due process rights under the U.S. Constitution.

The Parkers object to their child being presented in kindergarten and first grade with two books that portray diverse families, including families in which both parents are of the same gender. The Wirthlins object to a second-grade teacher's reading to their son's class a book that depicts and celebrates a gay marriage. The parents do not challenge the use of these books as part of a nondiscrimination curriculum in the public schools, but challenge the school district's refusal to provide them with prior notice and to allow for exemption from such instruction. They ask for relief until their children are in seventh grade.

Massachusetts does have a statute that requires parents be given notice and the opportunity to exempt their children from curriculum which primarily involves human sexual education or human sexuality issues. Mass. Gen. Laws ch. 71, § 32A. The school system has declined to apply this statutory exemption to these plaintiffs on the basis that the materials do not primarily involve human sexual education or human sexuality issues. . . .

. . . The [state education] statute mandates that the standards "be designed to inculcate respect for the cultural, ethnic and racial diversity of the commonwealth." Further, "[a]cademic standards shall be designed to avoid perpetuating gender, cultural, ethnic or racial stereotypes." The statute does not specify sexual orientation in these lists. . . .

[The state health curriculum establishes Learning Standards for different grades.] It is not until grades 6–8 that the Learning Standards under this component address "the detrimental effect of prejudice (such as prejudice on the basis of race, gender, sexual orientation, class, or religion) on individual relationships and society as a whole." There is also a Reproduction/Sexuality component under the Physical Health Strand [of the Learning Standards]. Within that component, the Learning Standards provide that by grade 5, students should be able to "[d]efine sexual orientation using the correct terminology (such as heterosexual, and gay and lesbian)." . . .

By statute, the actual selection of books is the responsibility of a school's principal, with the approval of the superintendent of schools. . . .

In January 2005, when Jacob Parker ("Jacob") was in kindergarten, he brought home a "Diversity Book Bag." This included a picture book, *Who's in a Family?,* which depicted different families, including single-parent families, an extended family, interracial families, animal families, a family without children, and—to the concern of the Parkers—a family with two dads and a family with two moms. The book concludes by answering the question, Who's in a family?: "The people who love you the most!" The book says nothing about marriage.

The Parkers were concerned that this book was part of an effort by the public schools "to indoctrinate young children into the concept that homosexuality and homosexual relationships or marriage are moral and acceptable behavior." Such an effort, they feared, would require their sons to affirm a belief inconsistent with their religion. [The Parkers met with the school principal to request notification class discussions of homosexuality, but the principal disagreed that the school had an obligation to notify them in advance of such class discussions.] . . .

As the 2005–2006 school year began, Paul Ash ("Ash"), the current Superintendent, released a public statement explaining the school district's position that it would not provide parental notification for "discussions, activities, or materials that simply reference same-gender parents or that otherwise recognize the existence of differences in sexual orientation." When Jacob entered first grade that fall, his classroom's book collection included *Who's in a Family?* as well as *Molly's Family,* a picture book about a girl who is at first made to feel embarrassed by a classmate because she has both a mommy and a mama but then learns that families can come in many different varieties. In December 2005, the Parkers repeated their request for advance notice, which Superintendent Ash again denied. . . .

. . . In March 2006, an Estabrook teacher read aloud *King and King* to her second grade class, which included Joseph Robert Wirthlin, Jr. ("Joey"). This picture book tells the story of a prince, ordered by his mother to get married, who first rejects several princesses only to fall in love with another prince. A wedding scene between the two princes is depicted. The last page of the book shows the two princes kissing, but with a red heart superimposed over their mouths. There is no allegation in the complaint that the teacher further discussed the book with the class. That evening, Joey told his parents about the book; his parents described him as "agitated" and remembered him calling the book "so silly." . . .

The plaintiffs argue that their ability to influence their young children toward their family religious views has been undercut in several respects. First, they believe their children are too young to be introduced to the topic of gay marriage. They also point to the important influence teachers have on this age group. They fear their own inability as parents to counter the school's approval of gay marriage, particularly if parents are given no notice that such curricular materials are in use. As for the children, the parents fear that they are "essentially" required "to affirm a belief inconsistent with and prohibited by their religion." The parents assert it is ironic, and unconstitutional under the Free Exercise Clause, for a public school system to show such intolerance towards their own religious beliefs in the name of tolerance. . . .

II.

. . . [The Supreme Court has held that] "a law that is neutral and of general applicability need not be justified by a compelling governmental interest even if the law has the incidental effect of burdening a particular religious practice." *Church of the Lukumi Babalu Aye, Inc. v. City of Hialeah,* 508 U.S. 520, 531 (1993). . . .

In contrast to the mere rationality standard for neutral laws of general applicability, [Free Exercise Clause cases] require a compelling justification for any law that targets religious groups. . . . [Here, the] school was not singling out plaintiffs' particular religious beliefs or targeting its tolerance lessons to only those children from families with religious objections to gay marriage. The fact that a school promotes tolerance of different sexual orientations and gay marriage when such tolerance is anathema to some religious groups does not constitute targeting. . . .

. . . Plaintiffs . . . rely on a Supreme Court decision recognizing a substantive due process right of parents "to make decisions concerning the care, custody, and control of their children." *Troxel v. Granville,* 530 U.S. 57, 66 (2000) (plurality opinion). *Troxel* is not so broad as plaintiffs assert. The cases cited by the Court in *Troxel* as establishing this parental right pertain either to the custody of children, which was also the issue in dispute in *Troxel,* or to the fundamental control of children's schooling, as in *Wisconsin v. Yoder* [406 U.S. 205 (1972)] . . .

Defendants respond that plaintiffs' argument runs afoul of the general proposition that, while parents can choose between public and private schools, they do not have a constitutional right to "direct *how* a public school teaches their child." *Blau v. Fort Thomas Pub. Sch. Dist.,* 401 F.3d 381, 395 (6th Cir.2005). That proposition is well recognized. . . .

Plaintiffs say, in response, that they are not attempting to control the school's power to prescribe a curriculum. The plaintiffs accept that the school system "has a legitimate secular interest in seeking to eradicate bias against same-gender couples and to ensure the safety of all public school students." They assert that they have an equally sincere interest in the accommodation of their own religious beliefs and of the diversity represented by their contrary views. Plaintiffs specifically disclaim any intent to seek control of the school's curriculum or to impose their will on others. They do not seek to change the choice of books available to others but only to require notice of the books and an exemption, and even then only up to the seventh grade. Nonetheless, we have found no federal case under the Due Process Clause which has permitted parents to demand an exemption for their children from exposure to certain books used in public schools. . . .

In *Mozert v. Hawkins County Board of Education,* 827 F.2d 1058 (6th Cir.1987), . . . the Sixth Circuit rejected a broader claim for an exemption from a school district's use of an entire series of texts. The parents in that case asserted that the books in question taught values contrary to their religious beliefs and that, as a result, the school violated the parents' religious beliefs by allowing their children to read the books and violated their children's religious beliefs by requiring the children to read them. The court, however, found that exposure to ideas through the required reading of books did not constitute a constitutionally significant burden on the plaintiffs' free exercise of religion. In so holding, the court emphasized that "the evil prohibited by the Free Exercise Clause" is "governmental compulsion either to do or refrain from doing an act forbidden or required by one's religion, or to affirm or disavow a belief forbidden or required by one's religion," and reading or even discussing the books did not compel such action or affirmation. . . .

The heart of the plaintiffs' free exercise claim is a claim of "indoctrination": that the state has put pressure on their children to endorse an affirmative view of gay marriage and has thus undercut the parents' efforts to inculcate their children with their own opposing religious views. The Supreme Court, we believe, has never utilized an indoctrination test under the Free Exercise Clause, much less in the public school context. The closest it has come is *West Virginia Board of Educ. v. Barnette,* [319 U.S. 624 (1943), where] the Court held that the state could not coerce acquiescence through compelled statements of belief, such as the mandatory recital of the pledge of allegiance in public schools. It did not hold that the state could not attempt to inculcate values by instruction, and in fact carefully distinguished the two approaches. We do not address whether or not an indoctrination theory under the Free Exercise Clause is sound. Plaintiffs' pleadings do not establish a viable case of indoctrination, even assuming that extreme indoctrination can be a form of coercion.

First, as to the parents' free exercise rights, the mere fact that a child is exposed on occasion in public school to a concept offensive to a parent's religious belief does not inhibit the parent from instructing the child differently. A parent whose "child is exposed to sensitive topics or information [at school] remains free to discuss these matters and to place them in the family's moral or religious context, or to supplement the information with more appropriate materials." *C.N. v. Ridgewood Bd. of Educ.,* 430 F.3d 159 (3d Cir. 2005). The parents here did in fact have notice, if not prior notice, of the books and of the school's overall intent to promote toleration of same-sex marriage, and they retained their ability to discuss the material and subject matter with their children. Our outcome does not turn, however, on whether the parents had notice.

Turning to the children's free exercise rights, we cannot see how Jacob's free exercise right was burdened at all: two books were made available to him, but he was never required to read them or have them read to him. Further, these books do not endorse gay marriage or homosexuality, or even address these topics explicitly, but merely describe how other children might come from families that look different from one's own. There is no free exercise right to be free from any reference in public elementary schools to the existence of families in which the parents are of different gender combinations.

Joey has a more significant claim, both because he was required to sit through a classroom reading of *King and King* and because that book affirmatively endorses homosexuality and gay marriage. It is a fair inference that the reading of *King and King* was precisely *intended* to influence the listening children toward tolerance of gay marriage. That was the point of why that book was chosen and used. Even assuming there is a continuum along which an intent to influence could become an attempt to indoctrinate, however, this case is firmly on the influence-toward-tolerance end. There is no evidence of systemic indoctrination. There is no allegation that Joey was asked to affirm gay marriage. Requiring a student to read a particular book is generally not coercive of free exercise rights. . . .

On the facts, there is no viable claim of "indoctrination" here. Without suggesting that such showings would suffice to establish a claim of indoctrination, we note the plaintiffs' children were not forced to read the books on pain of suspension. Nor were they subject to a constant stream of like materials. There is no allegation here of a formalized curriculum requiring students to read many books affirming gay marriage. The reading by a teacher of one book, or even three, and even if to a young and impressionable child, does not constitute "indoctrination." . . .

NOTES ON *PARKER v. HURLEY*

Doctrinally, *Parker* is an unremarkable case. As the First Circuit notes, it is well-established law that local school districts have great leeway in adopting curricular materials. Politically, however, *Parker v. Hurley* was a blockbuster—so much so that it may have determined the outcome of the Proposition 8 vote in California in November 2008.

One of the primary arguments made by proponents of Prop 8 was that legalization of gay marriage would lead to schoolchildren being taught that homosexuality is good. Several of the ads featured the *Parker* case, including interviews with the parents who brought that lawsuit. These interviews were introduced as proof that the fear of having young children being taught unacceptable things in school was not paranoia. The refrain was, it's already happened in Massachusetts, and it can happen here. Watch for yourself: http://www.protectmarriage.com/video/view/6.

How would you have responded to these arguments? Would an exemption for objecting parents be good policy even if not constitutionally mandated? See Martha Minow, *Should Religious Groups Be Exempt from Civil Rights Laws?*, 48 B.C. L. Rev. 781 (2007) (advocating negotiated rather than zero-sum outcomes in such disputes).

CHAPTER 8

FAMILIES WE CHOOSE: PRIVATIZATION AND PLURALITY IN FAMILY LAW

SECTION 2

THE EXPANSION OF MARRIAGE TO INCLUDE SAME–SEX COUPLES (AND OTHERS?)

Page 1086. Insert the following Cases and Notes at the end of Section 2, Part B:

Hillary Goodridge et al. v. Department of Public Health
Supreme Judicial Court of Massachusetts, 2003.

[Excerpted in Appendix 7 of the Casebook, pp. 1553–63]

Opinions of the Justices to the Senate, 802 N.E.2d 565 (Mass. 2004). Immediately after the Massachusetts Supreme Judicial Court's *Goodridge* decision (Casebook, pp. 1553–63), opponents focused on the mandated 180–day stay contained in the opinion, made "to permit the Legislature to take such action as it may deem appropriate in light of" the Court's holding that the state discrimination against same-sex couples was unconstitutional. Why had the Court included the stay? Why not put the decision into effect immediately, if not because the Court wanted to give the legislature some room to maneuver and provide a remedy other than marriage? Some commentators proposed that *Goodridge* left it open for the state to limit marriage to one man and one woman if they would state clearly the rational basis for such a limitation. See Hadley Arkes & Mary Ann Glendon, "Goodridge Case has Alternative to Gay Marriage," *Boston Herald*, January 8, 2004.

Another option, proffered by the Massachusetts attorney general and the Senate President, was to pass a bill creating civil unions for same-sex couples that had all the benefits of marriage but withheld the name "marriage." The State Senate requested an advisory opinion from the Supreme Judicial Court asking about the constitutionality of a civil union law in light of *Goodridge*. The question they submitted read (in part):

> Does Senate, No. 2175, which prohibits same-sex couples from entering into marriage but allows the to form civil unions with all 'benefits, protections, rights and responsibilities' of marriage, comply with the equal protection and due process requirements of the Constitution of the Commonwealth ...?

In another opinion by **Chief Justice Margaret Marshall**, the Court answered no. The stay was likely intended, not to induce a compromise, or to sway a weak fourth vote, but to encourage a legislative endorsement of the decision and to allow time for administrative adjustments in the wake of the decisions (none was made, but the decision went into effect May 17th notwithstanding).

The opinion summarized the holding in *Goodridge* and went on to say that the "same defects of rationality evident in the marriage ban considered in *Goodridge*" were evident in the Senate bill. The group classifications implied by the distinction between (heterosexual) marriage and (same-sex) civil unions were therefore "unsupportable." The strongest language of the opinion was against the idea, proposed by the dissent, that the difference in name was simply a semantic one, a difference in language that didn't make any real difference: "The bill's absolute prohibition of the use of the word 'marriage' by 'spouses' who are the same sex is more than semantic. The dissimilitude between he terms 'civil marriage' and 'civil union' is not innocuous; it is a considered choice of language that reflects a demonstrable assigning of same-sex, largely homosexual, couples to second class status. The demonstration of this difference by the separate opinion of Justice Sosman ... as merely a 'squabble over the name to be used' so clearly misses the point that further discussion appears to be useless. ... The bill would have the effect of maintaining and fostering a stigma of exclusion that the Constitution prohibits. It would deny to same-sex 'spouses' only a status that is specially recognized in society and has significant social and other advantages."

The Court's opinion concluded with an assertion that the distinction between civil unions and marriage is not merely a difference in tangible benefits, but in intangible benefits as well: "We recognize that the pending bill palliates some of the financial and other concrete manifestations of the discrimination at issue in *Goodridge*. But the question the court considered in *Goodridge* was not only whether it was proper to withhold tangible benefits from same-sex couples, but also whether it was constitutional to create a separate class of citizens by status discrimination, and withhold from that class the right to participate in the institution of civil marriage, along with its concomitant tangible and intangible protections, benefits, rights, and responsibilities. Maintaining a second-class citizen status for same-sex couples by excluding them from the institution of civil marriage *is* the constitutional infirmity at issue."

NOTES ON THE MASSACHUSETTS SAME-SEX MARRIAGE OPINIONS

1. *What's in a Name?* In dissent in the second marriage case, Justice Sosman wrote that both sides "appear to have ignored the fundamental import of the proposed legislation, namely, that same-sex couples who are civilly 'united' will have literally every single right, privilege, benefit and obligation of every sort that our State law confers on opposite-sex couples who are civilly 'married'" and quoted Shakespeare: "What's in a name? That which we call a rose/By any other name would smell as sweet." The proposed bill provided that a civil union will give "those joined in it a legal status equivalent to marriage and shall be treated under law as a marriage." The dissent noted, further, that there is a large difference between the situation the original *Goodridge* court confronted and the bill creating civil unions: it is the difference between no bundle of rights and benefits to same-sex couples and a bundle of rights and benefits that is equivalent to the rights and benefits conferred on a couple by marriage. Is the remaining name difference evidence of a desire to stigmatize gays, or is it evidence of good faith on the part of the legislature?

What are the intangible benefits of marriage? The dissent went on to say that the difference between civil unions and marriage is merely one of "form" and not of "content." The majority opinion, by contrast, seemed to suggest that the difference of form represents part of the good of marriage, the "intangible benefits" of marriage. As an *amicus* brief put it, *Goodridge* held that "the civil institution of marriage is indeed greater than the sum of its legal parts." But what are the "intangible" benefits of marriage? Why would the intangible benefits of civil unions be any less? If one of the intangible benefits of marriage is social recognition, as several of the *amicus* briefs maintained, is this something that the legislature can confer, just like that, by choosing one name for institution rather than another?

Consider again the debate over whether the distinction between "civil union" and "marriage" is merely a semantic one. The flip side of the intangible benefits of marriage claim is that denying the name "marriage" to same-sex unions entails stigmatizing gay and lesbians and giving them a second class status. Not only does marriage give intangible benefits, the deprivation of the title marriage constitutes an intangible harm. Or so says the majority in its response to the Senate. Could those in favor of the distinction claim that civil unions are not themselves stigmatizing and that the name "civil union" connotes no stamp of inferiority, and if it does, this is a construction that gays and lesbians have chosen to put on it? Cf. the majority in *Plessy v. Ferguson*? That is, is the act of limiting marriage to one man and one woman inherently discriminatory, especially if exactly the same benefits are given to same-sex couples, albeit under a different name? Is it saying that same-sex unions are worse (less stable?) than heterosexual marriages?

2. *A Possible Rational Basis?* Justice Sosman's opinion offered the following point in favor of distinguishing marriages from civil unions: even though same-sex marriages might be recognized in Massachusetts, they will not be recognized in other states, and not federally. Therefore, there will remain an ineliminable difference between straight and gay marriages. Justice Sosman wrote: "Those differences are real, and, in some cases, quite stark. Their very existence makes it rational to call the licenses issued to same-sex couples by a different name, as it unavoidably—and, to many, regrettably—cannot confer a truly equal package of rights, privileges, and benefits on those couples, no matter what name it is given." The distinction between civil unions and marriages, then, does not create a difference, but reflects a difference in status that is already there. The majority labeled this argument, "irrelevant," and wrote: "That there may remain personal residual prejudice against same-sex couples is a proposition all too familiar to other disadvantaged groups. That such prejudice exists is not a reason to insist on less than the Constitution requires." Who has the better of the argument? Is the argument by Sosman really just a *post hoc* rationalization (it was not offered by the legislature)?

3. *Getting the State Out of "Marriage"?* The *Goodridge* decision contemplated the possibility that the state may simply get out of the marriage business altogether. The "right to marry," it said, "is different form rights deemed 'fundamental' for equal protection and due process purposes because the State could, in theory, abolish all civil marriage while it cannot, for example, abolish all private property rights." But it went on to conclude that "[e]liminating civil marriage would be wholly inconsistent with the Legislature's deep commitment to fostering stable families and would dismantle a vital organizing principle of our society." What about keeping the institution but changing the name? In the Opinions of the Justices to the Senate, Justice Sosman raised this point, and it was also taken up by the majority. Sosman remarked that the legislature might simply rename the institution of heterosexual marriage, and that indeed "there is much to be said for the argument that the secular legal institution, which has gradually come to mean something very different from its original religious counterpart, be given a name that distinguishes it from the religious sacrament of 'marriage.'" Is this a possible solution to the disagreement between Sosman and the majority, i.e., doing away with the term marriage altogether, at least when talking about state supported unions (as opposed to, e.g., religiously sanctioned ones)? The majority opinion went so far as to suggest that if heterosexual marriages were given a name other than marriage, and same-sex marriages were called civil unions, the justification given by Sosman might pass constitutional muster. "What is not permissible," says the majority, "*is to retain the word* for some and not for others, with all the distinctions thereby engendered" (emphasis added).

Cote–Whitacre v. Department of Public Health, 844 N.E.2d 623 (Mass. 2006). Attempts were made not only to re-write the holding in *Goodridge* (by making it compatible with same-sex unions but not same-sex marriage) but also to limit its impact. In the wake of *Goodridge*, Governor Mitt Romney invoked a 1913 law that prevented marrying out-of-state couples if the marriage would be considered void under the laws of their home state. The relevant law reads:

> Section 11. No marriage shall be contracted in this commonwealth by a party residing and intending to continue to reside in another jurisdiction if such marriage would be void if contracted in such other jurisdiction, and every marriage contracted in this commonwealth in violation hereof shall be null and void.

Thus, those same-sex couples who came from outside Massachusetts but who resided in states which did not recognize same sex marriage would be barred from getting married.

Opponents of the law argued, *inter alia*, that the law had racist origins, passed originally (at least in part) to prevent black-white couples from getting married in Massachusetts, which permitted interracial marriage and it was an archaic law that was being selectively applied only to same-sex couples. (Town clerks since the late 1970s had not been asked to verify the residency of couples. This changed after *Goodridge*). Several towns, however, defied the governor and refused to ask couples for proof of residency. Provincetown had couples sign a statement that they knew of no impediment to their marriage in their own state, but did not make any effort to verify the statements. On May 18, the day after *Goodridge* went into effect, Romney demanded to see copies of the marriage applications from the cities that went against his order. Romney stated that he did not want Massachusetts to become "the Las Vegas of same-sex marriage," that is, one where couples might come for a "quickie" marriage with no intention of residing in the state where they were married.

In June 2004, eight same-sex couples filed a law suit seeking to enjoin the state from enforcing the 1913 law. The suit argued that Romney's application of the law was unconstitutionally selective; it also argued that the 1913 law ran afoul of the Privileges and Immunities Clause of the U.S. constitution. The Supreme Judicial Court denied the plaintiffs' motion.

The decision noted that *Goodridge* limited its holding to Massachusetts "residents" or "citizens," e.g., "[o]ur concern is with the Massachusetts Constitution as a charter of governance for every person properly within its reach." Moreover, the Court ruled that the plaintiffs had not proved the selective enforcement claim: the clerks were instructed to check for all couples and all impediments to marriage for out-of-state couples, not just same-sex couples, although it found "troubling the timing of the resurrection of the [1913 law] immediately after the Supreme Juridical Court declared the prohibition against gay marriages unconstitutional."

"Massachusetts has a legitimate interest in protecting the interest served by the Commonwealth's creation and regulation of the marriage relationship with the requirement that there be an approving state ready to enforce marital rights and duties for the protection of the public, the spouses, and their children. ... Thus, it is rational for the Commonwealth to require that in order to marry her, persons must reside here or in a jurisdiction where their marriage is similarly recognized and regulated. ... Safeguarding the benefits, obligations, and protections of the parties, including the children, of a marriage that the commonwealth has helped create, is a legitimate governmental objective."

The Court also denied that the right to travel from other states to Massachusetts in order to marry was a "fundamental right," and so the 1913 law did not violate the Privileges and Immunities Clause of the U.S. Constitution.

Postscript. The Massachusetts Legislature repealed the 1913 law in July 2008.

NOTE ON EFFORTS TO AMEND THE MASSACHUSETTS AND FEDERAL CONSTITUTIONS

1. *Proposals to Amend the Massachusetts Constitution.* Originally after *Goodridge*, opponents sought to pass a two pronged amendment to the Massachusetts constitution: civil unions for same-sex couples, but no gay marriage. That amendment passed the first round vote in March 2004 and was afterwards abandoned. The original amendment read in its relevant part:

> It being the public policy of this commonwealth to protect the unique relationship of marriage, only the union of one man and one woman shall be valid or recognized as a marriage in the commonwealth. Two persons of the same sex shall have the right to form a civil union if they otherwise meet the requirements set forth by law for marriage. Civil unions for same sex persons are established by this Article and shall provide entirely the same benefits, protections, rights, privileges and obligations that are afforded to persons married under the law of commonwealth.

Now (2007) running for President, former Governor Romney no longer endorses previous amendment, saying it was "somewhat confused or muddied" due to its support of civil unions.

Romney subsequently favored what he called a "clean, straightforward" amendment. The new amendment would simply have defined marriage as one man, one woman and would have left the issue of civil unions unaddressed. Because it was a "citizen's initiative" and not one proposed by the Legislature, the new amendment faced a lower threshold for going onto the ballot: the signatures of 65,825 residents and the support of one-quarter of the Legislature in consecutive sessions. In June 2007, the Legislature killed this second amendment, when it failed to achieve support from even one-quarter of the Legislature (50 members). Why did this measure fail so completely?

2. *The Proposed Federal Marriage Amendment.* On February 24, 2004, President Bush declared his support for a Federal Marriage Amendment. In his statement, Bush did not endorse any particular version of the amendment, but he was believed to have favored the language initially proposed by Representative Marilyn Musgrave of Colorado, which reads:

> Marriage in the United States shall consist only of the union of a man a woman. Neither this constitution or the constitution of any state, nor state or federal law, shall be construed to require that marital status of the legal incidents thereof be conferred upon unmarried couples or groups.

President Bush, in part, defended the amendment as necessary as a response to the decisions of state courts, in particular Massachusetts, which recognized gay marriage. He added that there was no assurance that the Defense of Marriage Act (DOMA) might not also be struck down by "activist courts." Hence, a federal amendment was needed.

The risk that DOMA might be overturned was echoed by Representative DeLay in his remarks during the Fall 2004 debate over the amendment in the House of Representatives:

> Those who know me know I am not a fan of constitutional amendments in general. And at first I resisted this amendment in particular. But the fact can no longer be denied. If marriage is to be protected in this country, it can only be protected by constitutional amendment. The timing, substance and necessity of the marriage protection amendment have been forced by the courts and their refusal to be bound by the clear and absolute limits of their constitutional authority to interpret the law. This amendment is the only way marriage will be protected.

Both President Bush and Members of Congress argued that the FMA was needed to defend the institution of marriage, the same argument underlying DOMA. There was a twist, however, in the 2004 congressional debates: the FMA proponents looked to experience abroad. Specifically, they argued that registered partnerships, close to marriage, for same-sex couples in Scandinavia had destroyed marriage in that region. Agreeing that the decline of marriage has several causes, Senator Rick Santorum maintained that same-sex marriage exacerbates the decline because it reinforces the notion that marriage is all about the pleasure and happiness of adults, and not about adult responsibility toward rearing children under the best possible circumstances. This is the reason, Santorum concluded, that the out-of-wedlock birth rate in Nordic countries is over 60%. 150 Cong. Rec. S7906–08 (July 12, 2004); for other statements to the same effect, see id. at S7926 (Senator Brownback); id. at S7967 (Senator Inhofe).

The Scandinavian argument against same-sex marriage originated with Stanley Kurtz, "The End of Marriage in Scandinavia," *Weekly Standard*, Feb. 2, 2004, and is empirically and normatively questioned by William Eskridge, Jr. and Darren Spedale, *Gay Marriage: For Better or For Worse? What We've Learned from the Evidence* chap. 5 (2006), which demonstrates that after same-sex "registered partnerships" (civil unions) were recognized in Denmark in 1989 the national marriage rate went up dramatically after two decades of steady decline, the divorce rate went down a little after two decades of increases, and the rate of non-martial births plateaued and then declined after two decades of geometric increases. In other words, Eskridge and Spedale argue, the defense of marriage argument, especially with the new Scandinavian twist, is a lavender herring.

3.   *The Defeat and Revival of the FMA.* In 2004, the Senate voted 48–50 against the FMA, well short of the two-thirds majority is needed to be approved by both chambers of Congress. The House voted in favor of the FMA, but not by the two-thirds needed to propose a constitutional amendment. Notwithstanding its failure in 2004, the Republican leadership brought the FMA back as the "Marriage Protection Amendment" in 2006, again shortly before the November elections. Again, the amendment failed to achieve anything close to the majorities needed under Article V.

These efforts, and their failure, reflect a familiar historical pattern. Edward Stein, "Past and Present Proposed Amendments to the United States Constitution Regarding Marriage," 82 *Wash. U.L.Q.* 611 (2004), demonstrates that for two hundred years Members of Congress have shown interest in amending the Constitution to "protect marriage" (usually against interracial couples in the past)—and never with any success. The impulse to amend the Constitution to enshrine traditional family law exclusions seems eternal—but that impulse runs up against arguments that such matters should be left to state-by-state policy and even experimentation.

Even with no chance of adoption, the FMA or the MPA might remain alive on the national political agenda if popular opinion remains hostile to same-sex marriages and people are nervous that courts will impose it upon unwilling populations. So far, the opposite seems to be occurring. Popular opposition to same-sex marriage is waning, and popular support for civil unions is waxing. And post-*Goodridge,* judges remain unwilling to require same-sex "marriage," even in jurisdictions that are gay-friendly. Consider the following case.

Daniel L. Hernandez v. Victor L. Robles et al.

New York Court of Appeals, 2006.
7 N.Y.3d 338, 855 N.E.2d 1, 821 N.Y.S.2d 770.

■ JUDGE R.S. SMITH (joined by JUDGES G.B. SMITH and by READ).

[Forty-four (44) lesbian and gay couples challenged New York's exclusion of them from civil marriage. Judge Smith asked whether there might be a rational basis for excluding them and then asked whether the New York or U.S. Constitution subjects this discrimination to heightened scrutiny requiring more than a rational basis.]

III. It is undisputed that the benefits of marriage are many. The diligence of counsel has identified 316 such benefits in New York law, of which it is enough to summarize some of the most important: Married people receive significant tax advantages, rights in probate and intestacy proceedings, rights to support from their spouses both during the marriage and after it is dissolved, and rights to be treated as family members in obtaining insurance coverage and making health care decisions. Beyond this, they receive the symbolic benefit, or moral satisfaction, of seeing their relationships recognized by the State.

The critical question is whether a rational legislature could decide that these benefits should be given to members of opposite-sex couples, but not same-sex couples. The question is not, we emphasize, whether the Legislature must or should continue to limit marriage in this way; of course the Legislature may (subject to the effect of the Federal Defense of Marriage Act, Pub. L. 104–199, 110 Stat. 2419) extend marriage or some or all of its benefits to same-sex couples. We conclude, however, that there are at least two grounds that rationally support the limitation on marriage that the Legislature has enacted. Others have been advanced, but we will discuss only these two, both of which are derived from the undisputed assumption that marriage is important to the welfare of children.

First, the Legislature could rationally decide that, for the welfare of children, it is more important to promote stability, and to avoid instability, in opposite-sex than in same-sex relationships. Heterosexual intercourse has a natural tendency to lead to the birth of children; homosexual intercourse does not. Despite the advances of science, it remains true that the vast majority of children are born as a result of a sexual relationship between a man and a woman, and the Legislature could find that this will continue to be true. The Legislature could also find that such relationships are all too often casual or temporary. It could find that an important function of marriage is to create more stability and permanence in the relationships that cause children to be born. It thus could choose to offer an inducement—in the form of marriage and its attendant benefits—to opposite-sex couples who make a solemn, long-term commitment to each other.

The Legislature could find that this rationale for marriage does not apply with comparable force to same-sex couples. These couples can become parents by adoption, or by artificial insemination or other technological marvels, but they do not become parents as a result of accident or impulse. The Legislature could find that unstable relationships between people of the opposite sex present a greater danger that children will be born into or grow up in unstable homes than is the case with same-sex couples, and thus that promoting stability in opposite-sex relationships will help children more. This is one reason why the Legislature could rationally offer the benefits of marriage to opposite-sex couples only.

There is a second reason: The Legislature could rationally believe that it is better, other things being equal, for children to grow up with both a mother and a father. Intuition and experience suggest that a child benefits from having before his or her eyes, every day, living models of what both a man and a woman are like. It is obvious that there are exceptions to this general rule—some children who never know their fathers, or their mothers, do far better than some who grow up with parents of both sexes—but the Legislature could find that the general rule will usually hold.

Plaintiffs, and *amici* supporting them, argue that the proposition asserted is simply untrue: that a home with two parents of different sexes has no advantage, from the point of view of raising children, over a home with two parents of the same sex. Perhaps they are right, but the Legislature could rationally think otherwise.

To support their argument, plaintiffs and *amici* supporting them refer to social science literature reporting studies of same-sex parents and their children. Some opponents of same-sex marriage criticize these studies, but we need not consider the criticism, for the studies on their face do not establish beyond doubt that children fare equally well in same-sex and opposite-sex households. What they show, at most, is that rather limited observation has detected no marked differences. More definitive results could hardly be expected, for until recently few children have been raised in same-sex households, and there has not been enough time to study the long-term results of such child-rearing.

Plaintiffs seem to assume that they have demonstrated the irrationality of the view that opposite-sex marriages offer advantages to children by showing there is no scientific evidence to support it. Even assuming no such evidence exists, this reasoning is flawed. In the absence of conclusive scientific evidence, the Legislature could rationally proceed on the common-sense premise that children will do best with a mother and father in the home. (*See Goodridge* [Sosman, J., dissenting].) And a legislature proceeding on that premise could rationally decide to offer a special inducement, the legal recognition of marriage, to encourage the formation of opposite-sex households.

In sum, there are rational grounds on which the Legislature could choose to restrict marriage to couples of opposite sex. Plaintiffs have not persuaded us that this long-accepted restriction is a wholly irrational one, based solely on ignorance and prejudice against homosexuals. This is the question on which these cases turn. If we were convinced that the restriction plaintiffs attack were founded on nothing but prejudice—if we agreed with the plaintiffs that it is comparable to the restriction in *Loving v. Virginia*, a prohibition on interracial marriage that was plainly "designed to maintain White Supremacy"—we would hold it invalid, no matter how long its history. As the dissent points out, a long and shameful history of racism lay behind the kind of statute invalidated in *Loving*.

But the historical background of *Loving* is different from the history underlying this case. Racism has been recognized for centuries—at first by a few people, and later by many more—as a revolting moral evil. This country fought a civil war to eliminate racism's worst manifestation, slavery, and passed three constitutional amendments to eliminate that curse and its vestiges. *Loving* was part of the civil rights revolution of the 1950's and 1960's, the triumph of a cause for which many heroes and many ordinary people had struggled since our nation began.

It is true that there has been serious injustice in the treatment of homosexuals also, a wrong that has been widely recognized only in the relatively recent past, and one our Legislature tried to address when it enacted the Sexual Orientation Non–Discrimination Act four years ago (L 2002, ch. 2). But the traditional definition of marriage is not merely a by-product of historical injustice. Its history is of a different kind.

The idea that same-sex marriage is even possible is a relatively new one. Until a few decades ago, it was an accepted truth for almost everyone who ever lived, in any society in which marriage existed, that there could be marriages only between participants of different sex. A court should not lightly conclude that everyone who held this belief was irrational, ignorant or bigoted. We do not so conclude.

[In Part IV, Judge Smith found that constitutional precedents did not require more than rational basis for the state's exclusionary rule. Part IV.A found no fundamental right, "deeply rooted in this Nation's history and tradition" (*Washington v. Glucksberg* (1997) (Casebook, pp. 74–76)), that would trigger strict scrutiny under the Due Process Clause.] The difference between *Lawrence* and *Glucksberg* is that in *Glucksberg* the relatively narrow definition of the right at issue was based on rational line-drawing. In *Lawrence*, by contrast, the court found the distinction between homosexual sodomy and intimate relations generally to be essentially arbitrary. Here, there are, as we have explained, rational grounds for limiting the definition of marriage to opposite-sex couples. This case is therefore, in the relevant way, like *Glucksberg* and not at all like *Lawrence*. Plaintiffs here do not, as the petitioners in *Lawrence* did, seek protection against State intrusion on intimate, private activity. They seek from the courts access to a State-conferred benefit that the Legislature has rationally limited to opposite-sex couples. We conclude that, by defining marriage as it has, the New York Legislature has not restricted the exercise of a fundamental right.

[In Part IV.B, Judge Smith concluded that the Equal Protection Clause also did not require strict scrutiny, because there was no "suspect classification." Judge Smith rejected plaintiffs' sex discrimination argument on the ground that both sexes were treated the same *and* there was no sex-based class subordinated by the sex-based classification (therefore completely unlike *Loving*). He then observed that the Court of Appeals had reserved the issue whether "sexual preference" is a suspect classification.] We resolve this question in this case on the basis of the Supreme Court's observation that no more than rational basis scrutiny is generally appropriate "where individuals in the group affected by a law have distinguishing characteristics relevant to interests the State has the authority to implement" (*City of Cleburne v. Cleburne Living Ctr., Inc.*, 473 U.S. 432, 441 (1985)). Perhaps that principle would lead us to apply heightened scrutiny to sexual preference discrimination in some cases, but not where we review legislation governing marriage and family relationships. A person's preference for the sort of sexual activity that cannot lead to the birth of children is relevant to the State's interest in fostering relationships that will serve children best. In this area, therefore, we conclude that rational basis scrutiny is appropriate. * * *

■ JUDGE GRAFFEO (joined by JUDGE G.B. SMITH) concurring. [Judge Graffeo also found strict scrutiny inapplicable under either substantive due process or equal protection precedents, largely for the reasons adduced by the plurality opinion. (Unlike Judge Smith, however, Judge Graffeo believed there was no "sexual preference" discrimination on the face of the statute.) The exclusion had a rational basis: "Since marriage was instituted to address the fact that sexual contact between a man and a woman naturally can result in pregnancy and childbirth, the Legislature's decision to focus on opposite-sex couples is understandable. It is not irrational for the Legislature to provide an incentive for opposite-sex couples—for whom children may be conceived from casual, even momentary intimate relationships—to marry, create a family environment, and support their children. Although many same-sex couples share these family objectives and are competently raising children in a stable environment, they are simply not similarly situated to opposite-sex couples in this regard given the intrinsic differences in the assisted reproduction or adoption processes that most homosexual couples rely on to have children."]

■ CHIEF JUDGE KAYE (joined by JUDGE CIPARICK) dissenting. [Chief Judge Kaye argued that strict scrutiny should apply, for three reasons: (1) Plaintiffs could invoke *Loving*'s "fundamental right to marry." It was circular for the majority to frame the fundamental right as "same-sex marriage," just as it would have been circular for the *Loving* Court to frame the right as "inter-racial marriage," also historically disapproved. (2) The exclusion falls upon sexual orientation minorities; sexual orientation is a "suspect classification" for the reasons developed in *Watkins* (Casebook, pp. 230–38), and this also triggers strict scrutiny. (3) The exclusion is on its face a sex discrimination, also triggering strict scrutiny. Chief Judge Kaye also argued that the discrimination did not even further a rational basis, for the following reasons.]

Defendants primarily assert an interest in encouraging procreation within marriage. But while encouraging opposite-sex couples to marry before they have children is certainly a legitimate interest of the State, the *exclusion* of gay men and lesbians from marriage in no way furthers this interest. There are enough marriage licenses to go around for everyone.

Nor does this exclusion rationally further the State's legitimate interest in encouraging heterosexual married couples to procreate. Plainly, the ability or desire to procreate is not a prerequisite for marriage. The elderly are permitted to marry, and many same-sex couples do indeed have children. Thus, the statutory classification here—which prohibits only same-sex couples, and no one else, from marrying—is so grossly underinclusive and overinclusive as to make the asserted rationale in promoting procreation "impossible to credit" (*Romer*). Indeed, even the *Lawrence* dissenters observed that "encouragement of procreation" could not "possibly" be a justification for denying marriage to gay and lesbian couples, "since the sterile and the elderly are allowed to marry." * * *

■ JUDGE ROSENBLATT did not participate.

Table 8–1. State Law Regarding Same–Sex Marriages, Unions, and Partnerships, 2009

State	Statute or Constitutional Limitation of Marriage to One Man, One Woman?	Constitutional Marriage Litigation (Appellate Level)?	Statewide Recognition?
Alabama	Statutory (1998) and Constitutional (2006) Limits	None	None
Alaska	Statutory (1996) and Constitutional (1998) Limits	None	None
Arizona	Statutory (1996) and Constitutional (2008) Limits	*Stanhardt v. Superior Court* (2004) (unsuccessful challenge)	None
Arkansas	Statutory (1997) and Constitutional (2004) Limits, including nonrecognition of relationships "substantially similar to marital status" (2004)	None	None
California	Statutory (2000) and Constitutional (2008) Limits	*Marriage Cases* (2008) (successful challenge, overridden by a Constitutional initiative)	Domestic Partnership* (1999, upgraded 2003)
Colorado	Statutory (2000) and Constitutional (2006) Limits	*Ross v. Denver Dep't of Health & Hosp.* (1994) (unsuccessful)	None
Connecticut	Statutory (2005) Limit	*Kerrigan v. State* (2008) (successful)	Marriage (2008)

State	Statute or Constitutional Limitation of Marriage to One Man, One Woman?	Constitutional Marriage Litigation (Appellate Level)?	Statewide Recognition?
Delaware	Statutory (1996) Limit	None	None
District of Columbia	None	*Dean v. District of Columbia* (1995) (unsuccessful)	Domestic Partnership* (1992, upgraded 2004–06)
Florida	Statutory (1997) and Constitutional (2008) Limits.	None	None
Georgia	Statutory (1996) and Constitutional (2004) Limits, including nonrecognition of same-sex "unions" as well as marriages (2004)	*Van Dyck v. van Dyck* (1993) (unsuccessful)	None
Hawaii	Statutory (1997) and Constitutional (1998) Limits, allowing Legislature authority to confine marriage to one man, one woman (1998)	*Baehr v. Lewin* (1993) (preliminary success, overridden by constitutional amendment [1998])	Reciprocal Beneficiaries (1997)
Idaho	Statutory (1996) and Constitutional (2006) Limits	None	None
Illinois	Statutory (1996) Limit	None	None
Indiana	Statutory (1997) Limit	*Morrison v. Sadler* (2005) (unsuccessful challenge)	None
Iowa	Statutory (1998) Limit	*Varnum v. State* (2009) (successful)	Marriage (2009)
Kansas	Statutory (1996) and Constitutional (2005) Limits, including nonrecognition of any relationship entitling parties to "rights or incidents of marriage" (2005)	*In re Estate of Gardiner* (2002) (unsuccessful suit by transsexual stripped of her marriage rights)	None
Kentucky	1998 (Statutory) and Constitutional (2004) Limits, including nonrecognition of "legal status identical or substantially similar to that of marriage for unmarried individuals" (2004)	*Jones v. Hallahan* (1973) (unsuccessful)	None
Lousiana	Statutory (1999) and Constitutional (2004) Limits, including nonrecognition of "legal status identical or substantially similar to that of marriage for unmarried individuals" (2004)	*In re Succession of Bacot* (1987) (unsuccessful)	None
Maine	None	None	Marriage (2009)
Maryland	Statutory (1984) Limit	*Conaway v. Deane & Polyak* (2007) (unsuccessful)	None
Massachusetts	None	*Goodridge v. Dep't Pub. Health* (2003) (same-sex marriages required)	Marriage (2004)
Michigan	Statutory (1996) and Constitutional (2004) Limits, including nonrecognition of "legal status identical or substantially similar to that of marriage for unmarried individuals" (2004)	None	None
Minnesota	Statutory (1997) Limit	*Baker v. Nelson* (1971, U.S. Supreme Court appeal denied, 1972) (unsuccessful)	None
Mississippi	Statutory (1997) and Constitutional (2004) Limits	None	None
Missouri	Constitutional (2004) Limit	None	None
Montana	Statutory (1997) and Constitutional (2004) Limits	None	None
Nebraska	Constitutional (2000) Limit, including nonrecognition of any "civil union, domestic partnership, or any other same-sex relationship"	*Bruning v. Citizens for Equal Protection* (10th Cir. 2006) (unsuccessful challenge to 2000 amendment)	None
Nevada	Constitutional (2002) Limit	None	None

State	Statute or Constitutional Limitation of Marriage to One Man, One Woman?	Constitutional Marriage Litigation (Appellate Level)?	Statewide Recognition?
New Hampshire	None	None	Marriage (2009)
New Jersey	None	*Lewis v. State* (2006) (successful challenge requiring equal treatment)	Civil Unions (2006)
New Mexico	None	None	None
New York	None	*Hernandez v. State* (2006) (unsuccessful challenge)	None
North Carolina	Statutory (1996) Limit	None	None
North Dakota	Statutory (1997) and Constitutional (2004) Limits. "No other domestic union, however denominated, may be recognized as a marriage or given the same or substantially equivalent legal effect." (2004)	*Jacobson v. Jacobson* (1981) (unsuccessful)	None
Ohio	Constitutional (2004) Limit, voiding any public act or judicial order extending "the specific statutory benefits of legal marriage to nonmarital relationships between persons of the same sex"	*Gajovski v. Gajovski* (1991) (unsuccessful)	None
Oklahoma	Statutory (1996) and Constitutional (2004) Limits	None	None
Oregon	Constitutional (2004) Limit	*Li v. State* (2004) (voiding local marriage licenses)	Domestic Partnership* (2007)
Pennsylvania	Statutory (1996) Limit	None	None
Rhode Island	None	None	None
South Carolina	Statutory (1996) and Constitutional (2006) Limits. State and political subdivisions can neither create nor recognize a "legal status, right or claim respecting any other domestic union however denominated" (2006).	None	None
South Dakota	Statutory (2000) and Constitutional (2006) Limits. "The uniting of two or more persons in a civil union, domestic partnership, or other quasi-marital relationship shall not be valid or recognized in South Dakota." (2006)	None	None
Tennessee	Statutory (1996) and Constitutional (2006) Limits	None	None
Texas	Statutory (2003) and Constitutional (2005) Limits. "This state or a political subdivision of this state may not create or recognize any legal status identical or similar to marriage." (2005)	None	None
Utah	Statutory (1995) and Constitutional (2004) Limits. "No other domestic union, however denominated, may be recognized as a marriage or given the same or substantially equivalent legal effect." (2004)	None	None
Vermont	None	*Baker v. State* (1999) (successful challenge requiring equal treatment)	Marriage (2009)

State	Statute or Constitutional Limitation of Marriage to One Man, One Woman?	Constitutional Marriage Litigation (Appellate Level)?	Statewide Recognition?
Virginia	Statutory (1997) and Constitutional (2006) Limits. "This Commonwealth and its political subdivisions shall not create or recognize a legal status for relationships of unmarried individuals that intends to approximate the design, qualities, significance, or effects of marriage." (2006)	None	None
Washington	Statutory (1998) Limit.	Andersen v. King County (2006) (unsuccessful challenge)	Domestic Partnerships* (2007)
West Virginia	Statutory (2001,2003) Limit.	None	None
Wisconsin	Statutory (1979) and Constitutional (2006) Limits.	None	None
Wyoming	Statutory Limit.	None	None

* "Domestic partnership" laws in California and Oregon are very similar to "civil unions," for they grant almost all the legal rights and duties of marriage to same-sex partners. The partnership laws of the District of Columbia and Washington are somewhat similar. See Table 8–2 below.

Sources: William Eskridge, Jr. & Darren Spedale, *Gay Marriage: For Better or For Worse? What We've learned from the Evidence* (2006); www.lambdalegal.org (viewed June 2007), and various media sources. Darsana Srinivasan (Yale Law School, Class of 2007) did most of the work compiling this table.

NOTE ON STATE RECOGNITION OF SAME–SEX RELATIONSHIPS (2009)

1. *The Dominant Pattern: State Judges, Legislators, and Voters Reject Marriage Equality.* As *Hernandez* illustrates, the press for same-sex marriage or civil unions does not necessarily attract the support of judges, even in gay-tolerant states such as New York. Generally, even gay-friendly courts are applying rational basis scrutiny and are finding some kind of rational basis, therefore not following *Baker* or *Goodridge*. As Table 8–1 demonstrates, the odds are so slim in many states that marriage equality for lesbian and gay couples has not even been worth litigating.

Table 8–1 also reveals that most states have adopted statutory bars to same-sex marriage. Problem 8–4 (Casebook, pp. 1092–93) raises interpretive questions relating to some of these marriage bars. Table 8–1 also shows that increasing numbers are amending their state constitutions to head off state constitutional litigation such as *Baker* and *Goodridge*. In every ballot initiative but one (Arizona, 2006), voters have endorsed anti-marriage constitutional amendments, usually by super-majorities of 60% or more.

2. *A New Rational Basis for Limiting Marriage to Different–Sex Couples.* Notice the new argument against same-sex marriage that surfaces in *Hernandez*. Rather than focusing on natural law definitions of marriage, or anti-homosexual stereotyping (homosexuals are promiscuous, predatory, etc.), or even the Clinton–Bush defense of marriage argument, the *new argument against gay marriage* is that the homosexuals just don't need the incentives and protections of marriage as much as heterosexuals, because they are less likely to have children. Marriage is much about children, and the state really needs to shore up those shaky heterosexuals-with-children relationships. Could the state be more gay-friendly than this? Sure, this justification is wildly over- and under-inclusive, especially as regards lesbians, who are raising children in large numbers. But genuine rational basis review allows a lot of over- and under-inclusion. (In *Hernandez*, this argument, made in the opinions of both Judges R.S. Smith and Graffeo, commands a majority. The child-needs-mother-and-father argument advanced by Judge R.S. Smith is only a plurality view; it might have been too close to sex or gender stereotyping for Judge Graffeo to join.)

3. *Equal Treatment, but Not the Name—Is this "Separate but Equal"?* A common pattern in gay-tolerant states is for judges to insist upon equal treatment of lesbian and gay couples by the state, but to leave the precise nature of the reform to legislatures, which have thus far eschewed the term "marriage" for such couples. This is the Vermont approach. In *Lewis v. Harris*, 908 A.2d 196 (N.J.2006), the New Jersey Supreme Court followed *Baker* to rule that denial of state marriage-based rights and duties to lesbian and gay couples *and* that the Legislature should have the first crack at a remedy. In dissent, Chief Justice Poritz argued that there was no valid reason not to grant lesbian and gay couples *full marriage equality*. No Justice took the position that the statewide discrimination was constitutional. In December 2006, the New Jersey Legislature enacted a civil unions law, without much controversy.

Other states have adopted civil unions laws *without* judicial prodding, namely, Connecticut in 2005 and New Hampshire in 2007. California's Legislature enacted a statewide domestic partnership law in 1999 and expanded it in 2003 to include almost all the same rights and benefits of marriage (Casebook, p. 1051). In 2007, both Oregon and Washington adopted domestic partnership laws after their state supreme courts refused to require same-sex marriage. As in California, these "domestic partnership" laws give almost all the legal rights and duties of marriage to same-sex partners—and so might usefully be thought of as "civil union" laws like those of Vermont and Connecticut in the East. Table 8–2 (below) provides some useful information about how much equality those laws actually provide.

Lesbian and gay couples—and a number of openly straight allies—have complained that civil unions and domestic partnerships constitute a "separate but equal" regime that denies full equality. This tag phrase seriously distorts the legal and political realities.

On the one hand, the "separate" institutions are generally *not* "equal" to marriage. Table 8–2 reveals some striking differences between marriage and domestic partnerships/civil unions in recent legislation. For example, in Maine and Oregon, "domestic partners" must cohabit before the state will recognize their relationships; such a prerequisite has never existed for marriage (indeed, it is inconsistent with the traditional notion of marriage). In DC, Maine, and Washington, domestic partnerships can be dissolved if one partner files a "notice of termination," with reasonable notice to the other party. Such an easy dissolution process assures that partnerships will be more short-lived than marriages, or New Jersey/New Hampshire civil unions and Oregon partnerships, which can only be dissolved by divorce proceedings in those states' marriage laws. Likewise, in Maine and Washington, the support rights of dependent partners is unclear upon dissolution, apparently left to state contract law.

On the other hand, notwithstanding different terminologies and these important legal distinctions, William Eskridge, Jr., *Equality Practice: Civil Unions and the Future of Gay Rights* (2002), argues that the "separate but equal" rhetoric must be abandoned. "Separate but equal" invokes apartheid, which was a violent regime designed to subordinate African Americans socially, economically, and legally. It is an inapposite comparison for civil unions, a major advancement for gay rights. Civil unions treat lesbian and gay couples with respect, not violent and systematic suppression. Professor Eskridge maintains that the more apt terminology is "equality practice": not complete equality now, but practice for possible equality in the future, after further normative persuasion of non-gay Americans, including at least some traditionalists. Note that "equality practice" laws in Vermont, New Hampshire, and Maine were all upgraded to marriage equality by state legislatures in those three states in 2009.

4. *The Symbolic Politics of Relationship "Upgrades."* Several of the new state relationship recognition laws provide for automatic switching between relationships regimes. In all instances, this automatic switching is unidirectional, in that it only allows for switching away from something less like marriage to something more like it. This phenomenon of "automatic upgrading" appears in Washington's, Maine's, and DC's's domestic partnership laws and in New Jersey's civil union law. All offer the ability to upgrade to something more like marriage but do not provide for the ability to move in the opposite direction. A relationship form that is less like marriage is, by implication, a "downgrade." New Jersey is particularly interesting in this regard. Since 2004, it has recognized lesbian and gay domestic partnerships, with some but not many of the legal features of marriage. If under the 2006 law two lesbian partners enter into a civil union, their domestic partnership is automatically terminated. But spouses joined in civil union cannot go in reverse, converting their union into a domestic partnership (which has the advantage for some couples of being easier to dissolve).

These arrangements may reflect the fact that marriage remains our society's normative anchor: the more "like" marriage a state institution is, the more beneficial, and rewarded, that institution is considered. This reflects the normalization of "committed relationship" in the United States, a normalization that is questioned by feminist theorists like Martha Fineman in the United States and Brenda Cossman in Canada. It also reflects the ways in which institutions called something else than marriage and offering fewer legal benefits and duties might be considered indicia of second-class citizenship.

5. *The Menu of Options for Straight Couples.* In DC, Maine, and (for older couples) Washington, domestic partnerships are available statewide to straight as well as gay couples. In those jurisdictions, much as in France, straight couples now have a menu of options: cohabitation, domestic partnership, and marriage. Eskridge, *Equality Practice*, argues that this is an important trend throughout western family law, with Europe and Canada leading the way. Eskridge's menu theory posits that the same options will ultimately be available to gay as well as straight couples, as they are in Canada and The Netherlands.

6. *How About Same-Sex Marriage?* Progressives have pressed for full marriage equality in civil union states. In recent years, lawsuits have been successful in California (2008), Connecticut (2008), and Iowa (2009). See *In re Marriage Cases* excerpted on pages 44–60 of this Supplement.

NOTE ON INTERPRETATION OF STATE ANTI-MARRIAGE
AMENDMENTS

As Table 8–1 demonstrates, 30 states now have constitutional provisions defining marriage as one man, one woman (or, in the case of Hawaii, allowing the Legislature to do so). The publicized effect of these provisions is to head off state constitutional marriage litigation such as *Goodridge* and *Hernandez.* Table 8–1 quotes the state constitutional provisions that go further, also barring the state from recognizing civil unions and other relationships that are not termed "marriage" but that are "similar" to marriage. A big issue in many of these states (such as Arkansas, Kentucky, Louisiana, Michigan, Nebraska, Ohio, South Carolina, South Dakota, Texas, Utah, and Virginia) is whether these new constitutional provisions foreclose domestic partnership benefits supplied by county and municipal employers.

In 2004, Michigan added a provision to its state constitution barring the state from recognizing or giving effect to same-sex marriage *or* any "legal status identical or substantially similar to that of marriage for unmarried individuals." On its face, this provision would head off not only constitutional marriage litigation (*Goodridge*), but also constitutional litigation seeking civil unions (*Baker*) or even legislation recognizing same-sex marriages or civil unions. As the decision below illustrates, however, Michigan judges have interpreted this provision to bar public employers from providing domestic partnership benefits to same-sex couples.

National Pride at Work v. Governor of Michigan

Michigan Supreme Court, 2008.
481 Mich. 56, 748 N.W.2d 524.

■ MARKMAN, J., for the Court [joined by the CHIEF JUSTICE and three other Justices].

We granted leave to appeal to consider whether the marriage amendment, Const. 1963, art. 1, § 25, which states that "the union of one man and one woman in marriage shall be the only agreement recognized as a marriage or similar union for any purpose," prohibits public employers from providing health-insurance benefits to their employees' qualified same-sex domestic partners. Because we agree with the Court of Appeals that providing such benefits does violate the marriage amendment, we affirm its judgment. * * *

On March 16, 2005, in response to a state representative's request for an opinion regarding the marriage amendment's effect on the city of Kalamazoo's ability to provide same-sex domestic-partner health-insurance benefits to its employees, the Attorney General issued a formal opinion, concluding that the city's policy did violate the amendment. The Attorney General asserted that "Const. 1963, art. 1, § 25 prohibits state and local governmental entities from conferring benefits on their employees on the basis of a 'domestic partnership' agreement that is characterized by reference to the attributes of a marriage." OAG, 2005–2006, No. 7,171, p. 17 (March 16, 2005), 2005 Mich. Reg. 5, p. 35.

[Kalamazoo's policy entailed health insurance for the "domestic partners" of municipal employees who:

- were of the same sex;
- were at least 18 years old and mentally competent to enter into a contract;
- shared a common residence and had done so for at least six (6) months;
- were unmarried and not related by blood closer than would prevent marriage;
- shared financial arrangements and daily living expenses related to their common welfare;
- filed a statement of termination of previous domestic partnership at least six (6) months prior to signing another Certification of Domestic Partnership.

The city required the employee and his or her domestic partner to sign a notarized certification of domestic partnership that affirmed these criteria. In addition, they were required to provide evidence of "mutual economic dependence," such as a joint lease or mortgage, and evidence of a "common legal residence," such as driver's licenses or voter's registrations. The city's official policy provided: "It is the intent of this program to provide insurance coverage and other benefits to domestic partners of the City of Kalamazoo identical to those provided to spouses of City employees."]

* * * [T]he primary objective of constitutional interpretation, not dissimilar to any other exercise in judicial interpretation, is to faithfully give meaning to the intent of those who enacted the law. This Court

typically discerns the common understanding of constitutional text by applying each term's plain meaning at the time of ratification. * * *

Plaintiffs argue that "the only thing that is prohibited by the [marriage] amendment is the recognition of a same-sex relationship as a marriage" and that the public employers here are not recognizing a domestic partnership "as a marriage." We respectfully disagree. First, the amendment prohibits the recognition of a domestic partnership "as a marriage or similar union. . . ." That is, it prohibits the recognition of a domestic partnership as a marriage or as a union that is similar to a marriage. Second, just because a public employer does not refer to, or otherwise characterize, a domestic partnership as a marriage or a union similar to a marriage does not mean that the employer is not recognizing a domestic partnership as a marriage or a union similar to a marriage.

* * * Plaintiffs and the dissent argue that because the public employers here do not bestow upon a domestic partnership all the legal rights and responsibilities associated with marriage, the partnership is not similar to a marriage. Again, we respectfully disagree. "Similar" means "having a likeness or resemblance, [especially] in a general way; having qualities in common [.]" *Random House Webster's College Dictionary* (1991). A union does not have to possess all the same legal rights and responsibilities that result from a marriage in order to constitute a union "similar" to that of marriage. If the marriage amendment were construed to prohibit only the recognition of a union that possesses legal rights and responsibilities identical to those that result from a marriage, the language "or similar union" would be rendered meaningless, and an interpretation that renders language meaningless must be avoided. Further, the dissimilarities identified by plaintiffs are not dissimilarities pertaining to the nature of the marital and domestic-partnership unions themselves, but are merely dissimilarities pertaining to the legal effects that are accorded these relationships. However, given that the marriage amendment prohibits the recognition of unions similar to marriage "for any purpose," the pertinent question is not whether these unions give rise to all the same legal effects; rather, it is whether these unions are being recognized as unions similar to marriage for any purpose.[5]

---

5. Indeed, we agree with plaintiffs and the dissent that marriages and domestic partnerships are dissimilar in many respects. Marriages give rise to many legal rights and responsibilities that domestic partnerships do not. However, we believe the pertinent question for purposes of the marriage amendment is not whether these relationships give rise to identical, or even similar, legal rights and responsibilities, but whether these relationships are similar in nature in the context of the marriage amendment. The dissent, post at 550 n. 50, fails to recognize that the pertinent question here is not whether marriages and domestic partnerships are similar in the abstract, but whether these relationships are similar for purposes of the marriage amendment, i.e., for the purpose of a constitutional provision that prohibits the recognition of unions similar to marriage "for any purpose." If they are, then there can be no legal cognizance given to the similar relationship.

All the domestic-partnership policies at issue here require the partners to be of a certain sex, i.e., the same sex as the other partner. Similarly, Michigan law requires married persons to be of a certain sex, i.e., a different sex from the other. MCL 551.1 ("Marriage is inherently a unique relationship between a man and a woman."). In addition, each of the domestic-partnership policies at issue in this case requires that the partners not be closely related by blood. Similarly, Michigan law requires that married persons not be closely related by blood. MCL 551.3 and MCL 551.4. Although there are, of course, many different types of relationships in Michigan that are accorded legal significance—e.g., debtor-creditor, parent-child, landlord-tenant, attorney-client, employer-employee—marriages and domestic partnerships appear to be the only such relationships that are defined in terms of both gender and the lack of a close blood connection. As discussed earlier, "similar" means "having a likeness or resemblance, [especially] in a general way; having qualities in common[.]" *Random House Webster's College Dictionary* (1991). Marriages and domestic partnerships share two obviously important, and apparently unique (at least in combination), qualities in common.[14] Because marriages and domestic partnerships share these "similar" qualities, we believe that it can fairly be said that they "resembl[e]" one another "in a general way." Therefore, although marriages and domestic partnerships are by no means identical, they are similar. Because marriages and domestic partnerships are the only relationships in Michigan defined in terms of both gender and lack of a close blood connection, and, thus, have these core "qualities in common," we conclude that domestic partnerships are unions similar to marriage.
* * *

The marriage amendment begins with a statement of its purpose that is effectively a preamble: "To secure and preserve the benefits of marriage for our society and for future generations of children. . . ." Plaintiffs argue that the marriage amendment does not prohibit public employers from providing health-insurance benefits to their employees' qualified same-sex domestic partners because health-insurance benefits do not constitute a benefit of marriage. However, the marriage amendment contains more than just a statement of purpose. In full, it states: "To secure and preserve the benefits of marriage for our society and for future generations of children, the union of one man and one woman in marriage shall be the only agreement recognized as a marriage or similar union for any purpose." The latter—the operative—part of this provision sets forth how the ratifiers intended to go about achieving the purposes set forth in the first part, "secur[ing] and preserv[ing] the benefits of marriage. . . ." This operative part specifies that public employers must not recognize domestic partnerships for any purpose. That is, the first part of the amendment states its

14. [The Court listed other features they have in common; each entails (1) two people; (2) mutual support obligations; (3) agreements or contracts as preconditions; (4) minimum age requirements; (5) relationships of indefinite duration; and (6) a common residence.

purpose, and the second part states the means by which this purpose is to be achieved. Doubtless, there are those who would disagree about the efficacy of achieving the former purpose by the latter means. However, it is not for this Court to decide whether there are superior means for "secur[ing] and preserv[ing] the benefits of marriage," or indeed whether the means chosen in the amendment are ineffectual or even counterproductive. The people of this state have already spoken on this issue by adopting this amendment. They have decided to "secure and preserve the benefits of marriage" by ensuring that unions similar to marriage are not recognized in the same way as a marriage for any purpose. * * *

Plaintiffs and the dissent argue that Citizens for the Protection of Marriage, an organization responsible for placing the marriage amendment on the 2004 ballot and a primary supporter of this initiative during the ensuing campaign, published a brochure that indicated that the proposal would not preclude public employers from offering health-insurance benefits to their employees' domestic partners. However, such extrinsic evidence can hardly be used to contradict the unambiguous language of the constitution. * * *

In *Michigan Civil Rights Initiative v. Board of State Canvassers*, 475 Mich. 903, 903, 716 N.W.2d 590 (2006) (Markman, J., concurring), in which it was alleged that numerous petition signatures had been obtained in support of placing the Michigan Civil Rights Initiative (MCRI) on the ballot by circulators who misrepresented the MCRI, it was emphasized that "the signers of these petitions did not sign the oral representations made to them by circulators; rather, they signed written petitions that contained the actual language of the MCRI." Similarly, the voters here did not vote for or against any brochure produced by Citizens for the Protection of Marriage; rather, they voted for or against a ballot proposal that contained the actual language of the marriage amendment.[22] * * * Moreover, like the Citizens for the Protection of Marriage, the Michigan Civil Rights Commission issued a statement asserting:

> If passed, Proposal 2 would result in fewer rights and benefits for unmarried couples, both same-sex and heterosexual, by banning civil unions and overturning existing domestic partnerships. Banning domestic partnerships would cause many Michigan families to lose bene-

---

22. As an aside, this brochure did not render a verdict on the instant controversy. Rather, it stated:

Marriage is a union between a husband and wife. Proposal 2 will keep it that way. This is not about rights or benefits or how people choose to live their life. This has to do with family, children and the way people are. It merely settles the question once and for all what marriage is-for families today and future generations.

We do not read this language as resolving that the marriage amendment would not prohibit domestic partners from obtaining health-insurance benefits. Moreover, statements made by other supporters of the amendment stated that partnership benefits would, in fact, be prohibited by the amendment.

fits such as health and life insurance, pensions and hospital visitation rights.[23]

Therefore, all that can reasonably be discerned from the extrinsic evidence is this: before the adoption of the marriage amendment, there was public debate regarding its effect, and this debate focused in part on whether the amendment would affect domestic-partnership benefits. The people of this state then proceeded to the polls, they presumably assessed the actual language of the amendment in light of this debate, and a majority proceeded to vote in favor. The role of this Court is not to determine who said what about the amendment before it was ratified, or to speculate about how these statements may have influenced voters. Instead, our responsibility is, as it has always been in matters of constitutional interpretation, to determine the meaning of the amendment's actual language. * * *

■ MARILYN KELLY, J., joined by CAVANAUGH, J., dissenting.

[The Citizens for the Protection of Marriage (CPM) spearheaded the petition campaign to add the marriage amendment.] During CPM's campaign, concerns arose regarding exactly what the amendment would prohibit. CPM attempted to address these concerns at an August 2004 public certification hearing before the Board of State Canvassers. Specifically, CPM addressed whether the amendment, which it had petitioned to place on the ballot, would bar public employers from providing benefits to their employees' same-sex domestic partners. CPM's representative, attorney Eric E. Doster, assured the board that it would not. Mr. Doster stated:

> [T]here would certainly be nothing to preclude [a] public employer from extending [health-care] benefits, if they so chose, as a matter of contract between employer and employee, to say domestic dependent benefits ... [to any] person, and it could be your cat. So they certainly could extend it as a matter of contract. * * *

> [A]n employer, as a matter of contract between employer and employee, can offer benefits to whomever the employer wants to. And if it wants to be my spouse, if it wants to be my domestic partner-however that's defined under the terms of your contract or my cat, the employer can do that. . . .

* * *

23. Other opponents made similar statements concerning the adverse consequences of the amendment. See, generally, amicus curiae brief of the American Family Association of Michigan, pp. 9–12. The dissent contends that "[i]t is reasonable to assume that the public relied heavily on the proponents of the amendment to explain its meaning and scope." We see no basis for this argument. Contrary to the dissent, it is no more likely that the voters relied on proponents' views rather than opponents' views of the amendment. Indeed, one might conceivably think that at least some of the people would be significantly more likely to rely on an assessment of the amendment from an official agency of the government than from a private organization with an obvious stake in the passage of the amendment. * * *

In its campaign to win over voters, CPM made a number of additional public statements that were consistent with Mr. Doster's testimony before the Board of State Canvassers. For example, Marlene Elwell, the campaign director for CPM, was quoted in *USA Today* as stating that "[t]his has nothing to do with taking benefits away. This is about marriage between a man and a woman." Similarly, CPM communications director Kristina Hemphill was quoted as stating that "[t]his Amendment has nothing to do with benefits. . . . It's just a diversion from the real issue."

CPM even distributed a brochure that asserted that the amendment would not affect any employer health-benefit plan already in place. The brochure stated:

> Proposal 2 is Only about Marriage
>
> Marriage is a union between a husband and wife. Proposal 2 will keep it that way. This is not about rights or benefits or how people choose to live their life. This has to do with family, children and the way people are. It merely settles the question once and for all what marriage is— for families today and future generations.

It can be assumed that the clarifications offered by CPM, the organization that successfully petitioned to place the proposal on the ballot, carried considerable weight with the public. Its statements certainly encouraged voters who did not favor a wide-ranging ban to vote for what they were promised was a very specific ban on same-sex marriage.

And a poll conducted shortly before the election indicates that CPM's public position was in line with public opinion. The poll results indicated that, whereas the public was in favor of banning same-sex marriage, it was not opposed to employer programs granting benefits to same-sex domestic partners. [In an August 2004 poll of 705 likely voters, 50% favored the amendment while only 41% planned to vote against it; but 70% disapproved of making domestic partnerships and civil unions illegal, and 65% disapproved of barring cities and counties from providing domestic-partner benefits.]

The majority attempts to justify its disregard of the extrinsic sources available by concluding that the "marriage amendment" is unambiguous. As can be discerned by any reader of the amendment, the vague language used is ambiguous in regard to the resolution of the question presented by this case. Clearly, the amendment does not unambiguously state whether public employers are barred from providing health benefits to their employees' same-sex partners. It says nothing about these benefits. Accordingly, it is necessary to engage in judicial construction to resolve that question.
* * *

It is clear that the employee-benefit programs at issue do not recognize same-sex marriage. Therefore, if the programs violate the amendment, it must be by recognizing a union similar to marriage. For a union to be "similar" to marriage, it must share the same basic characteristics or qualities of a marriage. Thus, in deciding whether the public employers violate the amendment by providing the benefits at issue, we must first consider what a marriage entails.

Marriage has been called "the most important relation in life...." [*Maynard v. Hill.*] It "is a coming together for better or for worse, hopefully enduring, and intimate to the degree of being sacred. It is an association that promotes a way of life, not causes; a harmony in living, not political faiths; a bilateral loyalty, not commercial or social projects." [*Griswold v. Connecticut.*] [Marriage is more than a private contract. Justice Kelly listed some of the 1000 + legal benefits and duties of marriage under state and federal law (such as spousal immunity, fidelity obligations, etc.).]

The employer benefit programs at issue do not grant same-sex couples the rights, responsibilities, or benefits of marriage. The most that can be said is that the programs provide health-insurance coverage to same-sex partners. But health coverage is not a benefit of marriage. Although many benefits are conferred on the basis of the status of being married, health benefits are not among them. Notably absent is any state or federal law granting health benefits to married couples. Instead, the health coverage at issue is a benefit of employment. And the fact that the coverage is conferred on the employee's significant other does not transform it into a benefit of marriage; the coverage is also conferred on other dependents, such as children.

But even if health coverage were a benefit of marriage, it is the only benefit afforded to the same-sex couples in this case. The same-sex couples are not granted any of the other rights, responsibilities, or benefits of marriage. It is an odd notion to find that a union that shares only one of the hundreds of benefits that a marriage provides is a union similar to marriage. It follows that the amendment is not violated because the employee-benefit programs do not constitute recognition of same-sex marriage or [a] similar union. * * *

Note on the 2004 Michigan Ballot Campaign. According to Professor Glen Staszewski, "The Bait-and-Switch in Direct Democracy," 2006 *Wis. L. Rev.* 17–74, the supporters of the marriage amendment repeatedly asserted *during* the campaign that the proposed amendment would *not* affect lesbian and gay employees' domestic partnership benefits. *After* the campaign, some leading proponents took a harder line and claimed that the new constitutional provision preempted domestic partnership benefits. Thus Professor Staszewski's charge of "Bait-and-Switch." This may be dirty politics, but should it affect the *legal* conclusion if the new constitutional text is as clear as Justice Markman found it? Note that the Michigan Attorney General took the position that the constitutional text was clear.

Different states may reach different results on this issue, depending on exactly how the constitutional provision is phrased. Alaska's Supreme Court, for example, ruled that its constitutional amendment could not be applied to bar domestic partnership benefits. *Alaska Civil Liberties Union v. Alaska*, 122 P.3d 781 (Alaska 2005). Ohio's trial and intermediate appeals courts have reached conflicting results in cases where different-sex as well as same-sex couples have sued to retain their domestic partnership benefits.

Page 1088. Insert the following new decision in *Langan* right after Justice Dunne's decision, which was reversed on appeal:

John Langan v. St. Vincent's Hospital, 25 A.D.3d 90, 802 N.Y.S.2d 476 (N.Y. App. Div. 2005), review denied, 850 N.E.2d 672 (N.Y. 2006). On appeal from Justice Dunne's judgment that plaintiff Langan was a "spouse" for purposes of New York's wrongful death statute, because he was joined in (Vermont) civil union with the decedent. Vermont calls each partner in a civil union a "spouse," and Justice Dunne concluded that New York would go along with that treatment. Writing for the panel majority, **Judge Lifson** rejected that construction of the wrongful death statute. "Included in th[e] class [of survivors entitled to bring wrongful death claims] is a surviving spouse. At the time of the drafting of these statutes, the thought that the surviving spouse would be of the same sex as the decedent was simply inconceivable and certainly there was no discriminatory intent to deny the benefits of the statute to a directed class. On the contrary, the clear and unmistakable purpose of the statute was to afford distributees a right to seek compensation for loss sustained by the wrongful death of the decedent." See also *Valentine v. American Airlines,* 791 N.Y.S.2d 217 (App. Div. 2005) (ruling that state workers' compensation law did not provide residual benefits to same-sex partners as statutory "spouses").

Judge Lifson also rejected Langan's claim that such a strict interpretation violated the federal or state constitutions. See *Baker v. Nelson*, 409 U.S. 810 (1972) (denying review of same-sex marriage claim on ground that it presented no "substantial federal question"). "The circumstances of the present case highlight the reality that there is a substantial segment of the population of this State that is desirous of achieving state recognition and regulation of their relationships on an equal footing with married couples. There is also a substantial segment of the population of this State that wishes to preserve traditional concepts of marriage as a unique institution confined solely to one man and one woman. Whether these two positions are not so hopelessly at variance (to all but the extremists in each camp) to prevent some type of redress is an issue not for the courts but for the Legislature. Unlike the court, which can only rule on the issues before it, the Legislature is empowered to act on all facets of the issue including, but not limited to, the issues of the solemnization and creation of such relationships, the dissolution of such relationships and the consequences attendant thereto, and all other rights and liabilities that flow from such a relationship. Any contrary decision, no matter how circumscribed, will be taken as judicial imprimatur of same-sex marriages and would constitute a usurpation of powers expressly reserved by our Constitution to the Legislature.''

Judge Fisher (joined by **Judge Crane**) dissented. However, Judge Fisher agreed with the majority that the "spouse" rights included in the wrongful death statute was limited to spouses in a valid "marriage," not a civil union of the kind Vermont had created. Judge Fisher also rejected the argument made by the New York Attorney General (then Elliott Spitzer) that New York was obligated, under the Full Faith and Credit Clause, to apply Vermont law. The FFC Clause has generally not been construed to force states to follow the laws of other states. Moreover, Vermont's own civil union law asserted no interest in protecting wrongful death or other rights of New York same-sex couples.

Judge Fisher dissented, because he found that New York's discrimination against committee same-sex couples joined in civil union was unconstitutional under *Romer*: it treated similar relationships differently, and the difference treatment reflected social animus.

"The purpose of the wrongful death statute is well-defined and firmly established. It is not intended to recompense the survivor for the loss of companionship or consortium, or for the pain and anguish that accompanies the wrongful and unexpected loss of a loved one. It is instead designed solely to make a culpable tortfeasor liable for fair and just compensation to those who, by reason of their relationship to the decedent, suffer economic injury as a result of the decedent's death. A person suffers economic injury in this context when the death deprives him or her of a reasonable expectation of future financial assistance or support from the decedent.

"The plaintiff argues that, with respect to that objective, the wrongful death statute classifies similarly-situated persons on the basis of their sexual orientation. Sexual orientation is a constitutionally cognizable characteristic, and therefore when legislation is challenged on the ground that it classifies and treats persons differently on the basis of sexual orientation, courts will 'insist on knowing the relation between the classification adopted and the object to be attained' (*Romer v. Evans*). * * *

St. Vincent's argued that the "discrimination" was based upon marital status, not sexual orientation. "Leaving aside the fact that opposite-sex couples who remain unmarried do so out of choice while same-sex couples have little choice but to remain unmarried, the classification here is not between unmarried opposite-sex couples who choose to live together in an informal arrangement, and unmarried same-sex couples who do the same. The classification at issue here is between couples who enter into a committed, formalized, and state-sanctioned relationship that requires state action to dissolve and, perhaps most important, makes each partner legally responsible for the financial support of the other. For opposite-sex couples, of course, the relationship is marriage, sanctioned and recognized by the State, requiring a divorce or annulment to dissolve, and obligating each spouse to provide for the support of the other. And, as relevant here, the relationship for same-sex couples is the Vermont civil union, sanctioned and recognized by the State, requiring a court proceeding to dissolve, and obligating each party to provide for the support of the other.

"With respect to the objectives of the wrongful death statute, spouses and parties to a Vermont civil union stand in precisely the same position. Marriage creates a legal and enforceable obligation of mutual support, and therefore the death of one spouse causes economic injury to the other because it results in the loss of an expectancy of future support created and guaranteed by law. And, in exactly the same way, because the state-sanctioned Vermont civil union gives rise to a legal and enforceable obligation of mutual support, the death of one party to the union causes economic injury to the survivor because it results in the loss of an expectancy of future support also created and guaranteed by law. Because no statute or authoritative holding in New York now permits or recognizes a marriage except between opposite-sex couples, and because Vermont civil unions are open only to same-sex couples, the operation here of New York's wrongful death statute to authorize a party to a marriage to recover damages for the wrongful death of his or her spouse, but not to permit a party to a Vermont civil union to recover damages for the wrongful death of his or her partner, in effect, affords different treatment to similarly-situated persons on the basis of sexual orientation.

"The question, then, is whether there is a rational relationship between that disparity of treatment and some legitimate governmental interest or purpose (*see Romer*). Ordinarily, when constitutional challenges are raised against laws prohibiting same-sex marriage, or laws favoring legal marriages over committed relationships between persons of the same sex, those who defend the challenged provisions do so on the basis of the traditional, religious, cultural, and legal understanding that marriage is the union of one man and one woman, and is the preferred environment for procreation and child-rearing. * * * The issue, therefore, is whether New York's interest in fostering traditional marriage, and in preferring it to any other relationship between unrelated adults, is in any conceivable way advanced or promoted by a law that authorizes a surviving spouse, but not a surviving member of a Vermont civil union, to sue for wrongful death. Two cases decided by the United States Supreme Court are instructive on this question, and both involve the right to sue for wrongful death.

"In *Levy v. Louisiana*, 391 U.S. 68 [1969], the Supreme Court struck down a statute which, because it was construed to authorize only legitimate children to maintain an action for the wrongful death of a parent, precluded five illegitimate children from suing for the wrongful death of their mother. The Supreme Court wrote:

> Legitimacy or illegitimacy of birth has no relation to the nature of the wrong allegedly inflicted on the mother. These children, though illegitimate, were dependent on her; she cared for them and nurtured them;

they were indeed hers in the biological and in the spiritual sense; in her death they suffered wrong in the sense that any dependent would.

And, in the companion case of *Glona v. American Guar. & Liab. Ins. Co.*, 391 U.S. 73 [1968], the Supreme Court struck down the same statute insofar as it was construed to bar a mother from maintaining an action for the wrongful death of her illegitimate child killed in an automobile accident. Here the court pointedly observed:

> We see no possible rational basis for assuming that if the natural mother is allowed recovery for the wrongful death of her illegitimate child, the cause of illegitimacy will be served. It would, indeed, be farfetched to assume that women have illegitimate children so that they can be compensated in damages for their death. A law which creates an open season on illegitimates in the area of automobile accidents gives a windfall to tortfeasors. But it hardly has a causal connection with the 'sin,' which is, we are told, the historic reason for the creation of the disability.''

In contrast, the Court did find a rational relationship between the classification and the statutory purpose when it considered a challenge to the constitutionality of Louisiana's intestate succession statutes which barred even publicly-acknowledged illegitimate children from sharing equally with legitimate children in the estate of their father when he died without a will. The Court upheld the statutes, noting, inter alia, that they clearly had a rational basis "in view of Louisiana's interest in promoting family life and of directing the disposition of property left within the State.''

'' * * * [J]ust as the Supreme Court could find no conceivable rational relationship between any governmental purpose promoted by a wrongful death law and a classification of wrongful death plaintiffs or victims according to their legitimacy, neither can I identify any reasonably conceivable rational basis for classifying similarly-situated wrongful death plaintiffs on the basis of their sexual orientation.

"Stated otherwise, I simply cannot reasonably conceive of any way in which New York's interest in fostering and promoting traditional marriage is furthered by a law that determines, based on a person's sexual orientation, whether he or she may have access to our courts to seek compensation for the loss of a pecuniary expectancy created and guaranteed by law (*cf. People v. Onofre* (Casebook, pp. 49–52) [statute permitting consensual sodomy between married persons but banning same conduct between unmarried persons bears no rational relationship to society's interest in fostering and promoting marriage]). And, tellingly, the majority's rejection of the equal protection claim does not include any hint or suggestion of how preventing the plaintiff from asserting a wrongful death claim promotes the State's interest in fostering the institution of marriage * * *. Indeed, the only real effect of the majority's position is to provide a windfall to a potential tortfeasor.''

NOTE ON *LANGAN* AND INTERSTATE RECOGNITION OF VERMONT CIVIL UNIONS

1. *The Full Faith & Credit Clause.* Attorney General (later Governor) Spitzer argued that the Full Faith & Credit Clause constitutionalized the conflicts celebration rule (relationship status is determined by the law of the place of the celebration) and *required* New York to recognize Vermont civil unions. All five *Langan* judges rejected this argument, as would most judges. The FFCC has generally *not* been given much coercive constitutional bite in matters of out-of-state licenses, laws, and records, and DOMA reinforces that traditional view with whatever additional authority (if any) Congress has under the FFCC. Contrast adjudicatory *judgments*, which the FFCC does give interstate mobility, with considerable coercive force backed up by Congress. See *Miller–Jenkins v. Miller–Jenkins*, 912 A.2d 951 (Vt. 2006), excerpted in Chapter 9 of this Supplement.

"Subsequent state appellate decisions declined to follow *Langan* and ruled that ordinary choice-of-law rules in New York required its courts to recognize valid out-of-state same-sex marriages, such as those in Massachusetts. *Martinez v. Monroe Community College*, 850 N.Y.S.2d 740 (App. Div. 2008) (appeal dismissed by the Court of Appeals). On May 14, 2008, immediately after the Court of Appeals denied review in *Martinez*, the counsel to Governor David Paterson (who succeeded Governor Spitzer) instructed all state agencies to follow *Martinez* and treat couples validly married out of state as "married" for purposes of New York law. Subsequent judicial decisions in New York have followed *Martinez* and the executive department memorandum, and not *Langan*. Why was the majority in *Langan* persuaded otherwise? Were they afraid of a backlash?"

2. *Assimilating Civil Unions into a State's Code?* Judge Dunne's strategy in the court below was to interpret the New York wrongful death statute to assimilate civil unions by considering the purposes of the statutory inclusion of "spouse" (Casebook, pp. 1086–88). This approach has had considerable success in New York, reflected in *Braschi v. Stahl Assocs.* (Casebook, pp. 1042–44), which interpreted a rent-control law purposively to include a surviving gay partner as "family." Perhaps surprisingly, none of the five appellate judges accepted this argument either, and none explained exactly why they were not inclined to expand *Braschi* to this situation. Probably the main reason is that the term "spouse" has such a fixed meaning in New York that, unlike "family," it would be usurpative rather than helpful for judges to interpret the term dynamically. Unlike the 1980s, moreover, judges everywhere feel much greater public and professional pressure to hew closely to the original meaning of statutory texts—and again "spouse" has a much narrower meaning than "family."

3. *Equal Protection Considerations.* Langan argued, and Judges Fisher and Crane agreed, that excluding him, a same-sex "spouse" with support obligations, represented a *Romer* equal protection problem. It is not clear why the majority rejected this argument, beyond the banal observation that lower courts have not been eager to read *Romer* or *Lawrence* broadly. And, as the majority observed, the matter is ripe for legislative attention. The New York Court of Appeals rejected constitutional demands for same-sex marriage (*Hernandez*, the previous case in this Supplement), and Attorney General Spitzer was elected Governor. In 2007, he proposed that the New York Legislature enact a same-sex marriage law. Spitzer's successor, David Paterson, has also pressed for same-sex marriage legislation.

CHAPTER 9

POLYPARENTING AND FAMILIES OF CHOICE

SECTION 1

SURROGACY, CUSTODY, AND VISITATION

Page 1155.   Insert the following materials at the bottom of the page:

K.M. v. E.G., 117 P.3d 673 (Cal. 2005). K.M. and E.G. were a romantically committed lesbian couple, registered as domestic partners in San Francisco in the 1990s. In 1995, K.M. agreed to donate her eggs so that E.G. could bear a child through in vitro fertilization. In the 1995 contract K.M. relinquished rights to any child born of this method, which was immediately successful. Twins were born in December 1995, and the couple celebrated a (non-legal) marriage ceremony shortly thereafter. The women's relationship ended in 2001, and K.M. sued to establish a parental relationship with the twins. The California Supreme Court, in an opinion by **Justice Moreno**, ruled that both women were the children's legal mothers.

Parental rights are governed by California's enactment of the Uniform Parentage Act, Family Code § 7600 et seq. The UPA defines the " '[p]arent and child relationship, [which] extends equally to every child and to every parent, regardless of the marital status of the parents.' " Id., § 7602. Just as the Court had previously ruled that the husband in *Johnson v. Calvert* (1979) was the presumptive parent of a child conceived through gestational surrogacy, so the Court ruled in K.M.'s case that the ovum-donor was a presumptive parent. *Johnson* "concluded that 'genetic consanguinity' could be the basis for a finding of maternity just as it is for paternity. Under this authority, K.M.'s genetic relationship to the children in the present case constitutes 'evidence of a mother and child relationship as contemplated by the Act.' "

Section 7613(b) states: "The donor of semen provided to a licensed physician and surgeon for use in artificial insemination of a woman other than the donor's wife is treated in law as if he were not the natural father of a child thereby conceived." The Court declined to extend this provision to the ovum donor. Dissenting **Justice Kennard** would have extended § 7613(b) to include ovum donors as well as sperm donors. Why should ovum donors have *more* rights than sperm donors? (One answer: the statutory language only denies rights to sperm donors. Is this an unconstitutional sex discrimination?)

In a separate dissent, **Justice Werdegar** would have followed *Johnson* to inquire as to the intent of the parties. In *Johnson*, the married couple and the ovum donor intended to create a family for the couple. In this case, even K.M. agreed that her donation was to enable E.G. to have children. The majority responded that an "intent of the parties" approach would create uncertainty in the law. (Also, K.M. disputed that she "intended" to renounce all rights to the twins when she was presented with the form in 1995.) Justice Werdegar responded that her approach was more predictable than the open-ended approach of the majority, which left many questions unanswered. For example, would the Court have recognized K.M. as a parent if she and E.G. had not raised the children within a domestic partnership? A committed relationship?

Because the Court neither overruled nor questioned *Johnson*, its rule did not apply to donors providing ova to different-sex couples. By creating a new rule applicable only to lesbian couples, the Court, argued Justice Werdegar, "confers rights and imposes disabilities on persons because of their sexual orientation. * * * I see no rational basis—and the majority articulates none—for permitting the enforceability of an ovum donation agreement to depend on the sexual orientation of the parties. Indeed, lacking a rational basis, the rule may well violate equal protection. (See *Romer v. Evans* (1996); *Gay Law Students Assn. v. Pacific Tel. & Tel. Co.* (1979).) Why should a lesbian not have the same right as other women to donate ova without becoming a mother, or to accept a donation of ova without accepting the donor as a coparent, even if the donor and recipient live together and both plan to help raise the child?"

Query: This issue may be decided differently in other jurisdictions, with different statutory and constitutional schemes. For example, most states now have constitutional amendments defining marriage as one man, one woman *and* refuse to provide legal recognition to lesbian unions. Would the Kennard or Werdegar position be more persuasive in those states?

ADOPTION AND DE FACTO PARENTING

Page 1194. Substitute the following for the lower court decision in *Lofton*:

Steven Lofton et al. v. Secretary of the Department of Children and Social Services et al.

United States Court of Appeals for the Eleventh Circuit, 2004.
358 F.3d 804, *petition for en banc review denied,* 377 F.3d 1275.

[Excerpted in Chapter 2 of this Supplement]

Page 1224. Add the following Note and Table at the bottom of the page, following the Notes:

NOTE ON THE REVOLUTION IN STATE RECOGNITION OF LESBIAN AND GAY FAMILIES

A March 2007 study authored by Gary Gates (Williams Institute) and Jennifer Ehrle Macomber (Urban Institute) report that one in three lesbians have borne or adopted one or more children and that one in six gay men have adopted a child. Four percent of all adopted children (about 65,500) are living with lesbian and gay parents, most of them in coupled family relationships. Three percent (about 14,000) of the nation's foster children are living with lesbian and gay parents, most of them in coupled family relationships.

Accompanying these sociological facts, there has been a legal revolution that has been unnoticed in the marriage-obsessed press and political process: a growing majority of American states now provide a formal mechanism for lesbian and gay couples to enjoy *joint parental rights* concerning the children they are raising in their same-sex households. As you have seen in Chapters 8 and 9, there are three mechanisms by which this has occurred, with one state (New Jersey) trying all three: (1) state recognition of same-sex marriage, civil unions, or sometimes domestic partnerships, tied in to state laws allowing step-parent adoption (Chapter 8, Section 2); (2) judicial recognition of de facto parenting (Chapter 9, Section

2B); and (3) second-parent adoption, either through judicial interpretation of adoption statutes or through their amendment (Chapter 9, Section 2C).

Table 9–1, below, demonstrates that a majority of states now allow one of these three mechanisms for legal recognition of lesbian and gay co-parenting. Notice that the geographical pattern demonstrated in Table 9–1 follows that of Table 8–1 (in Chapter 8 of this Supplement). States in the Northeast and Pacific Coast recognize lesbian and gay families and treat such parents with respect in custody disputes (often with former spouses of a different sex). States in the South, Border region, Great Plains, and Mormon West deny such rights, discriminate against lesbian and gay parents in custody disputes, and sometimes deny adoption rights entirely. States in the Midwest and non-Mormon West generally treat lesbian and gay parents with respect, allow individuals to adopt, but do not yet provide a legal structure for same-sex couples raising children.

Table 9–1. State Rules Relating to Adoption by Lesbian and Gay Persons and Couples, 2009

State	May Lesbians and Gay Men Adopt?	May a Gay Person Be a "Second Parent" with Her/His Partner?*	Do Judges Treat Gay Parents Neutrally?
Alabama	Yes	Sometimes (some lower courts have allowed second-parent adoptions)	Mixed
Alaska	Yes	Sometimes (Juneau's trial court)	Yes
Arizona	Yes	No	Mixed
Arkansas	No (2008 initiative)	No	No
California	Yes	Yes (*Sharon S.*, 31 Cal.4th 417 (2003); 2003 domestic partnership statute)	Yes
Colorado	Yes	Yes (2007 second-parent adoption statute)	Yes
Connecticut	Yes	Yes (2000 second-parent adoption statute)	Yes
Delaware	Yes	Yes (*In re Hart*, 806 A.2d 1179 (2001))	Yes
District of Columbia	Yes	Yes (*In re M.M.D. and B.H.M.*, 662 A.2d 837 (1995))	Yes
Florida	No (1977 statute)	No	Mixed
Georgia	Yes	Sometimes (some lower courts)	Mixed
Hawaii	Yes	Sometimes (some lower courts)	Yes
Idaho	Yes	No	Mixed
Illinois	Yes	Yes (*Petition of K.M.*, 653 N.E.2d 888 (1995))	Yes
Indiana	Yes	Yes (*Adoption of K.S.P.*, 804 N.E.2d 1253 (2004))	Yes
Iowa	Yes	Sometimes (some lower courts)	Yes
Kansas	Yes	No	Mixed
Kentucky	Yes	No	Mixed
Lousiana	Yes	No	Mixed
Maine	Yes	No	Yes
Maryland	Yes	Sometimes (some lower courts)	Yes
Massachusetts	Yes	Yes (2003 second-parent adoption statute; *Goodridge* [2003])	Yes

State	May Lesbians and Gay Men Adopt?	May a Gay Person Be a "Second Parent" with Her/His Partner?*	Do Judges Treat Gay Parents Neutrally?
Michigan	Yes	Sometimes (some lower courts)	Mixed
Minnesota	Yes	Sometimes (some lower courts)	Yes
Mississippi	No (only different-sex married couples)	No	No
Missouri	Yes	Sometimes (lower courts)	Mixed
Montana	Yes	No	Mixed
Nebraska	Yes	No (*Adoption of Luke*, 263 Neb. 365 (2002))	Mixed
Nevada	Yes	Sometimes (lower courts)	Yes
New Hampshire	Yes	Yes (2007 civil unions statute)	Yes
New Jersey	Yes	Yes (*Adoption by H.N.R.*, 666 A.2d 535 (1995); 2007 civil unions statute)	Yes
New Mexico	Yes	Yes (de facto parenting recognized, *A.C. v.C.B.*, 829 P.2d 660 (1992))*	Yes
New York	Yes	Yes (*In re Jacob*, 660 N.E.2d 397 (1995))	Yes
North Carolina	Yes	No	No
North Dakota	Yes	No	Mixed
Ohio	Yes	No (*Adoption of Jane Doe*, 719 N.E.2d 1071 (1998))	Yes
Oklahoma	Yes	No	No
Oregon	Yes	Yes (2007 domestic partnership statute)	Yes
Pennsylvania	Yes	Yes (*Adoption of R.B.F.*, 803 A.2d 1195 (2002))	Yes
Rhode Island	Yes	Yes (lower courts generally allow)	Yes
South Carolina	Yes	No	Mixed
South Dakota	Yes	No	Mixed
Tennessee	Yes	No	Mixed
Texas	Yes	Sometimes (some lower courts)	Mixed
Utah	Mixed (singles may adopt; non-marital couples may not)	No	No
Vermont	Yes	Yes (1995 statute; 2000 civil unions statute)	Yes
Virginia	Yes	Sometimes (some lower courts)	No
Washington	Yes	Yes (2007 domestic partnership statute)	Yes
West Virginia	Yes	No	Mixed
Wisconsin	Yes	Yes (recognizing de facto parents, *In re Custody of H.S.H.-K.*, 533 N.W.2d 419 (1995))*	Yes
Wyoming	Yes	No	Mixed

Source: www.lambdalegal.org (Updated as of March 2007).
* States recognizing de facto parenting but not second-parent adoptions. Wisconsin's Supreme Court handed down the leading decision declining to recognize second-parent adoptions, *In re Angel Lace M.*, 516 N.W.2d 578 (1994).

Lisa Miller–Jenkins v. Janet Miller–Jenkins

Vermont Supreme Court, 2006.
912 A.2d 951.

■ JUSTICE DOOLEY delivered the opinion for the Court.

[Lisa and Janet Miller–Jenkins were a cohabiting couple in Virginia. In 2000, they entered into a Vermont civil union and subsequently moved to that state. In 2002, Lisa gave birth to IMJ, who was conceived through artificial insemination from an anonymous sperm donor. Janet participated in this process, and the couple raised IMJ together until they separated in September 2003. At that point, Lisa moved to Virginia with IMJ.]

On November 24, 2003, Lisa filed a petition to dissolve the civil union in the Vermont family court in Rutland. In her complaint, Lisa listed IMJ as the "biological or adoptive child[]of the civil union." Lisa requested that the court award her custodial rights and award Janet parent-child contact. The family court issued a temporary order on parental rights and responsibilities on June 17, 2004. This order awarded Lisa temporary legal and physical responsibility for IMJ, and awarded Janet parent-child contact for two weekends in June, one weekend in July, and the third full week of each month, beginning in August 2004. The family court also ordered Lisa to permit Janet to have telephone contact with IMJ once daily.

[Now believing that she was not a lesbian and wanting no further contact with Janet, Lisa subsequently refused to comply with this order and was held in contempt. Lisa persuaded a Virginia state court to enter an order judging her to be IMJ's sole legal parent and cutting off all contact between IMJ and Janet. She also appealed the Vermont family court order.]

This case is, at base, an interstate jurisdictional dispute over visitation with a child. Lisa argues here that the Vermont family court should have given full faith and credit to the Virginia court's custody and parentage decision, which determined Janet had no parentage or visitation rights with respect to IMJ. The family court rejected this argument because it concluded the Virginia decision did not comport with the [Parental Kidnapping Prevention Act, 28 U.S.C. § 1738A (PKPA)], "which was designed for the very purpose of eliminating jurisdictional battles between states with conflicting jurisdictional provisions in child custody disputes." The Vermont court determined it had exercised jurisdiction consistent with the requirements of the PKPA and had continuing jurisdiction at the time Lisa's action was filed in Virginia. Therefore, it further concluded the Virginia court was prohibited from exercising jurisdiction by the PKPA, § 1738A(g), and the Vermont court had no obligation to give full faith and credit to the conflicting Virginia decision.

In analyzing Lisa's arguments, we note that she does not contest that if she and Janet were a validly married heterosexual couple, the family court's PKPA analysis would be correct. Because of her tacit acceptance of the family court's analysis with regard to jurisdiction under the PKPA, we provide only a summary description of why we believe that the family court was correct.

The purpose of the PKPA is to determine when one state must give full faith and credit to a child custody determination of another state, such that the new state cannot thereafter act inconsistently with the original custody determination. *Thompson v. Thompson,* 484 U.S. 174, 181 (1988). The PKPA follows on, and includes many of the provisions of, the Uniform Child Custody Jurisdiction Act (UCCJA), adopted in Vermont as 15 V.S.A. §§ 1031–1051. These acts were adopted to respond to "a growing public concern over the fact that thousands of children are shifted from state to state and from one family to another every year while their parents or other persons battle over their custody in the courts of several states." National Conference of Commissioners on Uniform State Laws, Uniform Child Custody Jurisdiction Act, Prefatory Note (1968). The PKPA embodies preferences "to leave jurisdiction in the state which rendered the original decree[,] ... to promote the best interests of the child[,] ... [and to] discourage[] interstate abduction and other unilateral removals of children for the purpose of obtaining a favorable custody decree." *Michalik v. Michalik,* 494 N.W.2d 391, 398 (Wis. 1993).

The PKPA applies equally to a visitation determination, requiring states to enforce "any custody determination or visitation determination made consistently with the provisions of this section by a court of another State." 28 U.S.C. § 1738A(a). Because the first custody and visitation determination with respect to IMJ was made by the Vermont court, we must first examine whether that court exercised jurisdiction "consistently with the provisions of" the PKPA. Id. If it did, and if it continued to have jurisdiction when Lisa filed her proceeding in the Virginia court, the Virginia court was without jurisdiction to modify the Vermont order. Id. § 1738A(g), (h).

In order for a Vermont court to exercise jurisdiction consistent with the PKPA, it must have jurisdiction under Vermont law, id. § 1738A(c)(1), and meet one of four conditions, id. § 1738A(c)(2)(A)–(D). In this case, it met the condition in subsection (c)(2)(A)(ii) that Vermont "had been the child's home State within six months before the date of the commencement of the proceeding and the child is absent from such State because of his removal or retention by a contestant or for other reasons, and a contestant continues to live in such State." Id. § 1738A(c)(2)(A)(ii). For purposes of this provision, "home State" is defined to mean "the State in which, immediately preceding the time involved, the child lived with his parents, a parent, or a person acting as parent, for at least six consecutive months." Id. § 1738A(b)(4). Because Vermont had been IMJ's home state within six months before Lisa filed her dissolution petition in November 2003, Lisa had removed IMJ from Vermont, and Janet lived in Vermont on the date the dissolution proceeding was commenced, the requirements of subsection(A)(ii) were met.

The PKPA also requires that the court have jurisdiction under Vermont law. Whether local jurisdiction is present is determined by the UCCJA. For the exact reason that the Vermont proceeding met the PKPA condition discussed above, it met the identically-worded provision of the UCCJA. Compare 15 V.S.A. § 1032(a)(1)(B) with 28 U.S.C.

§ 1738A(c)(2)(A)(ii). Thus, the family court had jurisdiction under Vermont law as required by 28 U.S.C. § 1738A(c)(1).

Because the Vermont dissolution proceeding was still pending in July 2004, when Lisa filed her action in the Virginia court, and the Vermont proceeding was consistent with the PKPA, the Virginia court lacked jurisdiction pursuant to § 1738A(g) of the PKPA. That section specified that the court could not exercise jurisdiction over a proceeding to determine the custody of, or visitation with, IMJ while the Vermont proceeding was pending. The Virginia court violated this section by exercising jurisdiction over the case filed by Lisa.

Because the Vermont court had issued a temporary custody and visitation order, the Virginia court was also governed by § 1738A(h) of the PKPA. That section prohibited the Virginia court from modifying the Vermont court's order unless the Vermont court "no longer [had] jurisdiction to modify such determination" or had "declined to exercise jurisdiction to modify such determination." Since the Vermont court continued to exercise jurisdiction over the Vermont proceeding, the Virginia court could have modified the order only if the Vermont court had lost its initial jurisdiction. Under the PKPA, a court that had initial jurisdiction to issue a custody or visitation order continues to have jurisdiction as long as it continues to have jurisdiction under state law and one of the contestants remains a resident of the state. Id. § 1738A(d). The latter requirement is met because Janet continues to reside in Vermont.

Again, the former requirement of continuing jurisdiction is met if it is authorized by the UCCJA. At the time the Virginia court acted, the Vermont court had jurisdiction to modify its own visitation order if:

> (2) it is in the best interest of the child that a court of this state assume jurisdiction because:

>> (A) the child and his parents, or the child and at least one contestant, have a significant connection with this state; and

>> (B) there is available in this state substantial evidence concerning the child's present or future care, protection, training, and personal relationships.

15 V.S.A. § 1032(a)(2). These provisions were met because IMJ had recently resided in Vermont and the evidence of IMJ's relationship with Janet was present in Vermont.

The Vermont court had continuing jurisdiction over the matter of Janet's visitation with IMJ. Therefore, the Virginia order extinguishing Janet's visitation right was issued in violation of § 1738A(h) of the PKPA. The Vermont court was not required to give full faith and credit to the Virginia order issued in violation of the PKPA.

[Lisa argued that the PKPA does not apply to *parentage* decisions such as Virginia's. Justice Dooley found no PKPA authority for a distinction between custody and visitation judgments *not* involving parentage determinations and those that *do* involve parentage determinations. The plain language of the PKPA applies to both the Virginia and Vermont judgments.] Lisa's second argument is that the PKPA has been superseded by the Defense of Marriage Act (DOMA), 28 U.S.C. § 1738C (2000), and DOMA requires that the Vermont court give full faith and credit to the Virginia decision and order. DOMA reads:

> No State, territory, or possession of the United States, or Indian tribe, shall be required to give effect to any public act, record, or judicial proceeding of any other State, territory, possession, or tribe respecting a relationship between persons of the same sex that is treated as a marriage under the laws of such other State, territory, possession, or tribe, or a right or claim arising from such relationship.

Lisa argues that a Vermont civil union is a relationship between persons of the same sex that is treated as a marriage under Vermont law and that Janet's right of visitation, if any, arises from that relationship. Thus, she argues that DOMA authorized the Virginia court to reject any right of visitation based on the Vermont court order, and the Vermont court must give full faith and credit to the Virginia order.

The family court concluded that DOMA would not provide Lisa the relief she sought:

> Nor is the application of the PKPA in this case, as Lisa's counsel has suggested, hindered by the more recently enacted Federal Defense of Marriage Act (DOMA).... Whether or not a Virginia court may be permitted under DOMA to decline to give effect to the judicial proceedings in Vermont in a Virginia court is not relevant to the essential question before this court, or before the court of Virginia as a prerequisite for exercising its jurisdiction, of whether this Vermont court had jurisdiction under Vermont law over this dispute before it was filed in Virginia. Clearly Vermont has jurisdiction and therefore the Commonwealth of Virginia's judgment is not entitled to full faith and credit.

* * *

Under Lisa's interpretation, we would be required to give full faith and credit to the Virginia court's decision not to give effect to the fully valid order of the Vermont court. Indeed, if we were to accept that argument, the Vermont biological parent of a child born to a civil union could always move to another state to make a visitation order unenforceable in every state, including Vermont. * * * [W]e will not give "greater faith and credit" to another state's judgment that is in conflict with a valid judgment of our own courts. Because we can affirm on this narrow ground, we need not reach the broader question [pressed by Janet] of whether DOMA, and not the PKPA, governs to determine the effect of a Vermont custody or visitation decision based on a civil union. * * *

Lisa next argues the civil union of her and Janet is void as a matter of law because it was entered into when both parties were residents of Virginia and would have been void if entered into in Virginia. She then argues that since the civil union is void, the temporary visitation order based upon the civil union is also void. In making these arguments, she relies first upon 15 V.S.A. § 6, which provides:

> A marriage shall not be contracted in this state by a person residing and intending to continue to reside in another state or jurisdiction, if such marriage would be void if contracted in such other state or jurisdiction. Every marriage solemnized in this state in violation of this section shall be null and void.

She argues that because same-sex legal unions are void in Virginia, Vermont must also find their union void. Lisa recognizes that § 6 alone, which applies to marriages, does not void the civil union. As we held in *Baker v. State*, a union between partners of the same gender is not defined by Vermont law as a marriage. The Legislature explicitly codified this holding in 15 V.S.A. § 8. 1999, No. 91 (Adj. Sess.), § 25. Thus, Lisa argues, § 6 applies to civil unions as well as marriages as a result of 15 V.S.A. § 1204(a), a section of the civil union statute, which states:

> Parties to a civil union shall have all the same benefits, protections and responsibilities under law, whether they derive from statute, administrative or court rule, policy, common law or any other source of civil law, as are granted to spouses in a marriage.

Accordingly, Lisa argues § 1204(a) incorporates § 6 and voids her union to Janet.

[Justice Dooley rejected this argument primarily because the Legislature apparently did not intend for the Civil Unions Law (2000) to incorporate § 6. The Law] specifically provided that any town clerk in the state could issue a license to applicants "if neither is a resident of the state." 18 V.S.A. § 5160(a). We take judicial notice that Vermont was the first state to offer civil unions. Thus, under Lisa's broad interpretation of 15 V.S.A. § 6, which she applies even to states with no explicit prohibition on civil unions, no resident of another state who intended to remain a resident of that state could have validly entered into a Vermont civil union because no other state allowed civil unions at that time. Section 5160(a) of Title 18 evidences the absurdity of that claim.

Moreover, where the Legislature intended to impose a residency requirement on couples in civil unions—that is, in the case of dissolution—it stated so explicitly. See 15 V.S.A. § 1206 ("The dissolution of civil unions shall follow the same procedures . . . that are involved in the dissolution of marriage . . . , including any residency requirements."). In addition, the Legislature specifically required town clerks to provide civil union applicants with information to advise them "that Vermont residency may be required for dissolution of a civil union in Vermont." 18 V.S.A. § 5160(f) (emphasis added). In this context, we take the absence of an explicit statement that residency would normally be required for civil union formation as a strong indication that the Legislature intended no such requirement.

Finally, the Legislature has charged the Secretary of State and the Commissioner of Health with providing public information about the requirements and procedures of the statute, and created and charged the Vermont Civil Union Review Commission with implementing a plan "to inform members of the public ... about the act," 1999, No. 91 (Adj. Sess.), § 40(c). We give some deference to the construction of the applicable statutes by these implementing agencies. The Secretary of State has created an online pamphlet, entitled "The Vermont Guide to Civil Unions" (revised Aug. 2005), which states in Part 3 that "[t]here are no residency or citizenship requirements for Vermont Civil Unions." http://www.sec.state. vt.us/otherprg/civilunions/civilunions.html (last visited July 31, 2006). The Commissioner of Health has also posted an online pamphlet entitled "Civil Unions in Vermont: Questions and Answers to Help you Plan your Vermont Civil Union." It states in response to the first question, "Who can form a civil union?," that "[y]ou do not have to be Vermont residents to form a civil union in Vermont." http://healthvermont.gov/research/records/civil.pdf (last visited July 31, 2006). Necessarily, these officials have adopted a different construction of the civil union statutes from that urged by Lisa in this case. [Moreover, an overwhelming majority of the 4371 civil unions entered by January 2002 were for out-of-state couples, a fact that did not dissuade the Commission from announcing that the law was working exactly as the Legislature had intended.]

NOTE ON THE VERMONT INTERSTATE CUSTODY CASE

Perhaps surprisingly, the Virginia Court of Appeals agreed with the Vermont Supreme Court and interpreted the PKPA to divest its state courts of jurisdiction to enter a judgment in conflict with the Vermont one. *Miller–Jenkins v. Miller–Jenkins*, 637 S.E.2d 330 (Va. App. 2006), appeal denied (Va. 2006), cert. denied (U.S. 2007).

The ability of judges in *both* Vermont (gay-friendly) and Virginia (traditionally anti-homosexual) to agree is evidence of the power of law to converge when statutes and precedents set forth bright-line rules. Not only is the PKPA relatively clear, as both courts emphasized, but the U.S. Supreme Court has interpreted Article IV's Full Faith & Credit Clause (FFCC) to require states to enforce *judgments* (but not laws) of sibling states. Virginia's Court of Appeals might have ruled the same way absent the PKPA.

But what to make of DOMA? It is a subsequent statute and might be read as trumping the PKPA. Moreover, Congress purported to act under its Article IV authority to "give Effect" to the FFCC. Justice Dooley and the

Vermont trial judge say that if the PKPA divests the Virginia judge of jurisdiction, then DOMA has nothing to say to the Virginia judge. But this response begs the question: Does DOMA (a subsequent statute) effectively amend the PKPA to create an exception for custody orders based upon a same-sex marriage? (The U.S. Supreme Court says that repeals by implication are not favored, but one might say that DOMA repeals/amends PKPA by its plain language.) Relatedly, does DOMA apply to a civil union? (In 1996, when Speaker Gingrich, Senator Dole, and President Clinton pushed DOMA through Congress and celebrated its family values in their respective political campaigns, no state recognized civil unions or domestic partnerships for lesbian and gay couples.)

If the DOMA–PKPA issue came before the U.S. Supreme Court, how would the Justices rule?

Transgender Issues: The Next Frontier

SECTION 3B

Discrimination Because of Sex

Page 1497. Add the following Case and Notes immediately after Note 3:

Diane Schroer v. James H. Billington, Librarian of Congress

U.S. District Court for the District of Columbia, 2008.
577 F.Supp.2d 293.

. . . Diane Schroer is a male-to-female transsexual. Although born male, Schroer has a female gender identity—an internal, psychological sense of herself as a woman. In August 2004, before she changed her legal name or began presenting as a woman, Schroer applied for the position of Specialist in Terrorism and International Crime with the Congressional Research Service (CRS) at the Library of Congress. The terrorism specialist provides expert policy analysis to congressional committees, members of Congress and their staffs. The position requires a security clearance.

Schroer was well qualified for the job. She is a graduate of both the National War College and the Army Command and General Staff College, and she holds masters degrees in history and international relations. During Schroer's twenty-five years of service in the U.S. Armed Forces, she held important command and staff positions in the Armored Calvary, Airborne, Special Forces and Special Operations Units, and in combat operations in Haiti and Rwanda. Before her retirement from the military in January 2004, Schroer was a Colonel assigned to the U.S. Special Operations Command, serving as the director of a 120–person classified organization that tracked and targeted high-threat international terrorist organizations. In this position, Colonel Schroer analyzed sensitive intelligence reports, planned a range of classified and conventional operations, and regularly briefed senior military and government officials, including the Vice President, the Secretary of Defense, and the Chairman of the Joint Chiefs of Staff. At the time of her military retirement, Schroer held a Top Secret, Sensitive Compartmented Information security clearance, and had done so on a continuous basis since 1987. After her retirement, Schroer joined a private consulting firm, Benchmark International, where, when she applied for the CRS position, she was working as a program manager on an infrastructure security project for the National Guard.

When Schroer applied for the terrorism specialist position, she had been diagnosed with gender identity disorder and was working with a licensed clinical social worker ... to develop a medically appropriate plan for transitioning from male to female. The transitioning process was guided by a set of treatment protocols formulated by the leading organization for the study and treatment of gender identity disorders, the Harry Benjamin International Gender Dysphoria Association. Because she had not yet begun presenting herself as a woman on a full-time basis, however, she applied for the position as "David J. Schroer," her legal name at the time. In October 2004, two months after submitting her application, Schroer was invited to interview with three members of the CRS staff ... [Charlotte] Preece, the Assistant Director for Foreign Affairs, Defense and Trade, was the selecting official for the position. Schroer attended the interview dressed in traditionally masculine attire—a sport coat and slacks with a shirt and tie.

Schroer received the highest interview score of all eighteen candidates. ... [T]he members of the selection committee unanimously recommended that Schroer be offered the job. ... Schroer accepted the offer, and Preece began to fill out the paperwork necessary to finalize the hire.

Before Preece had completed and submitted these documents, Schroer asked her to lunch on December 20, 2004. Schroer's intention was to tell Preece about her transsexuality. She was about to begin the phase of her gender transition during which she would be dressing in traditionally feminine clothing and presenting as a woman on a full-time basis. She believed that starting work at CRS as a woman would be less disruptive than if she started as a man and later began presenting as a woman.

When Schroer went to the Library for this lunch date, she was dressed in traditionally masculine attire. Before leaving to walk to a nearby restaurant, Preece introduced her to other staff members as the new hire who would soon be coming aboard. . . .

About a half hour into their lunch, Schroer told Preece that she needed to discuss a "personal matter." She began by asking Preece if she knew what "transgender" meant. Preece responded that she did, and Schroer went on to explain that she was transgender, that she would be transitioning from male to female, and that she would be starting work as "Diane." Preece's first reaction was to ask, "Why in the world would you want to do that?" Schroer explained that she did not see being transgender as a choice and that it was something she had lived with her entire life. Preece then asked her a series of questions, starting with whether she needed to change Schroer's name on the hiring documentation. Schroer responded that she did not because her legal name, at that point, was still David. Schroer went on to explain the . . . medical process for transitioning. She told Preece that she planned to have facial feminization surgery in early January and assured her that recovery from this surgery was quick and would pose no problem for a mid-January start date. In the context of explaining the Benjamin Standards of Care, Schroer explained that she would be living full-time as a woman for at least a year before having sex reassignment surgery. Such surgery, Schroer explained, could normally be accomplished during a two-week vacation period and would not interfere with the requirements of the job.

Preece then raised the issue of Schroer's security clearance, asking what name ought to appear on hiring documents. Schroer responded that she had several transgender friends who had retained their clearances while transitioning and said that she did not think it would be an issue in her case. . . .

Preece did not finish Schroer's hiring memorandum when she returned to the Library after lunch. Instead, she went to speak with Cynthia Wilkins, the personnel security officer for the Library of Congress. Preece told Wilkins that she had just learned that the candidate she had planned to recommend for the terrorism specialist position would be transitioning from male to female and asked what impact that might have on the candidate's ability to get a security clearance. Wilkins did not know and said that she would have to look into the applicable regulations. Preece told Wilkins that the candidate was a 25–year military veteran. She did not recall whether or not she mentioned that Schroer currently held a security clearance. Preece did not provide, and Wilkins did not ask for, the sort of information—such as Schroer's full name and social security number—that would have allowed Wilkins access to information on Schroer's clearance history. Had Preece requested her to do so, Wilkins had the ability to access Schroer's complete investigative file through a centralized federal database. . . .

[After her lunch with Schroer and the next day, Preece described the situation to a number of other officials at CRS. She and others repeatedly expressed concern about whether Schroer could qualify for a security clearance, but they took no steps to ascertain whether Schroer would in fact lose her clearance.] Preece . . . also testified, however, that she would have leaned against hiring Schroer even if she had no concerns regarding the security clearance, because her second candidate . . . presented "fewer complications"—because, unlike Schroer, he was not transitioning from male to female.

Later that same afternoon, Preece called Schroer to rescind the job offer. She said, "Well, after a long and sleepless night, based on our conversation yesterday, I've determined that you are not a good fit, not what we want." . . .

Since January 2005, Schroer has lived full-time as a woman. She has changed her legal name to Diane Schroer and obtained a Virginia driver's license and a United States Uniformed Services card reflecting her name change and gender transition. . . .

I.

Preece has claimed that her primary concern was Schroer's ability to receive a security clearance in a timely manner. It is uncontested that the ability to maintain or receive security clearance is a requirement for the terrorism specialist position. In light of the inquiry that the Library actually made into Schroer's clearance history and the specific facts affecting her case, however, I conclude that this issue was a pretext for discrimination. . . .

Although Preece knew that Schroer held a security clearance, she did not provide Wilkins with any of the information that might have been needed to see whether reciprocity would apply. Wilkins had the ability to access Schroer's entire security file, but she did not do so—because she was not asked to.

Without any specific information about Schroer—including whether she might have already addressed any issues arising out of her gender transition with the current holder of her security clearance (Benchmark)— Wilkins performed the most general kind of research. . . . [A supervisor] testified when an employee discloses such a disorder [as gender identity disorder], the proper procedure is for the personnel security officer to consult with the Library's Health Services. After interviewing the candidate and, potentially, his or her mental health providers, a Health Services officer determines whether or not the information raises a security concern. For an individual already holding a clearance, if Health Services is satisfied that the disorder raises no security concerns, the personnel security office proceeds to grant reciprocity.

The Library made no effort to determine whether Schroer's previous clearance would receive reciprocal recognition or to determine whether the agency previously holding Schroer's clearance already knew of, and had already investigated any concerns related to Schroer's gender identity disorder. ... Without being given a concrete time frame by Wilkins, and without speaking to anyone in Health Services, Preece simply "assumed" that it would take a year before Schroer would be fully cleared. This assumption was connected to no specific information about Schroer or her clearance history, and was not informed by the Library's own procedures for adjudicating possible security issues arising from a psychological disorder. . . .

II.

Schroer contends that the Library's decision not to hire her is sex discrimination banned by Title VII, advancing two legal theories. The first is unlawful discrimination based on her failure to conform with sex stereotypes. The second is that discrimination on the basis of gender identity is literally discrimination "because of . . . sex."

A. *Sex stereotyping*

Plaintiff's sex stereotyping theory is grounded in the Supreme Court's decision in *Price Waterhouse v. Hopkins,* 490 U.S. 228, 251 (1989). In that case, a female senior manager was denied partnership in a large accounting firm in part because she was perceived to be too "macho" for a woman. Her employer advised that she would improve her chances at partnership if she would "take 'a course at charm school' " and would " 'walk more feminine-ly, talk more femininely, dress more femininely, wear make-up, have her hair styled, and wear jewelry.' " Justice Brennan observed that it did not "require expertise in psychology to know that, if an employee's flawed 'interpersonal skills' can be corrected by a soft-hued suit or a new shade of lipstick, perhaps it is the employee's sex and not her interpersonal skills that has drawn the criticism." In ruling for the plaintiff, the Court held that Title VII reaches claims of discrimination based on sex stereotyping. "In the specific context of sex stereotyping," the Court explained, "an employer who acts on the basis of a belief that a woman cannot be aggressive, or that she must not be, has acted on the basis of gender." . . .

What makes Schroer's sex stereotyping theory difficult is that, when the plaintiff is transsexual, direct evidence of discrimination based on sex stereotypes may look a great deal like discrimination based on transsexuali-ty itself, a characteristic that, in and of itself, nearly all federal courts have said is unprotected by Title VII. Take Preece's testimony regarding Schroer's credibility before Congress. As characterized by Schroer, the Library's credibility concern was that she "would not be deemed credible by Members of Congress and their staff because people would perceive her to be a woman, and would refuse to believe that she could possibly have the credentials that she had." Plaintiff argues that this is "quintessential sex stereotyping" because Diane Schroer is a woman and does have such a background. But Preece did not testify that she was concerned that Members of Congress would perceive Schroer simply to be a woman. Instead, she testified that "everyone would know that [Schroer] had transitioned from male to female because only a man could have her military experiences."

Ultimately, I do not think that it matters for purposes of Title VII liability whether the Library withdrew its offer of employment because it perceived Schroer to be an insufficiently masculine man, an insufficiently feminine woman, or an inherently gender-nonconforming transsexual. One or more of Preece's comments could be parsed in each of these three ways. While I would therefore conclude that Schroer is entitled to judgment based on a *Price Waterhouse*-type claim for sex stereotyping, I also conclude that she is entitled to judgment based on the language of the statute itself.

B.   Discrimination because of sex

Schroer's second legal theory is that, because gender identity is a component of sex, discrimination on the basis of gender identity is sex discrimination. In support of this contention, Schroer adduced the testimony of Dr. Walter Bockting, a tenured associate professor at the University of Minnesota Medical School who specializes in gender identity disorders. Dr. Bockting testified that it has long been accepted in the relevant scientific community that there are nine factors that constitute a person's sex. One of these factors is gender identity, which Dr. Bockting defined as one's personal sense of being male or female.

The Library adduced the testimony of Dr. Chester Schmidt, a professor of psychiatry at the Johns Hopkins University School of Medicine and also an expert in gender identity disorders. Dr. Schmidt disagreed with Dr. Bockting's view of the prevailing scientific consensus and testified that he and his colleagues regard gender identity as a component of "sexuality" rather than "sex." According to Dr. Schmidt, "sex" is made up of a number of facets, each of which has a determined biologic etiology. Dr. Schmidt does not believe that gender identity has a single, fixed etiology.

The testimony of both experts—on the science of gender identity and the relationship between intersex conditions and transsexuality—was impressive. Resolving the dispute between Dr. Schmidt and Dr. Bockting as to the proper scientific definition of sex, however, is not within this Court's competence. More importantly (because courts render opinions about scientific controversies with some regularity), deciding whether Dr. Bokting or Dr. Schmidt is right turns out to be unnecessary.

The evidence establishes that the Library was enthusiastic about hiring David Schroer—until she disclosed her transsexuality. The Library revoked the offer when it learned that a man named David intended to become, legally, culturally, and physically, a woman named Diane. This was discrimination "because of . . . sex."

Analysis "must begin ... with the language of the statute itself" and "[i]n this case it is also where the inquiry should end, for where, as here, the statute's language is plain, 'the sole function of the courts is to enforce it according to its terms.' " *United States v. Ron Pair Enters.,* 489 U.S. 235, 241 (1989).

Imagine that an employee is fired because she converts from Christianity to Judaism. Imagine too that her employer testifies that he harbors no bias toward either Christians or Jews but only "converts." That would be a clear case of discrimination "because of religion." No court would take seriously the notion that "converts" are not covered by the statute. Discrimination "because of religion" easily encompasses discrimination because of a *change* of religion. But in cases where the plaintiff has changed her sex, and faces discrimination because of the decision to stop presenting as a man and to start appearing as a woman, courts have traditionally carved such persons out of the statute by concluding that "transsexuality" is unprotected by Title VII. In other words, courts have allowed their focus on the label "transsexual" to blind them to the statutory language itself.

In *Ulane v. Eastern Airlines,* the Seventh Circuit held that discrimination based on sex means only that "it is unlawful to discriminate against women because they are women and against men because they are men." The Court reasoned that the statute's legislative history "clearly indicates that Congress never considered nor intended that [Title VII] apply to anything other than the traditional concept of sex." 742 F.2d 1081, 1085 (7th Cir.1981). The Ninth Circuit took a similar approach, holding that Title VII did not extend protection to transsexuals because Congress's "manifest purpose" in enacting the statute was only "to ensure that men and women are treated equally." *Holloway v. Arthur Andersen Co.,* 566 F.2d 659, 663 (9th Cir.1977). More recently, the Tenth Circuit has also held that because "sex" under Title VII means nothing more than "male and female," the statute only extends protection to transsexual employees "if they are discriminated against because they are male or because they are female." *Etsitty v. Utah Transit Authority,* 502 F.3d 1215, 1222 (10th Cir.2005).

The decisions holding that Title VII only prohibits discrimination against men because they are men, and discrimination against women because they are women, represent an elevation of "judge-supposed legislative intent over clear statutory text." *Zuni Pub. Sch. Dist. No. 89 v. Dep't of Educ.,* 550 U.S. 81, 127 S.Ct. 1534, 1551, 167 L.Ed.2d 449 (2007) (Scalia, J., dissenting). In their holdings that discrimination based on changing one's sex is not discrimination because of sex, *Ulane, Holloway,* and *Etsitty* essentially reason "that a thing may be within the letter of the statute and yet not within the statute, because not within its spirit, nor within the intention of its makers." *Church of the Holy Trinity v. United States,* 143 U.S. 457, 459 (1892). This is no longer a tenable approach to statutory construction. Supreme Court decisions subsequent to *Ulane* and *Holloway* have applied Title VII in ways Congress could not have contemplated. As Justice Scalia wrote for a unanimous court:

> Male-on-male sexual harassment in the workplace was assuredly not the principal evil Congress was concerned with when it enacted Title VII. But statutory prohibitions often go beyond the principal evil to cover reasonably comparable evils, and it is ultimately the provisions of our laws rather than the principal concerns of our legislators by which we are governed.

Oncale v. Sundowner Offshore Services, Inc., 523 U.S. 75, 79 (1998).

For Diane Schroer to prevail on the facts of her case, however, it is not necessary to draw sweeping conclusions about the reach of Title VII. Even if the decisions that define the word "sex" in Title VII as referring only to anatomical or chromosomal sex are still good law—after that approach has been eviscerated by *Price Waterhouse*—the Library's refusal to hire Schroer after being advised that she planned to change her anatomical sex by undergoing sex reassignment surgery was *literally* discrimination "because of . . . sex."

In 2007, a bill that would have banned employment discrimination on the basis of sexual orientation and gender identity was introduced in the House of Representatives. *See* H.R. 2015, 110 Cong., 1st Sess. (2007). Two alternate bills were later introduced: one that banned discrimination only on the basis of sexual orientation, H.R. 3685, 110 Cong., 1st Sess. (2007), and another that banned only gender identity discrimination, H.R. 3686, 110 Cong., 1st Sess. (2007). None of those bills was enacted.

The Library asserts that the introduction and non-passage of H.R. 2015 and H.R. 3686 shows that transsexuals are not currently covered by Title VII and also that Congress is content with the status quo. However, as Schroer points out, another reasonable interpretation of that legislative non-history is that some Members of Congress believe that the *Ulane* court and others have interpreted sex in an unduly narrow manner, that Title VII means what it says, and that the statute requires, not amendment, but only correct interpretation. As the Supreme Court has explained,

> [S]ubsequent legislative history is a hazardous basis for inferring the intent of an earlier Congress. It is a particularly dangerous ground on which to rest an interpretation of a prior statute when it concerns, as it does here, a proposal that does not become law. Congressional inaction lacks persuasive significance because several equally tenable inferences may be drawn from such inaction, including the inference that the existing legislation already incorporated the offered change.

Pension Ben. Guar. Corp. v. LTV Corp., 496 U.S. 633, 650 (1990) (internal citations and quotation marks omitted).

Conclusion

In refusing to hire Diane Schroer because her appearance and background did not comport with the decisionmaker's sex stereotypes about how men and women should act and appear, and in response to Schroer's decision to transition, legally, culturally, and physically, from male to female, the Library of Congress violated Title VII's prohibition on sex discrimination. . . .

NOTES ON THE REASONING IN *SCHROER*

The *Schroer* decision is remarkable in many respects. First, it is one of the few decisions in the field of transgender employment law that resulted from a full-scale trial, rather than ruling on a motion to dismiss or summary judgment motion. Second, it is the only such case to find that discrimination based on gender identity is sex discrimination *per se*. Other judges have relied on a sex stereotyping theory, which the court here accepts, but only as an alternative ground.

In fact, in an earlier ruling in this case, Judge Robertson had expressed some reluctance to apply a stereotyping claim to the facts of this case. He hesitated to follow the lead of the Sixth Circuit, which has established that

> [D]iscrimination against a plaintiff who is transsexual-and therefore fails to act and/or identify with his or her gender-is no different from the discrimination directed against Ann Hopkins in *Price Waterhouse*, who, in sex-stereotypical terms, did not act like a woman. Sex stereotyping based on a person's gender nonconforming behavior is impermissible discrimination, irrespective of the cause of that behavior.

Smith v. Salem, 378 F.3d 566, 574–75 (6th Cir.2004); *see also Barnes v. City of Cincinnati*, 401 F.3d 729, 737 (6th Cir.2005).

Judge Robertson "expressed reservations about the Sixth Circuit's broad reading of *Price Waterhouse*, . . . explain[ing] that [n]either [its] logic nor [its] language establishes a cause of action for sex discrimination in every case of sex stereotyping. [W]hat *Price Waterhouse* actually recognized was a Title VII action for *disparate treatment,* as between men and women, based on sex stereotyping. . . . [A]dverse action taken on the basis of an employer's gender stereotype that does not impose unequal burdens on men and women does not state a claim under Title VII. . . . [A] plaintiff's transsexuality is not a bar to a sex stereotyping claim, [but] such a claim must actually arise from the employee's appearance or conduct and the employer's stereotypical perceptions." In other words, "a *Price Waterhouse* claim could not be supported by facts showing that [an adverse employment action] resulted *solely* from [the plaintiff's] disclosure of her gender dysphoria." (internal quotations omitted)

After hearing the evidence adduced at trial, the judge changed his view, in light of plaintiff's demonstration that her job offer was rescinded because of her failure to conform to gender conventions. Do you agree that in some cases, a disclosure of gender identity disorder followed by a firing would not state a case under *Price Waterhouse*?

For the back story on this case, see Sharon McGowan, *Litigating Trans Rights*, 45 HARV. C.R.-C.L. L. REV. (forthcoming 2010).

†